HIDDEN FOR CENTURIES

THE KEY TO THE ORIGINAL GOSPEL OF LUKE

HIDDEN FOR CENTURIES

THE KEY TO THE ORIGINAL GOSPEL OF LUKE

A Study Guide By Louise Banner Welch

iUniverse, Inc.

New York   Bloomington

Hidden for Centuries
The Key to the Original Gospel of Luke

iUniverse books may be ordered through booksellers or by contacting:

iUniverse
1663 Liberty Drive
Bloomington, IN 47403
www.iuniverse.com
1-800-Authors (1-800-288-4677)

Because of the dynamic nature of the Internet, any Web addresses or links contained in this book may have changed since publication and may no longer be valid. The views expressed in this work are solely those of the author and do not necessarily reflect the views of the publisher, and the publisher hereby disclaims any responsibility for them.

ISBN: 978-1-4401-4349-6 (pbk)
ISBN: 978-1-4401-4351-9 (dj)
ISBN: 9781440143502 (ebk)

Printed in the United States of America

iUniverse rev. date: 4/29/2009

PREFACE

Mystery and history are hidden in the Gospel According to Luke. Now that the secret is out, it can be yours with your Bible and this study guide. Jesus spoke of treasure hidden in a field. You have additional information hidden in your own Gospel of Luke. Equidistant Letter Sequencing was known to the author of the Gospel of Luke. Originally it was intended at Shiloh or before to enable scribes to detect missing or added letters. Only the Masoretic text has preserved the ELS in the Book of Isaiah, and only that text contains the ELS used in this study. Some would infer prophecy for the current time, but, but the author of this study assumes that some shaping of names and deeds was done to make them relevant. The author of the Gospel of Luke uses the ELS to designate identity of the testimony given. Sometimes this is harmonious with the Isaiah text, but it is used more as a tag than use its content. Since the point of the gospel is to compare Judaism and Christianity, the most probable timing would be the trial of Pontius Pilate in Rome in 37 c.e.

Eighteen was the number Kabbalists associated with the Messiah. Neither Mark nor Pilate were eyewitnesses. Eyewitnesses were called to Rome to determine if Christianity were a form of Judaism and therefore legal. Matthew had written his gospel so that it is a sequential commentary on the Ezra Cycle of the Pentateuch. After the eyewitnesses commented about Jesus to Luke, Luke's gospel was rearranged to make a similar commentary to facilitate comparison with Matthew's. For copyright reasons pertinent passages in Luke are given, but the reader needs a copy of the Gospel of Luke in hand for ready reference.

The author of this work has earned three Master's Degrees, one in Biblical studies at Perkins Theological School at Southern Methodist University in Dallas, Texas. Her attention to words was developed while teaching English to bilingual students. Her previous books are Luke's Twelve Eyewitnesses and Luke Knew Isaiah's ELS. At Perkins, Dr. William Farmer allowed her to see a German text of Rudolf Bultmann. It was marked to show repetition of words in the New Testament. She does not know why he did, but in light of her study thinks he was researching word patterns.

TABLE OF CONTENTS

Above the names of witnesses relate to their testimonies in Equidistant Letter sequencing in Isaiah 52-54. Each of the twenty testimonies has three parts but the three were not composed at the same time. The overall key word or its synonym occurs in most of the cited passages. Usually Parts I and III also have ten key words taken from Isaiah's Equidistant Letter Sequencing. These key words have ELS which begins in the same verse as the name of the eyewitness. Part II is often a word associated with the person of the eyewitness in a gospel . Each part has ten uses of the clue. Ten was used as a mnemotic device by Jewish speakers, five fingers on the one hand and five on the other. The enormity of the counting task may have inspired ancient computing machines.

OOS means "ordination of scribes". The texts of the Masorah, the only text using ELS to this degree, twice lists as a note eighteen words for ordination of scribes. (Psalm 106:20 and at the beginning of the Book of Numbers, McClintock, CBTEL, V, 861) DOT means that a dot or mark was placed on a letter in the Masoretic text. This notation allowed in texts was labeled 'corrections'. It lists 15 and 3 verses, 18 in all. (Bromiley, ISBE, IV, 807) Scribes could have used them to correct in this way: When checking to see whether or not he left out a letter, the scribe or his overseer could count letters using a given ELS pattern. As the scribe counts, the right letters turn up if he has not added nor left out a letter. Since vowels were not used, this was especially important. Above the DOT refers to the correction verses cited by Bromiley. OOS refers to the verses cited by McClintock. CT gives a few Carrington triads meaning a word used three times in no particular place or sequence within that one testimony. The use of ELS identifies by name eighteen eyewitnesses in the Gospel of Luke.

The reader is advised to have at least one copy of the Gospel of Luke in hand while reading this study. The content of verses in Isaiah seldom matters, for the words are clues regardless of meaning. Yacov Rambsel found the names of the eyewitnesses within Isaiah and the clue words in the testimony are taken from the same verse. The study has been reorganized as a Bible study so that the reader can judge current translations for himself.

Six genealogical charts are given to clarify some family names.

Scripture which the Samaritans called treasure is worth seeking. Jesus spoke of treasure hidden in a field. Letters in Isaiah and words in Luke must be sought like treasure, only some of the treasures have been broken into pieces. Casual reading is sufficient for salvation. Yet if there is more, seekers want to know how to find it. Using equidistant letter sequencing, Isaiah gives patterns to words that exist within the Gospel According to Luke. The contemporary order has been created to make it easier for a scholar to compare it with Matthew, Mark and John. The original order identifies the source (written work) or the identity of the eyewitnesses of Luke 1:2. Before that it was written so that the reader knew the name of the eyewitness. Contemporary copies of Luke are arranged as a commentary on the Ezra cycle which in turn is dependent on the order of the Pentateuch. (cf. Goulder in Spong, LTG). If so, the Synoptic Gospel is the result of careful comparison of each gospel to the Pentateuch's sequence. (cf. M.D. Goulder). Original Luke was the testimony of eighteen witnesses to Christ plus Mark and Pilate.. Then the testimony was rearranged to make comparison with the Gospel of Matthew easily possible. The editor was leaving a key to rediscovering who said what. In law repetition of the facts by two or three eyewitnesses is legally desirable. (cf. Numbers 35:30) Whoever rearranged the testimony had a Masoretic text of Isaiah. In it there was already a system of names and words which he could use to identify sources if he desired. If there is doubt, it should be directed toward any passage with a sole witness.

Equidistant Letter Sequencing can be found in the Masoretic text of Isaiah 52-54 which has relevance to the Gospel of Luke. Indeed eigthteen Old Testament verses were marked with a dot. Somehow it was once thought that these had been errors and were now corrected. (Bromiley, ISBE, IV, 807) These were first used to locate added or lost letters in manuscripts that only contained consonants. Since they correspond to the eyewitness testimony in Luke, scribal ingenuity on their part can be assumed. If it can be shown that the Gospel of Luke uses Isaiah's ELS, one first needs to ask what Isaiah's Equidistant Letter Sequencing is. Beginning with a verse in Isaiah, Yacov Rambsel notes that names, words and phrases are spelled out in a repeated interval from a particular verse. (Rambsel, HNJ, in passim.) The ones he found which are used in this study are from Isaiah 52-54. Some theorize that an earlier manuscript had had this copied onto the backside at one time. These chapters are neither at the beginning nor end of Isaiah. This gives support to the theory that the Book of Isaiah as it now is was not written at one time by one author. Most authorities would agree that it was not. In gospel times as now all of Isaiah was considered scripture.

What is Equidistant Letter sequencing? For example, the same number of letters can be counted to spell the name Mary: for example, MxxxAxxxRxxxY. Coincidence makes sense after it is seen as being intended. Some dimensional pictures look different from a different angle, but there does not have to be meaning in the difference. Rambsel's work applies to the Masoretic text, not to other texts. In Jewish tradition Moses was 'given' the Masora. (McClintock, CBTEL, V, 861) Huldah may have authenticated Hilkiah's find (Josiah's text) by checking equidistant letter sequencing. (II Kings 22). About 458 b. c. Ezra at Shiloh needed ways to preserve authenticity of scripture as he decentralized scribes into synagogues. A second set of mysterious notations may refer to appointment of scribes. It includes more than eighteen verses, and it is labeled the Ordination of Scribes. (McClintock, CBTEL, V, 861) This study also coordinates with the eighteen witnesses, eighteen being the number of the Messiah or blessings. At some point in time, the sopherim relocated to Tiberias where it was led by the Asher family. (Bromiley, ISBE, IV, 807) At Tiberias the Masoretic system preserved the earliest text whether it originated in the time of Moses or Ezra. The Cairo Codex of the Prophets is the earliest existing work associated with both Masora and Asher. (Bromiley, ISBE, IV, 799) Isaiah's ELS may have told them more than it tells readers today, possibly relating to calendars, locations around the temple, rights and\ or contributions. Within this study, the notes for the subdivisions are comments, not scripture per se. The meaning of the word may reflect its use in the Pentateuch. For example, Deuteronomy 5:21 refers to persons and things.

Stone tables supposedly used by scribes at Qumran had several troughs from ten to twenty inches long. The principle of a Catholic rosary is to count off and the principle of the Chinese abacus to use sets in counting off. If ELS were a device for correction of manuscripts, these troughs could have been useful in counting off. They could have held either small seeds or stones, an unstrung rosary of sorts. The discovery of the Antikythera computer creates the possibility it was used to facilitate using ELS. (New York Times, November 29, 2006)As one looks at of Part I, the stations of the cross comes to mind.

How can a study of the use of ELS further the study of the Gospel of Luke? It can produce a theory. . One possibility is that Parts I and III of Luke was first written to be used in the trial of Pontius Pilate in 37 c.e. The trial really did not happen because Tiberias died just before the eyewitnesses arrived. However, the brief would have been prepared prior to the trial. The point was whether or not Jesus was practicing a legal religion (Judaism) or not.). Pilate's life and career were at issue. Was 'Christianity' legal as a sect of Judaism or not?

Only someone with the capability of Seneca the Elder could have recombined all the evidence into the order in which Luke now exists. The purpose of this study is to return the jigsaw puzzle into the original eighteen testimonies. The Gospel of Luke did not surface until after the death of Marcion in Alexandria. He was Seneca's grandson and taught an abbreviated form of the Gospel of Luke in Alexandria. Probably he had the original given to him by Novatus, his uncle, who received it from his uncle Gallio who tried Paul. Seneca the Younger could have sent the manuscript to his brother Gallio for that trial.

To recap, Seneca's second wife Pomponia was a Christian. His sons were all called Lucius Annaeus Seneca. The first Novatus was adopted and renamed Gallio. He was judge when Paul was tried. He needed to know who said what. The original would furnish that information. His second son was Seneca the Younger or Secundus who was mysteriously absent from Rome for a time after 37 before 60 c.e. What he wrote forms part two describing each witness in this study. The third brother Mela at Sinope inherited the unpublished manuscript. Thus his son or nephew Marcion of Alexandria must have had access to it. Marcion's contribution was to chop out anything he considered Jewish. (Hultgren, ECH, 110) Upon his death, the full manuscript called the Alexandrian Papyrus was 'found'.

Orators used the fingers so the expression 'on the other hand' came into being. Masora was in three parts, magna, parva and finalis. The re-creation of Luke is also in three parts. Each part has ten uses of a word, phrase or synonym. This study notes that three sets of ten exist for each witness. Masora included three uses of the final word, but the meaning of the word 'final' is lost. (McClintock, CBTEL, V, 861) Moreover, Carrington triads may be intended as those final words. (Carrington, PCC, ATM, in passim.) Within this study, the overall word identifies all the testimony of the eyewitness, another unifies ten points of comparison of Jesus with a well-known Jew, a third unifies ten points of information about the eyewitness, and a fourth unifies a commentary on the Ten Commandments. By assuming that the present Gospel of Luke is now a jigsaw puzzle, modern man rebels that the same words are attributed to multiple witnesses. Yet multiple testimonies to the same event are essential to jurisprudence.

Mathew 5:17-18 states that there are dots used which should not be removed. In the Table of Contents they are labeled DOT. Computers allow easier location of ELS, for Yacov Rambsel found some ELS to be separated by as much as 700 spaces. Yacov Rambsel's book, His Name Is Jesus, gives the names of persons whose names are spelled out by ELS within Isaiah 52-54. Modern minds find the idea repulsive until they realize that Jewish families used the same names over and over. In several instances names were changed to fit. For example, Zacchaeus becomes Matthias. Peter becomes Simon bar Jonah. In the Masoretic version, the names for the eighteen eyewitnesses are all spelled out. Rambsel then gives other words, phrases and other names that can be spelled out using ELS from the same verse that had ELS for that person's 'name'. Luke used the name and the words spelled out from that particular verse to write the Gospel of Luke. These words, their homonyms and synonyms become the unifying words within the testimony of the named eyewitness. Furthermore, oratorial repetitions internal within one testimony are cited relying on the American

Bible Society for authority. Rudolf Bultmann was intrigued with the repetition of words as a mnemonic devise, but he did not relate them to separate witnesses as far as is known.. (Aland, NT, in passim).

Structural analysis is not new. M. D. Goulder found that the Gospel of Matthew is a sequential commentary on three years of scriptural readings. They correspond to the content of the Ezra Cycle. (Goulder, MLM, in passim.) The Palestinian readings of the Law and the Prophets took three years. (Bromiley, ISBE, IV, 807) Aileen Guilding found that the Gospel of John appears to be notes taken at Jewish–Christian feasts over three years. These meetings often occurred after the proscribed Jewish feasts listed in Leviticus 23. John's chapters 1, 8, 15 are more or less a journal of thoughts following Passover. John's chapters 2, 9, 16 are more or less a journal of thoughts following the Feast of Unleavened Bread. John's chapters 3, 10, 17 refer to Firstfruits, a term relating to resurrection to the Christians. John's chapters 4, ll, 18 relate more or less to the Holy Spirit to be revealed at Pentecost. John's chapters 5, 12, 19 relate to the returns from Babylon, Egypt and death. John's chapters 6, 13, 20 relate to the Day of Atonement. God's divine retribution was the issue. John's chapters 7, 14, 21 relate to the founding of the Messianic Kingdom and Feast of Tabernacles. (after Guilding, FGJW, in passim.) Austin Farrar considered the Gospel of Mark as a series of dialogues in the sequence of the Pentateuch. (Farrar, SAG, in passim.)

In a study of this kind, the bibliography of each chapter needs to be handy. It is given herein in alphabetical order by the author or editor's name at the end of each chapter. Within the text, reference to the bibliography is given: First the author's last name, then a few initials taken from the title, and last the location in pages and/or volumes. The index at the end of the study shows pagination according to the name of the witness, the name of the person compared with Jesus, and the name of the most likely religious group represented.

Illustrations are treasures found by Matthaus Merian of Basel as woodcuts in Spain. He first published them as Iconum Biblicarum in 1630 adding titles. (Strasburg,:1630). Titles to the woodcuts are omitted so that the reader can have a treasure hunt of his own. Sufficent information is given in this Bible study for him to identify all.

BIBLIOGRAPHY

Aland, Kurt, et. al., ed. The Greek New Testament. American Bible Society (New York:1975)

Bromiley, Geoffrey W, The Internation al Standard Bible Encyclopedia. 4 vols. William B. Eerdmans Publishing Company (Grand Rapids, Michigan:1979)

Carrington, Philip. The Primitive Christian Calendar. University Press (Cambridge:1952)

Farrar, Austin. Seekers After God. A. L. Burt (New York:n.a.)

Goulder, M. D. Midrash and Lection in Matthew. SPCK (London :1974)

Guilding, Aileen. The Fourth Gospel and Jewish Worship. Clarendon Press (Oxford:1960)

Hultgren, Arland, and Steven A. Haggmark, eds. The Earliest Christian Heretics. Pb. Fortress Press (Minneapolis:1996)

McClintock, John and James Strong, eds. Cyclopedia of Biblical, Theological, and Ecclesiastical Literature. 12 vols. Baker Book House (Grand Rapids, Michigan:1981)

Rambsel, Yacov. His Name Is Jesus. Pb. Word Publishing (Nashville:1999)

Spong, John   Shelby. Liberating the Gospels. HarperSanFrancisco (Morristown, New Jersey: 1996)

THE FAMILY OF HEROD

```
xxxxxxxxxxxxxxxxxxxxxxxxxxxxxxxxxxxxxxxxxxxxxxxxxx
x                              x
HEROD ANTIPATER                JOSEPH HEROD PHILIP
   x

      xxxxxxxxxxxxxxxxxxxxxxxxxxxxxxxxxxxxxxxxxxx
x                              x
HEROD THE GREAT                ALEXANDRA SALOME
md. MARIAMNE BERAT             md. 1. JOSEPH H.P.
BOETHUS                        md. 2. JOSEPH A.
   x
xxxxxxxxxxxxxxxxxxxxxxxxxxxxxxxxxxx

x               x              x                        x
HEROD PHILIP II  DEACON PHILIP  OTHER MARY
   (1 OF 70)       (1 OF 7)     md. APOSTLE PHIILP
md. SALOME, DAUGHTER            (1 of 12) son of Jacimus (Jacob)
OF HEROD PHILIP I AND             xxxxxxxxxxxxxxxxxxxx
HERODIAS            x                            x
            JUDAS THADDEUS    JAMES OF ALPHAEUS
```

ALEXANDRIAN ZADOKITES

H.P. SIMON BEN BOETHUS (22-5 b.c.)
md. MARIAMNE THE HASMONAEAN

```
      xxxxxxxxxxxxxxxxxxxxxxxxxxxxxxxxxxxxxxxxxxxxxxxxxxxx
x             x            x              x             x
MARIAMNE    ELEAZAR    MARIAMNE      MARIAMNE      DAUGHTER
md. HEROD THE .LAZARUS md. ZACCHAEUS md. JOSHUA  md. JONATHAN
GREAT         H.P. 16-17  (MATTHIAS)   BEN GAMLA  ANNAS H.P. 37
x                         H.P. 65-67      x         SON OF ANNAS
x                                         x         H.P. 6-15
x                                      DRUSILLA
x

HEROD PHILIP II                              md. FELIX
md. SALOME
```

9

II. JOHN BEN ZEBEDEE-VIRGIN MARY-JESUS

From the cross, Jesus asked John the son of Zebedee to take care of his mother. (Matthew 27:56). Only Matthew describes a difference between John and James. (Matthew 20:20-28) The spirit of this testimony is found in Psalm 150:6. Isaiah 53:10 contains ELS for John, Mary, Passover, and Yeshua. (Rambsel, HNJ, 7, 20, 44) The author of Luke uses "pass" as the unifying word for all the testimony, but in Part one, the words "blessed" and "beloved" unify it.

Zechariah was a descendant of Barak (thunder) who once saved Israel. (Matthew 23:35, Judges 4:5-6) James and John are called 'sons of thunder', so Zebedee and Zechariah, father of John the Baptist, were probably kin, perhaps brothers to Escha. Carved on the monument to Absalom the son of David, the names Zebedee and Zechariah have the words "ben Phabes" added. Zechariah was known as Ishmael ben Phabes when he served as a priest in 15-16 c.e. (Jeremias, JTJ, 377). Escha was first wife to Joseph of Nazareth. John cared for the mother of Jesus until her death. (McBirnie, STA, 110 and Matthew 23:35) As an evangelist John worked with Philip in Ephesus. The spirit of the testimony is found in Psalm 150:6.

Kabbalism was taught in John's time. Indeed the Gospel of John can be read as a rewriting of the personification of the Infinite Mind. References to Jesus are added for sake of revealing who Jesus truly was. (Hall, STAA, 397) Perhaps this has relevance to the Book of

Revelations which is generally attributed to him. John's biographer Prochoros wrote earlier than the third century. (McBirnie, STA, 111) From another point of view written in the twentieth century, Aileen Guilding finds that the Gospel of John is a sequential commentary on Jewish feasts for three years.

PART ONE: STATIONS OF THE CROSS

Part One is a dual biography of the Virgin Mary and her son Jesus. The prophecy given to Mary was that Jesus would be born. He was to fulfil the prophecy given to David. "Blessed" becomes the unifying word for Part One.

SUBJECTS (Luke 11:27-28, blessed, pass, John 1:1) Aland notes that Luke 11:271:28, 42, 48. When John wrote the Gospel of John, he said that he had read another gospel and would only add to it, not replace it. The short repetitions between John and Luke are to be expected, for it is generally believed that the Gospel of John was written after the Gospel of Luke.

This witness is that of John ben Zebedee. The theory of two John's compares John ben Zebedee and John the Presbyter. It seems to be supported by the ELS. John the Presbyter may have been Jochanan ben Zakki, grandson of High Priest Annas. (McClintock, CBTEL, IV, 942) John the Presbyter would judge John ben Zebedee at Jabneh for the healing of the lame man. John the Presbyter used the pseudonym of Elijah ben Asira. His ELS is Isaiah 53:11, but the ELS for John ben Zebedee is 53:10. Elijah was called a thunderer for God, and John was called a son of thunder.

Although it is not necessarily so, the crowd could have been at Passover.

FAMILY (Luke 1:38-55, blessed, pass, John 13:13, Psalm 111:9) Aland notes that Luke 1:42-48=11:27. The report of the census was left out. David commited a sin when he allowed a census, the numbering of the people. (II Samuel 24) In gospel times, the census was grounds to affirm that Jesus was indeed of the lineage of David. Matthew states that

Joseph was of the lineage of David. (Matthew 1:18). Many prophecies are known. (Jeremiah 30:9, Hosea 3:5, Amos 9:11) The king prophecy is found in II Samuel 7:12.

Jacim (Alcemis) was the last of the Zadokite priests (162-159 b.c.). His lineage was highly disputed. (Jeremias, JTJ, 182) Mary was the daughter of Joakim (a form of Alcemis) and Anna. At the age of two Mary was taken to live at the Temple. When she was twelve, Zachariah chose Joseph of Nazareth to be her husband. (Barnstone, OB, 385-387) He was of the lineage of David through Nathan.

GENEALOGY (Luke 3:21-23, beloved, pass, John 1:32) Aland notes that Luke 3:22=9:35. The Virgin Mary sings the Magnificat which was first sung by Hannah, the mother of Samuel. (I Samuel 2:1-10) In gospel times it had become a battle song which had been used by the Maccabees.

Salome, the mother of John, had been a midwife for the Virgin Mary. When she touched Mary without believing, her hand withered. Then it was restored. (Barnstone, OB, 390-391)

John the Baptist baptized Jesus in the River Jordan. A voice from heaven said, "This is my beloved son." On theIsle of Patmos John would hear that voice again. (Book of Revelation 1:10)

SERMON (Luke 10:23-38, blessed, pass, John 8:56) Aland notes that Luke 10:32=22:13. However, Jesus may have been referring to Barak who saved Israel. He was an ancestor of Zechariah (Matthew 23:35) and his name means 'thunder.' When James and John ben Zebedee are called 'sons of thunder,' it may refer to the same Barak. (Mark 3:17)

A lawyer asks Jesus about eternal life. He tells the Parable of the Good Samaritan. It is about a Roman named Stephanus who was helped by either Herod Philip or Herod Agrippa I. John would have despised all three. Even so, Jesus told John to become as charitable as they were.(cf. Schurer, LTJM, I, 2. 172)

MARVEL (Luke 7:11-18, idea of blessing, idea of passing, John 12:49) Aland notes that Luke 7:15=2:47 and Luke 7:16=1:68, 19:44. Jesus restored Maternus son of Leah to life. Later Maternus became a believer. He built a Christian church beyond the Alps and named it to honor the Virgin Mary. (McBirnie, STA, 60-61)

FAME (Luke 18:35-43, idea of blessing, pass, cf. John 14:23) Aland notes that Luke 18:38=17:13 and Luke 18:42=7:50, 17:19. Bartimeus (Baba ben Buta) was Herod the Great's physician. He angered Herod so Herod ordered that he be blinded immediately after the death of his two sons. He was blinded, but Joseph of Arimathea hid the sons in Samaria. (Edersheim, LTJM, I,.pp. 120, 126, 370, 372) Baba became an enthusiastic follower of Jesus. Herod Antipas had come into power. He heard that his sons were alive and killed them.

PROPHECY (Luke 20:9-18, beloved, come=pass, John 5:18, 7:30, Psalm 118:22) Aland notes that Luke 20:19=19:47-48, 22:2.) Since the time of Ezekiel, Israel had been compared to a vine or vineyard. When no longer useful, vines were destroyed. Jesus says that the owner of the vineyard was absent. He sent several other messengers before he sent his beloved son. The prophecy was that he would give the vineyard to others if they did not accept his son.

Josephus tells a story about Philip very much like this. (Josephus, 3)

LAST WEEK (Luke 19:28-40, blessed, pass, John 12:12-19, Psalm 118:26) Aland noted that Luke 19:32=22:13 and Luke 19:38=2:14. Jesus sent Peter and John into Jerusalem to find a place for the Last Supper. They found all as he said it would be. Jesus called himself the bridegroom, for the Messiah was likewise long-awaited. At the beginning of Jesus's career, John and Jesus had attended a wedding at Cana. The bride may have been Jesus's friend Martha ben Boethus. She married Joshua ben Gamla about that time.

The Virgin Mary was not only present. She asked Jesus to provide wine.

DEATH (Luke 9:28-36, beloved, pass, John 14:8-11) First there was the Lord's Supper. John was on one side of Jesus. They went up on the Mount of Transfiguration. John and the other disciples fell asleep. Jesus spoke with Moses and Elijah about his death-to-be. Again a voice from heaven said, "This is my beloved son."

When they got to the tomb, Mary Magdalene would take off, and Salome left to speak to the guards. Finally, Bethany is the site of the Ascension. One was Our Lord who would take off, and the other as the other John would be left to take care of Mary. The eagle became the symbol associated with John. He wrote a gospel, and the words for 'eagle=aiteas' and 'lesson=aeteas' sound alike.

AFTER THE DEATH (Luke 24:50-53, blessed, pass, John 14:28, 16:22) When Lazarus died, Jesus asked for an act of faith, 'moving the stone away'. In speaking of the tomb of Jesus, John says the stone was moved away. The Virgin Mary was present at the crucifixion. Jesus asked that John take care of Mary. (Mark 15:40)

A tradition exists that John was told to drink poison, but the poison took the form of a snake and came out of the cup. (McBirnie, STA, 116) One recalls that Jesus once asked him if he could drink from the same cup that Jesus would. (Matthew 20:22)

PART TWO: THE LORD'S PRAYER

In Part Two, it is as if the prayer were to be said by John ben Zebedee himself. The unifying word for Part Two is the name John. The unifying word for all three parts is "pass". John said that he would not include in his gospel what had. already been told in another gospel. References may refer to phrasing found in John rather than content.

OUR (Luke 6:12-16, John, pass, John 6:70, 8:1, 19:26-27, Matthew 10:1-4) Jesus called twelve disciples and each served him in his own way. John's wholehearted belief made him different (cf. 'holy'). Others saw what he saw but they did not understand the significance. From the cross Jesus gave him charge of his mother the Virgin Mary.

Zebedee was of the Tribe of Levi and he called one son James Levi. Salome was of the Tribe of Judah and she called John Judah. (McBirnie, STA, 101-102) The Tribe of Judah was the first tribe to follow David. (Peloubet, PBD, 336) Because Zechariah was a priest, he was of the Tribe of Levi as Zebedee was. Markings on the monument of Absalom say they are both "ben Phabes" (sons of Fabatus, Josephus, 359, 464).

FATHER (Luke 5:1-11, John, pass, John 213-8, Matthew 4:18-22) Zebedee could have been Governor of Nabatea as his name relates to worship and Edom. If so, he was also Treasurer of the Temple at Jerusalem. Peter, James and John were fishing when Jesus came by. He told them to lower their nets once more, and a miraculous catch of fish followed. Using Mandaean terminology, Jesus said he would make them fishers of men. (Mead, GJB, 14) John the Baptist was honored by the Mandaeans. James and John were followers of John the Baptist.

NAME (Luke 9:51-56, John, pass, John 4:9) Aland notes that Luke 9:51=17:11.and 9:52=17:11, 9:51. John was impatient with Samaritans and wanted Jesus to force them to 'listen'. Jesus said that he came with a spirit different from that of Elijah. (II Kings 1:10, 12) At the time there were zealots who watched the road to Jerusalem from Elijah's Roost. It was on a barely accessible cliff. The signal that someone was coming was making a sound like the cooing of a dove. (cf. Charlesworth, OTP, I, 744)

KINGDOM (Luke 18:15-17, when=it came to pass, Matthew 19:13-15) When John was old, he would be carried into worship on a stretcher. He would always say, "Little children, love one another." He was chided for his simplicity and replied, "It is a good start." The people would ask for another saying of Jesus. He would reply, "It is the Lord's command. If this alone be done, it is enough." Another source said, "It is the beginning." (McBirnie, STA, 118)

Salome, John"s mother, had once asked Jesus if he could be on his right hand when Jesus became king. Jesus said that position was not his to give. (Matthew 20:20-28)

EARTH (Luke 8:19-25, John present, pass, I John 1:25) One can note that Luke 8:21 is similar to Luke 11:27-28. The disciples which included John were in a boat. Perhaps thunder was heard. Fishermen are used to boats, so the sea must have been stormier than usual. Jesus is asleep, but they waken him. He stills the water.

BREAD (Luke 8:40-56, John , pass, John 13:21-30) Aland notes that Luke 8:48=17:19. John is amazed when the daughter of Jairus rises up. What is shocking is that Jesus does not recommend vegetarianism. He says to give her meat.

When the Virgin Mary was taken to the Temple to live while still a child, Mary of Cleopas came to live with Joakim and Anna. Perhaps she was a sister to Lazarus. This passage is attributed to the sisters of Lazarus. Jesus said that only one thing (dish) is needful. At At Qumran, it was the custom to serve only one dish.

EVIL (Luke 22:7-13, John, Passover, John 2:6-10) Aland notes that Luke 22:13=19:32.

Many religious Jews blamed women for all the evil. Soon they could be associated with good. At Ephesus, Philip and John may have begun an order of nuns. Philip had no children, but he had several daughters. If male followers are called sons, it follows that nuns could be called daughters. (Acts 21:9) John was caring for the aging Mary. At Jerusalem, the temple supported a group of aging widows. A fund was set up for this purpose.

Early Christianity sought to Christianize paganism, so the advocates of paganism sought to paganize Christianity. Some critics say that the Book of Revelation is their satire that reveals truth inadvertently. (cf. Hall, STAA, 609)

FORGIVE (Luke 12:11-15, John, when=it came to pass, John 1:32-33, Matthew 20:20-28) Aland notes that Luke 12:11-12=21:12-15. Jesus disappointed his disciples who thought his was an earthly kingdom. Salome asked if her sons could sit on either side when he came into his kingdom Both James and John said they could drink from the same cup he would. Then James was the first of the twelve to die. John was forced to drink from a cup of poison but survived the rest of the twelve. They needed forgiveness for lack of understanding.

AS WE (Luke 9:49-51, John, pass, cf. Mark 9:38-40) Verse 51 is included in two places. Recalling the sermon about the Good Samaritan, Herod Philip and Herod Agrippa I cared for exiles from the territories of Herod Antipas and Aretas IV. John already did not like Samaritans. Jesus told John to be more like the ones who helped others . The victim the Samaritan helped was a Roman named Stephanus, and Jews were also prejudiced against Romans. (Schurer, HJP, I. 2. 172) In 44 c. e., Agrippa would kill James, the brother of John.

AMEN (Luke 5:33-35, John present, idea of these things will pass, John 2:1-12) Early in the ministry of Jesus, he went to a wedding in Cana. At Mary's request, he changed water into wine. This passage mentions a bridegroom who will be taken away. When the Apostles Creed was written, John was associated with the words, 'maker of heaven and earth.' (Hone, LBB, 91)

PART THREE: THE TEN COMMANDMENTS

The unifying word is Yeshua (Jesus) or "he" is a reference to Yeshua.

ONE LORD

(Luke 17:11-19, Jesus, pass, John 8:3-11) Aland notes that Luke 17:11=9:51. John had a problem accepting Samaritans. When other Jews were sent into Babylon, those Jews unable to work and the Samaritans stayed behind. They took over some property which was lying idle. They wished to keep it after the Jews returned. The Jews then refused to let Samaritans help them restore the temple. In gospel times, Samaritans were second-class citizens. They could contribute money to the temple, but not worship in it. So they worshiped on Mount Gerizim as the ancients had. Jesus sent the lepers he had cured to Jerusalem, but one was a Samaritan. God can be worshiped in a temple, but God also needs to be worshiped from the heart.

IDOLS

(Luke 16:14-17, he=Jesus, another John, pass used twice, cf. John 8:3-11) Anything can be an idol if you want it more than God's Will. John was troubled when he learned that an artist had made a portrait of him. (Kraeling, TD, 144) John the Baptist taught repentance. He revered the Law. John ben Zebedee followed John the Baptist before Jesus.

18

HOLY NAME

(Luke 21:7-19, he=Jesus, pass, John 16:2) Aland notes that Luke 2112-15=12:11-12. Jesus warns John and the others that they might face prison for his name's sake. Indeed John would be banished to Patmos. He would return to Ephesus safely in time. (McBirnie, STA, 112)

SABBATH

(Luke 14:1-6, Jesus, pass, cf. John 5:14) Aland would note that 41=11:37, 14=6:9 and 14:5=13:15. Jesus calls himself Lord of the Sabbath. It was humorous because Saboath was the Lord's army. (Unger, UBD, 939) Armies gleaned from their crops which they resented.

The Sabbath was to be a day of rest. John was criticized for petting a partridge. He replied that a bowstring is kept loose so that it will have more power when stretched. (Kraeling, TD, 147

PARENTS

(Luke 2:41-52, Jesus, Passover, John 2:16, 7:15) From the cross, Jesus asked John to take care of the Virgin Mary as if she were his mother. He agreed and took her with him to Ephesus. (John 19:26-27) Although it may not have any relation here, John had a protégée which he saved. Many years later John returned to find the man a sinner. He saved him again. This brings up several theological questions.

When Jesus was twelve, his parents took him to Jerusalem to celebrate Passover.He astounded the doctors with his knowledge.

KILL

(Luke 6:6-11, Jesus, pass, John 18:20) Aland notes that Luke 6:8=5:22 an d Luke 6:9=14:3. Some were astounded with the miracles of Jesus. He knew their hearts and knew some were merely being entertained. A man with a withered hand came to Jesus. One legend is that he was from a priestly family. He had cut his own hand so that he would not have to serve as priest. Perhaps he was the Clitus who was later a Christian leader in Rome. Sometimes he was called Anaclitus. Perhaps he was a citizen of Clitae, a city involved in the question of Jews being numbered in a census. (Schurer, HJP, I, 2, 123)

A legend says that when Salome acted as midwife for the Virgin Mary, she doubted and her hand withered. Then she believed and the hand was healed.

John met a young man who had killed his father. He was on his way to kill his paramour and her husband before he killed himself. John restores the father to life. (Kraeling, TD, 146)

ADULTERY

(Luke 7:36-8:1, Jesus, pass, feet, cf John 8:3) Aland notes Luke 7:48-49= 5:20-21 and Luke 7:36=17:19, 18:42. The woman who had been caught in adultery took her precious ointment and anointed Jesus for his burial. Judas Iscariot objected, saying it should have been sold and the money given to the poor. (John 12:5)

Adultery was a part of the worship of Artemis. John was invited to the Temple of Artemis. Although others did not dress in black, he wore the color of mourning. The indignant crowd threatened to kill him. He challenged them to pray that he die because he would be praying to his god for mercy. (Kraeling, TD, 146)

STEAL

(Luke 19:11-27, he=Jesus, pass) Taking riches for ones own self and not caring about the poor keeps one from entering heaven. The thief has something more valuable taken from him, his possible future, eternal life.

One is reminded of John 1:1 which calls Jesus a Word. This parable has many homonyms: Minas=coins, Minyehs=villages, Minyahs=quorum for worship and minim=curses.

John found a youth that he cared for. When he left, he left him in the care of a bishop. The young man became a thief. John returned and forgave him. Durer put a reference to John's favorite verse on a painting of John. It is I John 4:1, "Test the spirits..." (Kraeling, TD, 129, 144)

LIE

(Luke 5:17-26, Jesus, pass, John 10:38) Aland notes that Luke 5:20-21=7:48-49 and Luke 5:22=6:8, 9:47. Either Nicodemus or his brother Ptolemy was carried upon a roof. He was let down in front of Jesus. Jesus first forgave his sins. The crowd called Jesus a blasphemer (liar) because only God can forgive sin. Even so, Jesus healed him.>

COVET

(Luke 16:14-18, he=Jesus, pass, John 19:7) Jesus did not explain the Law the way that the Pharisees did. Some say they "hedged the Torah"; that is, required more than God did. Jesus remnds his followers that God's Law is to be obeyed, not changed.

In the Fourth Century, Prochoros wrote the Apocryphon of John which relates several stories of covetousness. None are more poignant than the request of John to benefit more than his brother. (Matthew 2:20-28)

BIBLIOGRAPHY

Aland, Kurt. The Greek New Testament. United Bible Societies (Nashville:1975)

Barnstone, Willis. The Other Bible. Pb. Harper Collins (San Francisco:1984) Contains the Acts of John.

Berlin, Adele and Marc Zvi Brettler, eds. The Jewish Study Bible. Oxford University Press (New York:2004)

Charlesworth, James and Loren Johns, eds. The Old Testament Pseudepigrapha. 2 vols. (Garden City, New York:1985)

Edersheim, Alfred. The Life and Times of Jesus the Messiah. 2 vols. Wm. B. Eerdmans (Grand Rapids, Michigan:1976)

Guilding, Aileen. The Fourth Gospel and Jewish Worship. Clarendon Press (Oxford:1960)

Hall, Manly P. The Secret Teachings of All Ages. Pb. Pen guin (New York:2003)

Hone, William. Lost Books of the Bible. Bell Publishing (New York:1979)

Kraeling, Emil G. The Disciples. Rand McNally and Company (USA:1966)

McBirnie, William Steuart. The Search for the Twelve Apostles. Pb. Tyndale House Publishers (Wheaton, Illinois:1977)

McClintock and James Strong. Cyclopedia of Biblical, Theological and Ecclesiastical Literature. 12 vols. Baker Book House (Grand Rapids,Michigan:1981)

Mead, G. R. S. The Gnostic John the Baptizer. John M.Watkins (London:1924)

Rambsel, Yacov. His Name Is Jesus. Pb. Word Publishing (Nashville:1999)

Schurer, Emil. A History of the Jewish People in the Time of Christ. Hendrickson (Peabody, Massachusetts:1994)

III. THADDEUS (ADDAI)-JESUS (SHILOH)-ISAIAH

Shiloh was the Jewish central sanctuary before Jerusalem. All the tribes had fought for the Promised Land. Most had been taken before the land was parceled out to the Sons of Jacob at Israel at Shiloh. (cf. Joshua 18:8). Shiloh was the name the coming Messiah would be called. He was prophesied in Deuteronomy 18:18. One of the four sects of Essenes in gospel times was called the Children of Light.

The name Thaddeus is spelled out in ELS from Isaiah 53:12. Other words and phrases in ELS originating from Isaiah 53:12 are Mary, come (roam, wander, like a serpent), Leban, My Holiness, My God, bridegroom, Shiloh, disciple and bread. (Rambsel, HNJ, 16, 24, 29, 35, 36, 37, 44, and 45) Thaddeus was the brother of James. (Luke 6:16) Some homonyms for Thaddeus were "thanks" and "breast". He was also called Lebbaeus (courageous) with"heart" as a homonym.

.... At Bethel the Sons of Jacob (Israel) had been promised the land in four directions. (Genesis 28:14) Utopian freedom from allearthly government was their hope that Shiloh could fulfil. Those who believed that there should be no king were organized as the Fourth Philosophy which may or may not have been the Children of Light. Rome occupied the land, but allowed Herod to rule on many matters. Genesis 49:10 about Shiloh the Temple uses words seeming to authorize the Sceptre and Scroll Society. Theudas is the Greek form of the name Thaddeus. Three with similar names were its masters or leaders: Judas of Galilee, son of Gamaliel, was its first leader. In Aramaic Theudas is a near-homonym for Mathetes (disciple or learner). (Kitto, 853) The second was Thaddeus brother of James, the eyewitness who was the source of this testimony. After the Ascension of Jesus, Thaddeus and Bartholomew went to heal King Abgar of Edessa. He was in Armenia when the third Theudas became leader of the Sceptre and Scroll Society. That Theudas led 400 Jews to the Jordan River, expecting it to part like the Red Sea. They died in the attempt to free Jerusalem from Roman rule. (Acts 5:35-39) One of the main tenets of zealots (barjonim) was that God alone was to be their leader. (Purves, CAA, fn. 50) Herod Agrippa mistakenly identified the third Theudas as James and had James ben Zebedee killed in 44 c.e. (Acts 12:2)

Daniel in Persia had inspired a movement called the Sceptre (King) and the Star (disciple). King Gondophares formerly of Persia ruled in India. He was probably one of the Wise Men who believed that the signs Shiloh had come. His own brother Legion (Fortunatus, Gad) had once been a Theudas (possibly a librarian-astronomer in Persia, Thiering, J&DSS, 214,224), but later he was mentally ill. Jesus cured him at Gadara. (Luke 8:28-35)

Valentinus claimed to be a disciple of Theudas, but one would have to ask which one. (Ehrman, LC, 235) The 600 c.e. version of the Apostles Creed assigns "resurrection of the body" to Jude of James. (Hone, LBB, 91)

Thaddeus was called a physician and sent by Jesus to heal King Abgar of Edessa. (Kraeling, TD, 195-196) Enoch had written a book of medicine which Noah took aboard the Ark. Then in thedays of Hezekiah the book was destroyed. Hezekiah thought the people had made idols of the book and the rod of Moses. (Schurer, HJP, II, 153f and Numbers 2:4-9) Instead of crediting Hippocrates as being the father of medicine, the honor might belong to Hermes. The Emerald Tablet (which may have been his) is a chemical formula. (Hall, STAA, 344) Hermes was better known as a librarian. Many of his books were lost when the Alexandrian Library burned. (Ibid.., 96) Thaddeus either studied medicine at Alexandria where all priests who studied there were or at the Island of Cos, a teaching hospital. Essenes treated with herbs, set bones, advised enemas from gourds, and ate mostly organic vegetables.

The overall unifying word is 'come' as in the Coming One. Genesis 49:10 uses the phrase, 'til Shiloh come'.

PART ONE: STATIONS OF THE CROSS

This is an encomnia (dual biography) about the coming of the Messiah (Shiloh) and Isaiah. In Part One the unifying word are taken from ELS beginning at Isaiah 53:12. A Carrington triad exists for the word 'revealed'. Once Thaddeus had asked Jesus, "Why do you reveal yourself to others and not to us?" (John 14:22) References are made to the Book of Revelations when appropriate. The phrase "said unto them" has been associated with Philip because it appears in the Gospel of Philip. It is so-called because no other name of a disciple appears in it. Philip fathered Jacimus who fathered Thaddeus. Then James the brother of Jesus married the rich widow of Judas of Galilee. (Eisenman, **JJ, 250**) **She** was the Mary of Cleopas who was raised by Joseph of Nazareth. That made Joseph his father-in-law and Thaddeus was brother-in-law to Joseph's son James. Since the Children of Light called their church a brotherhood, they were brothers in church fellowship also. (cf. Luke 6:16)

SUBJECTS (Luke 8:19-21, come, see, Mary, said unto, Isaiah 1:10, Gospel of the Essenes 41, 51, Psalm 19:14) Aland compares Luke 8:19-21 to 11:27-28. Joseph had six children by his first wife Escha. Among them were Jude, the ascribed author of the Book of Jude, and James (Jacob) who became leader of the Circumcision Party in Jerusalem. Since Jude (Thaddeus) was older than the Virgin Mary, he probably was offended by her and her son Jesus. To be turned away would be an additional affront to him.

The central sanctuary for the sons of Jacob was at Shiloh. A prophecy said that Jerusalem would fall because of its sin as Shiloh had fallen for its sin. (Jeremiah 25:5-9) The Messiah would be called Shiloh after an earlier central sanctuary. Genesis 49:10 seems to promise earthly reunion of all of God's people, "The sceptre shall not depart from Judah, nor a lawgiver from beneath his feet until Shiloh come;

and unto him shall the gathering of the people be." (cf. II Samuel 7:16, Acts 1:9, Genesis 3:15) The Coming One is said to return after Daniel's seventieth week in the Old Testament (Psalm 2, Zachariah 14, Isaiah 11) and in the New Testament (Revelation 19:11-16.)

FAMILY (Luke 2:35-52. come, eyes sword, thanks, revealed, doctors, Gen. 28:10, Isaiah 42:6-7. Rev. 14:13, II Maccabees 15:16 (holy sword), said unto, Gospel of the Essenes, 68, Psalm 57:4) Aland notes that Luke 2:38=23:51, Luke 2:40=2:52. The Patriarch Jacob struggled with an angel at Peniel. He saw a vision of a ladder reaching up to heaven. In Egypt, the steps on the sides of a pyramid were called a ladder. Jacob built an altar to God at Beth-el. (Genesis 35:3) The Book of Revelation describes God as up in heaven sitting on a throne and judging

The Children of Light called their gospel the Gospel of Peace. (Szekely, GOE, 52-72) They called thieir church a brotherhood. (Szekely, GOE, 85) Ironically, the desire to put one's feet on the path of peace has often caused revolt. An uprising was led by Judas of Galilee the year that Jesus was twelve. Thaddeus refers to the family of Abraham, Isaac and Joseph. As Eli had recognized Samuel, Samuel recognized David, so Simon recognized the infant Jesus as Shiloh. He uses the word 'sword' a near homonym for 'word'. (cf. Genesis 49:10 and Isaiah 1:10) One should also note I Timothy 5:5.

GENEALOGY (Luke 20:26-38, come, Isaiah 54:6. Abraham, Isaac and Jacob, sword, come, Judges 21:19-21, Revelations 22:11, 7:9-10, Gospel of Essenes 102, Psalm 126:6) Genealogy was important, especially to the Sadducees. In the days of Shiloh, the tribe of Benjamin had been decimated by war. They were allowed to date-rape-marry women at the required festivals. Most of the women were Jews from other tribes, but some were pagans. The descendants of the lineage of David could not claim a pure blood line in gospel times. Jesus was of the lineage of David.

The genealogy of Jesus is given at Luke 3:21-38. Although the Virgin Mary was accused by some of adultery, an angel appeared to Joseph to assure him she was innocent and blessed. (Matthew 1:24) Later Jesus would teach that there is no marriage in heaven. In the meantime, marriages of priests were highly important. Alcemis (Jacimus, Joakim) was the last Zadokite priest (162-159 b.c.). He was taken out of office because of his genealogy. (Jeremias, JTJ, 182) Jacimus was the name of the father of Thaddeus. Using all consonants with a silent J makes for confusion between the names James and Jacimus. Joakim was the name of the father of the Virgin Mary.

SERMON (Luke 4:16-23, come, blind, physician, said unto, Isaiah 61:1-2, 58:6, Gospel of the Essenes 150, Psalm 66:5) Aland notes that Luke 4:18=7:22. The family of Joseph would have been in the service when Jesus preached and said the prophesied day had arrived. Whether or not the revolt was caused by the barjonim, the sons of Joseph would have known the revolt occured. (Luke 4:24-29) Its leader was Judas of Galilee, husband of Mary of Cleopas. James the son of Joseph had married the rich widow of Judas of Galilee. (Eisenman, JBJ) Ebionites claimed this James as the source of their faith. He had been head of the Circumcision Party. Ebionites claimed James the brother of Jesus as their source. Paul showed animosity toward the Children of Light when he said the devil poses as an angel of Light. (II Corinthians 11:14)

MARVEL (Luke 7:19-35. come, blind, said unto, Isaiah 61:1-3, Gospel of Essenes 129, Psalm 103:3)) Aland notes that Luke 7:22=4:18. John the Baptist sent his disciples to see Jesus. Perhaps Thaddeus was the spokesman who asked Jesus if he were the Messiah (Master, Shiloh). Jesus praises John, but accepts his own role. He seems to refer to the Temple at Shiloh that burned. Jesus omits an allusion to the day of vengeance which would refer to God's vengeance inburning that Temple.

FAME (Luke 7:1-18, come, said unto, saw, Joshua 20, Isaiah 26:19, Psalm 115:17, Rev 13:3) A centurion asks Jesus to heal his servant. Often Jesus healed with a touch, but this time he healed from a distance. In his time Hezekiah had feared that the people idolized the Book of Cures. Jesus might have feared that the people think the touch was essential. Only God's Will is essential to His healing.

As Jesus and the disciples are traveling, they meet Leah whose only son if being buried. His importance was that he was the last of the

Hasmonaeans. Leah daughter of Laban was the wife of Jacob, and the sons of that Leah worshiped at Shiloh. Jesus restores Maternus to life. In the years to come, Maternus preached and built a church beyond the Alps. In time Maternus along with three other pupils of Peter in Rome went to Trier to preach. He built a little church beyond the Alps dedicated to the Virgin Mary. (McBirnie, STA, 60-61) He was the sole surviving Hasmonaean. (Jeremias, JTJ, 190)

Thaddeus had a companion in evangelism called Simon Zelotes, son of Joseph of Arimathea. He must have must have met Simon Zelotes as the infant son of Joseph of Arimathea, at the balsam groves. Joseph of Arimathea or his brother Sylleus had hired Simon Magus, the father of Judas Iscariot, to be the overseer of the groves. (Schneemelcher, NTA, I, 555) So it is likely these three of the twelve disciples, Thaddeus, Simon Zelotes and Judas Iscariot, more or less grew up together in Nabatea (Edom).

PROPHECY (Luke 13: 22-30, come, see, Abraham, Isaac and Jacob, I Kings 9:7-8, Rev. 22:11, I Maccabees10:43, Isaiah 41:4, Gospel of the Essenes 87, said unto, Psalm 32:6, Isaiah 55:6) Aland notes that Luke 13:29=14:15. Jesus is asked who will be saved. He answers that the faithful of ancient times will be at the final banquet. The banquet was an important part of Essene worship. Some who know him in the flesh will not be able to come in. He then uses an Essene phrase "first and last". If Alcemis were called the last Zadokite priest relative to time, Jesus could have been called the first relative to importance.

The people expected King Shiloh to come. Some thought either Elijah or John the Baptist was the Coming One (the messiah). Judas Thaddeus relates the teaching of Jesus in two parts, first the fall of Jerusalem and then Jesus's return upon the clouds. His comment about Gentiles reflects that Thaddeus is a Gentile.

LAST WEEK (Luke 22:35-53, sword, come, sight of angel, Isaiah 2:4, Daniel 8:23, Genesis 49:10, Isaiah 53:12, I Mc 9:73, Revelation 7:12, Sirach 35:18, Gospel of the Essenes 138, said unto, Psalm 116:13) Aland finds that Luke 22:36=22:49 and 22:37=22:52. Also Luke 23:48=18:13, Luke 23:49=8:2, Luke 22:49=22:36. Mindful of the scriptures about Shiloh, and Isaiah 53:12, Jesus asks his disciples for readiness and self-sufficiency, not revenge. (Bock, L, II, 1746) Jesus intentionally makes it obvious that his own death when it occurs is God fulfilling prophecy.

Isaiah predicts a time when nation shall not lift up a sword against other nations. Daniel's vision had been of a time when transgressors would rule and stand against the Prince of Princes (the Son of Man).

DEATH (Luke 21:20-28, sword, come, signs of sun and moon, Isaiah 53, Isaiah 65:12-15, 63:18, said unto, Genesis 31:52, Rev 6:12-13, 16:10. II Chronicles 36:1-21, Gospel of the Essenes 94, Psalm 121:6) This passage is heavily dependent on the Book of Daniel. Aland notes that Luke 21:24=Daniel 9:26, 12:7, and Luke 21:27=Daniel 7:13.

Jacob was tricked by his father-in-law Laban. A stack of stone was to be witness that Jacob would not go into Laban's land again. (Genesis 31:52) This was not the altar mentioned in Genesis 28: 10 at Peniel intended to praise God. In the Book of Revelations, the souls of the martyrs ask, "How long..". An ELS for Laban occurs in the same verse as the ELS for Thaddeus. Another name for Thaddeus was Lebbeus.

Again the term Son of Man is used, a term associated with Enoch. Perhaps those who sought to kill Jesus included zealots, but Luke 22:2 cites chief priests and scribes. Jesus promises what is now called the Second Coming. One legend is that Thaddeus used medication to aid the resuscitation of Jesus. (Thiering, JDSS, 397)

A. D. (Luke 24:25-35, come, bread,, eyes, said unto, Isaiah 33:16, Gospel of the Essenes, 159, Psalm 119:18) Aland notes that Luke 24:25-27=17:31 and Luke 24:30=22:19. Thaddeus was the disciple who asked, "Why do you reveal yourself to others and not to us?" (John14:22) At the Ascension, Jesus was revealed to all. After the Resurrection and before the Ascension, Jesus gave the teaching of the scripture. Although Thaddeus was called Adas the teacher, Thaddeus was there. (Gospel of Nicodemus, XIV. 1 in Barnstone, OB, 369)

PART TWO: THE LORD'S PRAYER

This refers to what Thaddeus might have prayed. The Thanksgiving Hymn was written at Qumran. Some near homonyms to the name Thaddeus are 'breasts,', 'thanks', and "praise".

OUR (Luke 4:1-13, return=come back, bread, said unto, Revelation 20:10, Gospel of Essenes 173, Psalm 91:11, 12) The split between "saddok (Sadducees)" over the high tax issue and appointment of priests made the 'sadducee movement' and the Fourth Philosophy compatible if not identical in 4 b.c. (Eisenman, DSS&FC,121-122)

Revelation 7:4-8 lists tribes, the first being Judah. Many Jews were named Judas, including Jude who wrote a book in the Bible, most likely the son of James ben Zebedee. Judas Iscariot was the son of Simon Magus, not Zelotes. Judah as a tribal name means "may he be praised". (Harrison, UNUBD, 719) "Praise" was a synonym for "thanks".

FATHER (Luke 11:5-10, bread, thank, come, revealed, 158, Genesis 35:4, Isaiah 55:6,, Wisdom 2:15, said unto, Gospel of the Essenes 158, 181, Psalm 104;15) Aland notes that Luke 11:8=18:5. As in Luke's account, the Essene gospel teaches that one should love they neighbor as thyself.

Joseph of Nazareth often gave bread to the hungry. On the anniversaries of his death, he was honored by the giving of bread to the poor. He raised Mary of Cleopas as a daughter. By marrying Mary of Cleopas, James became a brother-in-law to Thaddeus, the son of Jacimus. (Luke 6:16) The Essenes or Children of Light called all believers brothers. James was an Ebionite.

NAME (Luke 11:33-36, come, light, said unto, heart, Isaiah 2:5, Gospel of Essenes 78, 185, Psalm 4:6) Aland notes that Luke 11:33=8:16. Thaddeus was a healer, either an Egyptian Zadokite or an Essene. (Thiering, JRDSS, 59, 71) At the trial of Thaddeus, the accusation was in regard to the heading of Psalm 100:1, "A psalm for thanksgiving" which became a reason to "sacrifice Todah (praise)". The decision was based on Psalm 50:23, "Whoso offereth Todah honoreth me." The second half of this verse was apparently ignored. (Dalman, JCT, 72)

Lebonah (frankincense) is the name of a town near Shiloh, so a person whose perspective centered on Shiloh might be called Lebbeus (courageous). (Harrison, NUBD, 767-768) The name Lebbaeus could refer to Laban, the father of Jacob's wife Leah.

KINGDOM (Luke 14:7-15, come, bread, blind, said unto, Isaiah 33:17, Gospel of the Essenes 81, 98, I Mc 1:32, Psalm 22:29) Aland notes that Luke 14:15=13:29, 22:16.When the time came, it was believed that Shiloh would host a Messianic Banquet. As the Jews waited for the Coming One, Jesus told them that he would be coming again on clouds. Clouds symbolyzed armies and multitudes of people, but also God's Judgment Day. (Harrison, NUBD, 243) The people at Qumran called themselves the Many, a word often translated as 'multitude'.

Shiloh was the site of Israel's central sanctuary in the time of Judges. Its history and central location made it ideal for a secret military group like the Sceptre. (Judges 5:14) The scepter-and-sword people may have thought that the Messiah (Shiloh) would come again at Shiloh. A War Scroll was found at Qumran. One report is that the Therapeutae met at Qumran to prepare for war. (Thiering, JTDSS, 59). It is more likely that this was the third Thaddeus, not the second who was a disciple.

EARTH (Luke 9:1-9, come=go, said unto, bread, vision of Herod, Revelation 14:6, Psalm 65:6) Aland notes that Luke 9:4=10:5-7 and Luke 9:5=10:10-11. Thaddeus was one of the twelve so these were instructions from Jesus to them. The word "feet" may allude to yet another ELS which issues from Isaiah 53:12, and relies on Genesis 49:10..

BREAD (Luke 22:14-23, come, thank, bread, behold=look, said in verse 17, cf Genesis 19:3, Isaiah 61:8, I Mc 1:22, Psalm 116:13) Aland notes that 22:19=24:30 Jesus inspired communion when he offers in ceremony, bread for his body and wine for his blood. .

Thaddeus served communion with bread which he said was leavened with that of the Last Supper. (McBirnie, STA, 198) The Treasurer of the Temple (Governor of Edom Joseph of Arimathea or Aretas IV) was in charge of the Holy Lump. After Passover, theoretically no one had any leaven except what came from that single lump that had been saved. Thaddeus may have meant 'spirit' instead of leaven, for Jesus had said, "This is my body" at the Lord's Supper. Later he had risen.

The Old Covenant required that on the first day of the seventh month, Jews were to celebrate an additional Sabbath by the blowing of horns. The trumpets were to announce the prophecy about the regathering of Israel. (Isaiah 18:3, 27:13 (in context), all of chapter 58 and Joel 2:1-3:21) Some of these ideas are in the War Scroll. There seems to be no separation of promise for Jews and Gentiles.

Melchisedek had performed the equivalent of the Lord's Supper. (Hall, STAA, 583)

Students under Pythagoras studied Melchisedek. Pythagoras sought to relate theology and scholasticism. (Hall, STAA, 27)

EVIL (Luke 11:10-13, "come to you", said unto in verse 5, Isaiah 1:23, Gospel of the Essenes 38, Psalm 68:5, Rev 6:12,) Thirsty children traveling in the desert were given stones to suck on. It seemed to relieve the thirst. In the desert, the stones appeared to be loaves of bread, but they were not. The fish was the sign of the Christian and the serpent the sign of the devil. One religious sect compared the creation to the hatching of a giant egg. If someone asks about that, to give him a scorpion (whipping) would not be a good answer.

FORGIVE US (Luke 15:1-7 re 5:30, come=draw near, said unto, eat, heaven, Psalm 119:176) Aland notes that 15:2=7:34. With his background, Thaddeus once thought that Israel needed military salvation. Jesus asked him to be patient and let God win the victory over sin and death..

"As the Israelites stood assembled at the foot of Mount Sinai to enter into their solemn covenant with God, there suddenly descended from heaven and remained suspended beside it, one of the Sword. 'Choose!' commanded the Bat Kol from heaven. 'You can have one or the other, but not both-either the Book or the Sword! If you choose the Book, you must renounce the Sword. Should your choice be the Sword, the Book will perish." (Ausubel, BJK, 39)

AS WE FORGIVE (Luke 7: 30-35, come, bread, said, cf. Isaiah 35:5, the whole Gospel of the Essenes, Psalm 60:1) Thaddeus belonged to the Children of Light. Their gospel of peace shows reverence for life, beauty and nature. God is their Creator. (Szekely, GE, in passim.)John comes along asking people to repent. Jesus comes for those that need a physician. (Luke 5:31-32) The general public is blind and does not appreciate either.

AMEN (Luke 24:18-24, come, bread, said unto, 17:11-19, stranger, thank, come, feet, Lev 13:46, I Esdras 4:60, Gospel of Essenes19, 24, Psalm 78:25) Aland notes that Luke 24:21=2:38. According to the Essene Gospel, the most ancient revelation was when God spoke to man. The name of the stranger was Allogenes. (Robinson, NHL, 490) Since James married Mary of Cleopas, he may have been one of the two. He told Jesus he would eat bread with him after the.resurrection if it occurred. When Jesus saw him again, he said, "Bring the table."

PART THREE: THE TEN COMMANDMENTS

The Gospel of the Essenes (page 41) translates all Ten Commandments, so the reader can know that they believed all ten to be the word of God. The key word for Part Three is "disciples" found in ELS for Isaiah 53:12, which Yakov Rambsel found was the same beginning verse as for the ELS of the name Thaddeus. The Aramaic form of Theodotus is Mathetes, a homonym for the Hebrew word disciple. (Kitto, 853) The phrase "said unto them" is associated elsewhere with the disciple Philip. (Isenberg, NHL, 138) One twenty-first century denomination of Christians calls itself the Disciples of Christ.

ONE GOD

(Luke 11:1-4, come, said unto, bread, disciples, Psalm 72:15) Aland notes that Luke 11:l = 5:33. James had a throne which he stood before to pray. He prayed so much that he had "camel knees". That was an allusion to his wife's first husband, Judas of Galilee, son of Gamaliel (camel). Essenes prayed to the East, the rising of the Sun. Other Jews faced in the direction toward the Temple at Jerusalem. Jesus offers the short form of a prayer. Its original form was used on the anniversary of the death of a loved one. When the Apostles reed was formed, the phrase associated with Thaddeus was "life everlasting.

IDOLS

(Luke 10:1-12, come, said unto,disciples, Isaiah 57:21, Psalm 35:13) Aland notes that Luke 10:5-7=9:4 and Luke 10:10-11=9:5.Thaddeus was one of the twelve disciples, but Jude, son of James ben Zebedee, was one of the seventy.

To avoid breaking the law against idols, Essenes took what developed into the vow of poverty.

HOLY NAME

(Luke 5:30-35, disciple, come, eat, physician, said unto, Ex 20:3, Isaiah 62:5, Psalm 19:5, Tobit 14:7). Thaddeus was a healer who refused to take silver and gold in payment. (Kraeling, TD, 207) The woman Jesus healed had spent all her living on doctors. (Colossians 4:14) Thaddeus's ancestor Hezir was named for Hezekiah. Hezekiah destroyed Moses's bronze serpent and Book of Cures. Instead of praising God, he thought his people were simply worshiping objects including Moses staff and a book of cures. (Numbers 21:4, II Kings 18:4)

SABBATH

(Luke 6:1-5, come, disciples, said unto, showbread, cf, Psalm 132:15) Ebionites recognized the second Sabbath as a makeup day for those who had not worshiped on the Sabbath. Jesus took (harvested) grain on that day. The listeners would know that Sabaoth meant "armies". Farmers resented armies that fed themselves on their unharvested crops.

PARENTS

(Luke 14:25-33, disciple, come, Exodus 20:12, cf Numbers 14:18, Isaiah 8:16, Psalm 27:10) Aland notes that Luke 14:26=18:29. Jesus demanded first allegiance. Otherwise followers could not become disciples. When Tiberius was told about this, he became angry. The Roman people respected their parents.

KILL

(Luke 21:7-19, come, heart, sign, said unto, disciples,Isaiah 19:2, 9:15, Revelation 6:5, 6, 12, Gospel of the Essenes 213, Psalm 37:19) Aland notes that Luke 21:12=12:11. Jesus warns his disciples that they might be betrayed and killed. Their souls will be safe.

Thaddeus died on Mount Ararat tied to a cross. He was stabbed by a javelin and/or arrows. (McBirnie, STA, 202) This was not known at the time Luke was written.

ADULTERY

(Luke 18:9-15, come, thank, breast, said unto, Isaiah 10:6, Psalm 35:16, Gospel of the Essenes 62,) Aland notes that Luke 18:13=23:48 and Luke 18:14=14:11. James thanks God that he is not like the adulterers.

STEAL

(Luke 16:1-9, told to come, said unto, disciples, Isaiah 42:22, Psalm 23:5, Gospel of Essenes 81, Enoch 63:10) The persons Thaddeus wanted to save may have been thiefs.

LIE

(Luke 12:1-12, disciples, come, leaven, said unto , Exodus 20:13, Isaiah 28:15-18, Psalm 49:16, I Macc 1:1) Aland notes that Luke 12:11=21:12, Luke 12:11-12=21:14-15 and Luke 12:7=21:18. Hypocrisy is the leaven of the Pharisees. Jesus tells the disciples not to fear those who might kill them as much as they fear God. Judas Thaddeus and Simon Zelotes were in Parthia (Persia). They approached the Babylonian General Varadach. He said he would listen to their prediction about salvation after a battle the next day. Simon told him that at the third hour on the morrow he would have good news. His diviners had predicted bad news. Even so, it was as Simon said. The general ordered a fire to burn the false diviners, but Judas and Simon protested that they wanted to bring salvation to all, including the diviners. (Kraeling, TD, 210)

COVET

(Luke 12:15-34, come=many years, disciples, eat, Revelation 1:6, Gospel of Essenes 206-207, Psalm 49:15, 16) Aland notes that Luke 12:24=12:7. Although James was not rich in his own right, his wife was rich. Jesus preached this sermon about Solomon's riches which is very much like another sermon found in the Gospel of the Essenes.

BIBLIOGRAPHY FOR THADDEUS (ADDAI)

Aland, Kurt, ed. et al. The Greek New Testament. American Bible Society (New York:1975)

Ausubel, Nathan. The Book of Jewish Knowledge. Crown Publishers (New York:1964)

Barnstone, Willis, ed. The Other Bible. Harper Collins (San Francisco:1971)

Bock, Darrell L. Luke. 2 vols. Baker Book House (Grand Rapids, Michigan:1996)

Bromiley, Geoffrey W. The International Standard Bible Encyclopedia. 4 vols.

William B. Eerdmans Publishing Company (Grand Rapids, Michigan:1979)

Charlesworth, James H. and Loren L. Johns, eds. Hillel and Jesus. Fortress press (Minneapolis::1997)

Dalman, Gustaf et al. Jesus Christ in the Talmud, Midrash, Zohar and the Liturgy of the Synagogue. Deighton, Bell and co. (New York:1893)

Ehrman, Bart D. Lost Christianities. Oxford University Press. (New York:2003)

Edersheim, Alfred. The Life and Times of Jesus the Messiah. 2 parts. Wm. B. Eerdmans Publishing Company (Grand Rapids, Michigan:1976)

Eisenman, Robert. James the Brother of Jesus. Viking Press (New York:1996)

"Epistles of Jesus Christ and King Abgarus of Edessa" in Lost Books of the Bible.

Hall, Manly P. The Secret Teachings of All Ages. Pb. Penquin (New York:2003)

Harrison, R. K., ed. The New Unger"s Bible Dictionary. Moody Press (Chicago:1988)

Hastings, James, ed. Dictionary of the Bible. 5 vols. Charles Scribner's Sons (New York:1909)

Hengel, Martin. The Zealots. T & T Clark (Edinburgh:1989)

Isenberg, Wesley W., tr. "The Gospel of Philip" in Robinson, James M.,ed., The Nag Hammadi Library in English. Harper & Row (New York:1988), pp. 139-160.

Jeremias, Joachim. Jerusalem in the Time of Jesus. Pb. Fortress Press (Philadelphia:1969)

Josephus. Complete Works. William Whiston, tr. Kregel (Grand Rapids, Michigan:1985)

Kitto, The History of Palestine. Adam and Charles Black (Edinburgh:1853)

Kraeling, Emil G. The Disciples. Rand-McNally (USA:1966)

Lawlor, John Irving. The Nabateans in Historical Perspective. Pb. Baker Book House (Grand Rapids, Michigan:1974)

McBirnie, William Stewart. The Search for the Twelve Apostles. Pb. Tyndale House Publishers (Wheaton, Illinois:1977)

McClintock, John and James Strong. Cyclopedia of Biblical, Theological and Ecclesiastical Literature. 12 vols. Baker Book House (Grand Rapids, Michigan:1981)

Pick, Bernard. The Life of Jesus According to Extra-Canonical Sources. John B.

Alden, Publisher (New York:1887)

Hultgren, Arland J., ed. The Earliest Christian Heretics. Pb. Fortress Press (Minneapolis:1996)

Rambsel, Yacov. His Name is Jesus. Word Publishing (Nashville:1999)

Robinson, James H. The Nag Hammadi Library. Harper & Row (San Francisco: 1978)

Schneemelcher, Wilhelm. New Testament Apocrypha. 2 vols. James Clarke (Westminster:1992)

Schurer, Emil. A History of the Jewish People. Hendrickson (Peabody,

Massachusetts:1994)

Szekely, Edmond Bordeaux. The Gospel of the Essenes. Pb. Saffron Walden (USA:1974)

Thiering, Barbara. Jesus and the Riddle of the Dead Sea Scrolls. pb. (HarperSanFrancisco:1992)

IV. THOMAS BEN BOETHUS-JESUS-JOB (TROUBLE)

Since the name Thomas means 'trouble' and Didomi can mean 'twin', Thomas could be one of two disciples. The name of Bartholomew is on one list, and Nathanael on the other as the twin, so the name Thomas may very well be used to intend either one. Cantheras (Akantha=thorn) was one of the last Priests of an order (Josephus,414) Nevertheless Herod the Great imported his descendant, Simon ben Boethus to be High Priest (22-25 B.C., Jeremias, JTJ, 377) Both of Simon's sons Joezer and Eleazar ben Boethus served as High Priest in Jerusalem before 5 B.C. (Ibid.) The Equidistant Lettering Sequence begins at Isaiah 53:2 for Thomas, and other words that their ELS begins at that verse are Joseph, Levites, Job (trouble, suffer=didomi), and Prophets of God. (Rambsel, HNJ, 8, 17, 39, 40, 45) Thomas is herein Eleasar (Lazarus), brother to Joseph (Joezer) Levi, a former high priest and son of Simon ben Boethus, also a High Priest. Their educational background was at the temple at Alexandria, Egypt. With Osiris as a god pattern, reincarnation and salvation by the divine were already accepted in Egypt. The Jews were divided on all three beliefs.

Since Simon's daughter was a marriageable age in Egypt, Thomas grew up in Egypt even though of Babylonian descent. In Egypt, Naasene doctrine concerning the Trinity faces the same questions Job faced. Two words used in this testimony (touch and kiss) translate from

Nashaq (sounds like serpent). Egyptians taught that man's only hope is to become androgenous. Jews blamed the serpent in Eden for trouble. Chaldeans taught that Noah was androgenous like Seth. (Blavatsky, IU, II, 413) Others claim that the Holy Spirit is female and wants to be revealed to mankind. The male as expressed by the Hebrew Jehovah tries to conceal truth in order to control mankind. Marcion in Egypt knew the Naasene doctrine. (Hastings, DOB, Extra, 425) Isis beguiled Osiris in Egyptian lore by making a serpent to poison him. (Budge, EBD, lxxxix-xci) The testimony of Thomas is that the three members of the Trinity are one and the same. (Schneemelcher, NTA, I, 455) In contrast, Nestorians centuries later taught that Christ had a physical body with two (twin) natures (human and divine). (Ferguson, EEC, 645)

PART ONE: STATIONS OF THE CROSS

This is a dual biography about Job (Trouble) and Jesus. The word touch (kiss) refers to Nashaq and the Naasenes. Job (trouble) has the a letter in same verse for the beginning of its ELS as the verse for name Thomas. (Rambsel, HNJ, 8, 24, 25). Job believed and served God, but he did not understand why bad things happen to good people. Temptation for vengeance and resentment are part of the human experience. Jesus says that it is not trouble that determines our futures, but our response to the trouble.

SUBJECTS (Luke 7:11-18, touch, arose, trouble, Job 3, I Kings 17:17) Aland notes that Luke 7:12=8:42. Egyptians focused on the meaning of death in the Egyptian Book of the Dead. They believed in the resurrection of Osiris who rose from death to become king of the underworld and judge of the dead. (Budge, ER, 61) When Jesus rose from the dead, they would have no trouble believing he did. The problem for the Jews was separating him from Osiris a pagan god.

God has agreed with Satan that he can test Job, but not to the death.

Satan said to God, "Put forth thine hand now, and touch all that he hath, and he will curse you to your face." In due time, God blessed

Job more at the end than at the beginning. (Job 42:12-15) God gave his daughters as well as his sons an inheritance.

Jesus met a funeral procession and took pity on the widowed mother named Leah. He raised Maternus from the dead. As Elijah had when he raised the son of a widow woman (I Kings 17:17), Jesus showed his divine power. He would raise Lazarus (Eleasar) after he was three days in a tomb.

FAMILY (Luke 18:1-17, trouble, touch, heaven, Job 1:21, Log 22) Aland notes that Luke 18:5=11:7-8. Jesus tells of a woman who has faced injustice for a long time. For example, Elizabeth's personal property was confiscated when her husband Zechariah was killed. Because of her patience and persistence, the property was eventually restored by Felix.

Job was told of several tragedies in Job 1. He says, "Naked came I out of my mother's womb, and naked shall I return thither: the Lord gave, and the Lord taketh away; blessed be the name of the Lord."

The people brought infants for Jesus to touch them. He said that those who entered heaven entered with the faith of a child.

GENEALOGY (Luke 1:1-59, trouble, perfect, seed, touch, arise, Job 1:1) Aland notes that Luke 1:28, 42, 48=11:27. Job was perfect. The Naasene or Kabbalistic approach was to blame women for evil. Indeed Herodias could be blamed for the beheading of John. However, the death of Jesus was a blessing to mankind. As the Patriarch Joseph once said, "God meant for good what mankind meant for evil." (Genesis 50:20) Celibacy was a step in the right direction. The Naasene belief was that becoming androgenous was a step of faith. Seth was not born of woman, and Sethites claimed Noah was descended from Seth. (Blavatsky, IU, II, 459)

The virgin birth was predicted by the translators of the Bible at Alexandria. As Samuel had been a gift from God, Jesus was a gift from God. Mary sings Hannah's song.

At Alexandria, the teachings of Osiris were also embedded in song to make them easier to remember. (Budge, ER, 65) John the Baptist was born at summer solstice, and Jesus at winter solstice. (Darlison, GTZ,

30) In the time of Moses, the winter solstice brought a prediction that caused the Pharoah to order midwives to kill Jewish sons.

Job lived in the land of Uz. Possibly this was on Mount Seir. (Peloubet, PBD, 716) He was an upright man, perfect, one who feared God and eschewed evil. A surviving quotation from the Naasenes is, "The knowledge of man is the beginning of perfection, and the knowledge of God is perfection accomplished." (Petrement, ASG, 116)

Naasenes gave Seth special consideration because he was not born of woman.

Jesus was born of woman, but not born of fornication. When the Septuagint Bible was translated at Alexandria, Egypt, Isaiah 7:14 was translated 'born of a virgin'. The Hebrew Bible was translated 'born of a young woman.' The Virgin Mary was told that her kinswoman Elizabeth who had been barren was now with child. It was said that the hand of an angel brought Mary bread and wine three years before Christ was born. (Schneemelcher, NTA, I, 544-545) She was probably twelve. The child to be born to Elizabeth and Zacharias was John. He would turn the hearts of the fathers to their children. (Malachi 4:5) Zacharias said that this was the Lord's doing.

SERMON (Luke 8:4-15, sow seed=touch, wither, thorn, Job 21:7-9, Log 24) Aland notes that Luke 8:8=14:35. The quotation, "He that has ears to hear, let him hear", recall a time that the ears of some Levitical Jews were cut off so that they might not ever serve as priests again. (Harrison, NUBD, 796) Job questions why the wicked seem to flourish while God does nothing. His friends believe in divine retribution and have said that God is punishing Job for his sin. Job asks God to reveal to him his sin.

Osiris "sowed seed" when he taught the Egyptians how to cultivate and improve fruits of the earth, how to rule by law and how to pay reverence to the gods. (Budge, ER, 64) Basically Osiris taught cause-effect but Jesus introduces the idea of being gifted (promise and chance).

Jesus also tells the Parable of Sowing Seed. Several homonyms occur: fowls=Arabians and Assyrians, rock=Petra or Tyrus, moisture=baptism, thorns=name Cantheras.

MARVEL (Luke 8:40-56, trouble, touch, hand, arise, Job 14:1)

Aland notes that Luke 8:42=7:12, Luke 8:48=17:19, 7:50 and 18:42 and Luke 8:56=5:14. Job states that any man born of woman has few days and those are full of trouble. Job's children died, but in time, he had other children. (Job 42:13)

Bernice (Veronika) had tried to get help from many physicians. When she touched the hem of the garment Jesus wore, technically she sinned. Even so, that hem had a fringe tied with knots, each tied while a scriptural promise was recited. Jesus said, "Thy faith hath made thee whole. Go in peace." Works like Pistis Sophia praised revelation and not just legalistic obedience to the law. (cf Schneemelcher, NTA, I, 361ff)

Jair was the son of Eleazar ben Hyrcanus and Imma Shalom of Bathyra. If so, he was a nephew to Joezer ben Boethus, another name for Thomas. When Lazarus died, Thomas said, "Let us also go that we may die with him." (John 11:16) Jairus asks Jesus to heal his daughter. Friends said she was dead, but they were as mistaken as the friends of Job.

The healing of the daughter of Jairus has many of the same details as an Oriental tale about the God Krishna. (Blavatsky, IU, II, 241-242) When the Seventy translated the Bible at Alexandria, they gathered religious books from many nations. The behavior of a god was described in scripture in many lands. This is consistent if God had tried to reach mankind over and over, but that until Jesus, it was not successful. In the Book of the Dead, Set (Seth?) hacks the body of Osiris. (Budge, ER, 101)

FAME (Luke 5:12-26, rise up, touch, hand, Job 42:11-12) Aland notes that Luke 5:14=8:56, Luke 5:20-21=7:48-49 and Luke 5:22=6:8. Simon ben Boethus became a high priest in Jerusalem after Herod the Great had killed Mariamne the Hasmonaean. Herod wanted to replace her with Simon ben Boethus's daughter Mariamne. Herod made Simon High Priest to give him more prestige. (Jeremias, JTJ, 69) First her brothers were former High Priests Eleazar and Joezer, then Herod made her father High Priest. One recalls the restitution of Job's family.

Thomas was a carpenter, and he may have been kin to Ptolemy, brother of Nicodemus. Cana was the hometown of Thomas, and Jesus performed a miracle at the wedding in Cana. (John 4:47) God asked Job, "where were you when…the morning stars sang together…" Egyptians looked to the heavens to see the serpent dragon that they thought determined their fate. (Doresse, SBEG, 51)

PROPHECY (Luke 11:5-13, serpent, trouble, Job 19:21) Aland notes that Luke 11:7-8=18:5. Job asks for mercy, "Have pity upon me. Have pity upon me, O ye my friends, for the hand of God has touched me."

Jesus taught that his followers should ask God to supply their needs. In the second part of the teaching, there is a play on words. Boys were told to put stones in their mouths in the desert to placate the feeling of thirst. The word fish meant Christian, and the letter A (alpha) looked like a fish when it was drawn in the sand. If a son asks for a Christian, would his father give him a scribe (tannaim=serpent)? If he asks for an egg, the Hindu symbol of infinite chaos and darkness, (Blavatsky, IU, I, 91), will he give him a scorpion (whipping)?

LAST WEEK (Luke 13:29-35, kiss, perfect, Job 1:1) Aland notes that Luke 13:29=14:15.

Judas Iscariot identified Jesus with a kiss (touch). Someone cut the ear of Malchus, son of Aretas IV. Jesus touched the ear and healed it. As God had not allowed Satan to kill or maim Job, Jesus did not allow Malchus to be harmed on his behalf.

Jesus taught that the patriarchs of old would sit at the banquet. People would come to it from the four directions. Jesus invited all others after the chosen ones had chosen not to come. Samaritans were not allowed to attend worship services at the Temple in Jerusalem. During the exile of many to Babylon, they had intermarried with Gentiles.

Twin pillars at the entrance of Christian churches do not deliberately refer to Gemini, the sign of the twins, but other temples used twin pillars to do so. (Hall, STAA, 159)

DEATH (Luke 23:46-53, body, smote breasts, righteous=perfect, Job 1:1) Aland notes that Luke 23:51=2:25, 38. Longinus, the centurion, called Jesus a righteous man. The people grieved. Joseph of Arimathea wrapped the body in linen that had once covered the scriptures. (Lightfoot, CNT, III, 214)

Eleazar ben Hyrcanus (Lazarus) was brother to Mary and Martha, friends of Jesus. When he died, they sent for Jesus. It was Thomas (Joezer?) who asked, "Let us go also that we may die with him. (Eleazar=Lazarus)" (John 11:16) The rich man in hell may have been a Herodian or a member of the Chanina family because of his having five brothers. Eleazar (who could be called Thomas) was asked to bring him some water. Then Jesus says that justice which is not given in this life may be served after death. God's way is not mankind's way. Eleazar is returned to life, and it is said that he lived to be sixty years old. The allusion to leprosy may be a clue to the sound of the family name of Sirach or Asira. Despite his trouble, Job lived to see the fourth generation, 140 years.

AFTER THE DEATH (Luke 6:43-49, thorn, trouble, mouth, Job 42;16)

Jesus taught that the heart which is good brings forth good. Those who build on temporal things, which are like sand, may face disaster as a house built on sand. As a builder, Thomas was aware of the necessity of better foundations on sand.

Egyptians thought Osiris controlled the flow of the waters of the Nile. It was both the bane of Egyptian existence and a blessing. Their crops depended on the Nile. When Moses claimed to make the water flow red because his God had caused it. Pa-Ramses called his bluff. He knew seasonal red water in the Nile was natural. (Osman, CAER, 163) Since Moses believed in God as a god of history, this was not a problem to him.

PART TWO THE LORD'S PRAYER

This is as if Thomas the Eyewitness (Luke 1:2) were praying. The unifying word in Part two is finger or hand with a sub-theme of death. It is said that Thomas added to the Apostles Creed, "He descended into hell, the third day he rose again from the dead." (Blavatsky, IU, II, 514)

OUR (Luke 24:50-53, hands, heaven) Simon ben Boethus (one of the seventy) lived at Nob Hill or Bethany the estate provided for Samuel and his progeny. Simon's children included at least two sons, the daughter Mary who married Matthias (Zacchaeus), and the daughter Martha who married Joshua ben Gamla. They were called the Bethany Band. (McBirnie, STA, 289) Possibly also living there was the Mary who married Herod the Great but returned to Bethany after his death. Simon ben Boethus took in Joseph of Arimathea and his son Simon Zelotes when Joseph was replaced as Governor of Edom.

Jesus ascended into the heavens at Bethany with his hands held high.

FATHER (Luke 2:25-38, arms, Isaiah 9:6) Simon ben Boethus was father to Eleazar (Lazarus), Joezer, Mary and Martha. He naturally had little jug-ears which reminded all of the Maccabaean plight when their enemies cut off their ears. It made them unfit to be priests. Nevertheless Simon ben Boethus, a descendant of Cantheras, was made High Priest in Jerusalem because Herod the Great wanted to marry his daughter Mariamne. Simon or Symeion blessed the infant Jesus. (Josephus, 414)

Anna also had a revelation of the true identity of the infant Jesus. She was from the tribe of Asher which may mean Asira. The passage Luke 18:1-8 may refer to her. The Asira family of Tiberias is believed to be associated with the use of ELS.

NAME (Luke 16:19-31, finger, hell) Eleazar ben Boethus was High Priest around 4 b.c. (Jeremias, JTJ, 377) When Herod Archelaus came into power, he accused Joazar ben Boethus of sedition and gave his office of high priest to his brother Eleazar. (Josephus, 375) Within a year, Eleazar too was replaced. As Eleazar ben Hyrcanus he married Imma Shalom, and they named their son Jair. No reason is given for his death. (John 11:1-44) Upon hearing of his brother's death, Thomas (Joezer) said, "Let us also go that we may die with him." (John 11:16) In Malabar of India, Bartholomew is remembered by folk-songs and Thomas remembered for his martyrdom . (McBirnie, STA, 158)

The story of Jesus's Descent into Hell is attributed to Charinus and Lenthius, also called sons (followers?) of Simon ben Boethus. ("Gospel of Nicodemus", LBB, 80) Lenthius may be Longinus. Longinus was the centurion who called Jesus righteous after his crucifixion. (Luke 23:47)

KINGDOM (Luke 11:14-20, finger, heaven, Log 22) Jesus taught that Beelzebub (Satan) was strong, but that the finger of God was more powerful.

The Bible translation made in Egypt during the third or second centuries b.c. was not accepted in Jerusalem. Some Egyptian Christians like Marcion in Alexandria were filled with hate for the Jews. From hate the Samaritans refused to share their text of the Old Testament scriptures. They accepted most prophets. Jerusalem had scriptures, but no proof they had not been tampered with. Even so, both Jerusalem and Alexandrian translations were known at the Babylonian-exile academy at Bathyra (Araq el-Emir) led by Hillel and Gamaliel. Jesus would say that he kept the original intent.

The Trinity according to John is closest to that of Thomas. (John 1:1-2) Dositheos, a Samaritan, wrote the Three Stelae of Seth, a Revelation. Simon Magus, father of Judas Iscariot, was once a disciple of one Dositheos. (Doresse, SBEG, 188-189)

Marcion may have confused the Judaism of Samaria and that of Jerusalem.

EARTH (Luke 11:42-52, finger, sepulcre) Jesus noted that they had not lifted a finger to support those carrying heavy loads. When a load becomes unbalanced on one's head or back, another could easily rebalance it. Jesus refers to the keys of knowledge. Scripture was placed on scrolls which were wound up. To make it easier to unroll them when being held up to be read, a long stick with a knobbed end was used. It was called God's finger. The thought of death was everpresent. Elkesaites expressed disapproval by the pointing of the finger. Sometimes a ruler pointing a finger meant death.

BREAD (Luke 7:36-50, kiss, feet, prophet) Aland notes that Luke 7:36=11:37 and Luke 7:48-49=5:20-21. One of Simon ben Boethus's daughters married Herod the Great. That Mary was sister or stepsister to Eleazar (Lazarus) and Joezer. The presence of a Simon is mentioned when she anointed the feet of Jesus in whom she had faith. Judas said the perfume should have been sold to feed the poor. Jesus replied that the perfume was against the day of his burying. (John 12:7-8) Egyptians took elaborate care of their dead.

EVIL (Luke 15:11-32, kiss, arise, heaven, hand) Joseph of Arimathea (Obodas II) was part of the Bethany Band. Although every detail does not fit, Joseph was the younger brother of Sylleus. Sylleus was the older brother who refused to marry Herod the Great's sister Alexandra Salome, the Queen of Edom. Joseph married her. As Governor of Edom, Joseph was Treasurer of the Temple at Jerusalem. He neglected his duties in Nabatea and in Jerusalem. He traveled many years and thus improved the economic status of Edom. In time Sylleus wanted to take his brother's wife and kingdom, so he had him declared dead. (Lawlor, NHP, 91-118)

FORGIVE US (Luke 24:36-48, hands, trouble, handle=touch) Thomas finds himself accepted even though he doubted and went away from the other disciples for a time. Job found peace within himself after he humbled himself. John reports that Thomas said he would not believe unless he saw Jesus alive with nailprints. (John 20:24-25)

Luke reports that Thomas did see the hands and his life shows that he believed.

AS WE FORGIVE (Luke 8:26-39, torment=trouble, feet, madness) Aland notes that Luke 28=4:34. Thomas forgave Fortunatus and went to India with him. Earlier Thomas had believed that illness (madness) was divine retribution. Fortunatus (Legion, Troop) had a name that recalled history. Zilpah, the maid of Jacob's wife, had a son by Jacob. Leah said, "A troop (legion) cometh", and she named him Gad saying she was happy (fortunate). (Genesis 30:11-13) Fortunatus, the brother of King Gundaphorus of India, was one of the Wise Men. (Schneemelcher, NTA, II, 345-347)

In India, the King would ask Thomas to build a palace for him. Being a disciple he gave some of the funds away, but Fortunatus convinced his brother that Thomas was building him a home in heaven. Perhaps as Wise Men, the brothers had come to Gadara looking for the Christ Child. Whether by natural disaster or torture, Fortunatus had gone mad. (Schneemelcher, NTA, II, 197, 199f) Years later, Fortunatus allowed the corpse of Drusiana to be defiled. He died from snakebite.

Drusiana was raised from the dead, and she begged that Fortunatus be raised from the dead again. As the years passed, he was snake-bitten several times and died from the last. John said, "Devil, thou hast thy son." (Schneemelcher, NTA, 200-201)

AMEN (Luke 6:6-11, hand, wither, arise, madness) Josephus tells of an event at Tiberias. Joseph of Nazareth once worked there, and his son Joseph Justus went to the academy there. Josephus says that Pistis (Faith)'s son had had his hands cut by the Galileans. (Josephus, 9) Herod Agrippa II employed Joseph to help him write a history, but Joseph was also writing a history of his own . He wrote of the Kings of Israel. Joseph was accused of extortion and murder, but Bernice persuaded Herod Agrippa II to help him. (Josephus, 17, 20) As an irony of fate, in 37 c.e. Joseph Justus was in Rome to testify for Herod Agrippa II.

Possibly Mark Kolobodactylis was cured by Jesus. He did not wish to be a priest under certain conditions, so it was said that he had severed a nerve in his own hand. (Josephus, 9) Mark Kolobodactylis invited Christians to Pella when Jerusalem fell.

One legend says that he later went to Rome and served Christ as Clitus or Anaclitus.

PART THREE THE TEN COMMANDMENTS

Luke only has the phrase "ears to hear' in two places, but it can be found in Luke many times associated with other teachings from the Gospel of Thomas. (Guillamont, in passim.) Legend says that Matthias (Zacchaeus) was the one who wrote down what Thomas said Jesus said. The relevant Logion number is given below.

ONE GOD

(Luke 14:34-35, ears to hear, rhetorical question, Exodus 20:3, Logion 9,8,21, etc., Isaiah 6:9,10) Aland notes that Luke 14:35=8:8. A pun exists between salt and praise. If praise does not reflect the heart, it is fit only to be shouted (cast out as dung).

IDOLS

(Luke 21:1-4, ears to hear, rhetorical question, Exodus 20:4, Logion 38) The receptacles for money for charity were shaped like ears. It prevented givers from retrieving their gifts. While others like Annas were condemning the coins with images, she just gave.

HOLY NAME

(Luke 12:1-7, ears to hear, rhetorical question, Exodus 20:7, Logion 33, Psalm 49:16...) Aland notes that Luke 12:2=8:17. Beware of hypocrisy which uses the Holy Name without having the spirit along with obedience. Fear the one who can cast you into hell.

A pun exists between sparrows and Assyrians.

SABBATH

(Luke 12:31-34, ears to hear, rhetorical question, heaven, Exodus 20:8, Logion 27...) The Sabbath was a time of preparation for the coming of the Savior. Believers have their treasure in heaven. Samaritans called their scriptures the treasure.

PARENTS

(Luke 11:27-28, womb, Exodus 20:12, Logion 99) True followers are those who hear the word and keep it. These words were first said about Eleasar ben Hyrcanus's mother, but in this instance refer to the Virgin Mary.

KILL

(Luke 13:6-9, ears to hear, dung, rhetorical question, Exodus 20:13, Logion 8,40, Isaiah 5:1-7) Again there is a reference to the third year. The meaning seems to be lost opportunity. If a plant does not bear fruit, it should be cut down. Israel is that plant. However, the Gospel of Thomas relates more often to individuals than to governments. (John

1:45) Reading under the fig tree should be reminding Thomas to act on what he has learned.

ADULTERY

(Luke 8:16-21, ears to hear, ask, Log 5, Psalm 90:8) Aland notes that Luke 8:17=12:2, cf. 8:18. Passion can be compared to a fire. Often the mattress on a bed was stuffed with hay. Trouble could come quickly if a lit candle were placed under the bed. When the virgin Mary was accused of adultery, some said Panthera, a Roman soldier was father to Jesus. Others said Panthera was an Alexandrian priest who had befriended the Holy Family in Egypt. The name Pantheras may have been an error for Cantheras, an ancestor of High Priest Boethus. (Eisenman, DSSFC. 53) Boethus said that Mary was still a virgin.

STEAL

(Luke 20:9-19, ears to hear, rhetorical question, Exodus 20:15, Logion 65, 66, Isaiah 5:1-7) Josephus gives a similar vineyard story. Philip, the son of Jacimus, a governor under Agrippa, was in a foreign land. He needs money and sends to Agrippa and Bernice for help. They have temporarily left their estate in the hands of Varus. Varus kills the messengers Philip sent, for he hopes to become governor himself. Eventually Philip, Agrippa and Bernice all return. Varus is removed. (Josephus, 3-4)

LIE

(Luke 14:16-24, ears to hear, rhetorical question, to taste, Exodus 20:16, Logion 64, Isaiah 30:15) Thomas did not come to see Jesus immediately when he heard Jesus was alive. He as a disciple had promised to follow Jesus. He saw the hands and feet before he believed. Then the disciples were sent on missions. Thomas did not like his assignment of India. He was told he was a slave and had to go. He overcame his doubt and went to India as Bartholomew. He took the scriptures called the Gospel of Matthew to India. (McBirnie, STA, 167)

COVET

(Luke 12:16-21, ears to hear, rhetorical question, death, Exodus 20:17, Logion 63, Sirach 11:19) For a disciple, the old rules of possessions became new rules. One thinks of Ananias and Sapphira who did not understand the spirit. (Luke 9:44-45) Imagine how Eleazar would have responded to the question, "If you die tomorrow, whose will all this be?" Once Eleazar (Lazarus) had been dead, but Jesus had restored him.

PART FOUR BIBLIOGRAPHY

Aland, Kurt, et al. eds. The Greek New Testament. American Bible Society (New York:1975)

Blavatsky, Helen P. Collected Writings. 2 vols. Pb. Theosophical (Wheaton, Illinois:1972)

Budge, E. A. Wallis. The Egyptian Book of the Dead. Dover (New York:1967)

Budge, E. A. Wallis. Egyptian Religion. Gramercy (New York:1996)

Darlison, Bill. The Gospel and the Zodiac. Duckworth Overlook (New York:2007)

Doresse, Jean. The Secret Books of the Egyptian Gnostics. MJF Books (New York:1986)

Ferguson, Everett, ed. Encyclopedia of Early Christianity. Garland Publishing, Inc. (New York:1990)

"Gospel of Nicodemus", Lost Books of the Bible. Bell Publishing (Cleveland, Ohio:1979)

Guillaumont, A. et al. trs. The Gospel According to Thomas. Harper and Row (New York: 1959)

Hall, Manly P. The Secret Teachings of All Ages. Pb. Penquin (New York:2003)

Hastings, James, ed. Dictionary of the Bible. 5 vols. Charles Scribner's Sons (New York:1909)

Jeremias, Joachim. Jerusalem in the Time of Jesus. Pb. Fortress Press (Philadelphia:1969)

Josephus. Complete Works tr. By William Whiston. Kregel (Grand Rapids, Michigan:1985)

Harrison, R. K., ed. The New Unger's Bible Dictionary. Moody Press (Chicago;1988)

Lawlor, John Irving. The Nabateans in Historical Perspective. Pb. Baker Book House. (Grand Rapids, Michigan:1974)

Lightfoot, John. A Commentary on the New Testament from the Talmud and Hebraica. 5 vols. Hendrickson (n.a.: 1995)

McBirnie, William Stewart. The Search for the Twelve Apostles. Pb. Tyndale House Publishers (Wheaton, Illinois:1977)

Osman, Ahmed. Christianity, an Ancient Egyptian Religion. Pb. Bear and Company (Rochester,Vermont:2005)

Peloubet, F. N. Peloubet's Bible Dictionary. Universal Book and Bible House.

(Philadelphia, Pennsylvnia:1947)

Petrement, Simone. A Separate God. Pb. HarperSanFrancisco (USA:1990)

Rambsel , Yacov. His Name is Jesus. Pb. Word Publishing (Nashville: 1999)

Schurer, Emil. A History of the Jewish People. 5 books in 3 vols. Hendrickson (Peabody, Massachusetts:1994)

Schneemelcher, Wilhelm , ed. New Testament Apocrypha. 2 vols. (Westminster:1992)

LEVITES AND MANDAEANS

FABATUS (involved in beheading of Herod Antipater)

x
x
x
JESUS BEN PHABES (H.P. 22 b.c., PHIABI, FABATUS)

xxxxxxxxxxxxxxxxxxxxxxxxxxxxxxxxxxxxxxxxxxxxxxxxxxxxxxxxxxx

x   x   x
ZECHARIAH BEN PHABES ZEBEDEE   ESCHA
md. ELIZABETH   md. SALOME   md. JOSEPH OF
NAZARETH
x   xxxxxxxxx   xxxxxxxxxxxxxxxxxxxxxxxxx
x   x   x   x   x   x   x   x
YAHYA (JOHN   JAMES   JOHN   SIMON JOSEPH JUDE LYDIA JAMES
THE BAPTIST)   (LEVI) (JUDAH)
    x

ISHMAEL

H.P. 61 C.E.

SAMARITANS

xxxxxxxxxxxxxxxxxxxxxxxxxxxxxxxxxxxxxxxxxxxxx

            x   x
FELIX ANTONIUS JULIANUS   PALLAS, TREASURER TIBERIUS
xxxxxxxxxxxxxxxxxxxxxxxxxxxxxxxxxxxxxxxxxxxxxxxx

I md.   2 md,   3 md.
md. RACHEL   DRUSILLA,   SELENE, RELATIVE OF.
    x   x   DAUGHTER OF   CLEOPATRA, THE
SIMON   JOSEPH   JOSHUA BEN   EGYPTIAN
 MAGUS   CAIAPHAS   GAMLA
md.   md. DAUGHTER
CYBOREA   OF ANNAS
    x   x
JUDAS   SARAH

V.JOSEPH CAIAPHAS-JESUS-JUDAS ISCARIOT (SATAN)

Samaritans and Christians differ concerning the nature of worship and the role of blood sacrifice in sacrifice. Cain killed Abel in an ironic blood sacrifice. Abraham was willing to sacrifice Isaac, but God provided a sacrifice in the bushes. The synagogue at Philadelphia was organized for blood sacrifice of Satan in the second century.,

Its premise was that Satan was trying to bless mankind in the Garden of Eden.(Bromiley, ISBE, IV, 344) Cain had sacrificed his own brother to God in a blood sacrifice, so Judas Iscariot participated in the sacrifice of Jesus. Whether his own motive was faith or not, Seth (Dositheos) declared himself the Messiah according to Deuteronomy 18:18. His follower Simon Magis, father of Judas Iscariot and brother of Joseph Caiaphas, betrayed him, took his consort Cyborea, and then took over his following. Simon used the money he had offered to the disciples to buy the Holy Spirit to buy Cyborea. (Acts 8:19) The Dositheans had dropped the commandment against adultery while adding more legalistic requirements to Sabbath worship. (McClintock, CBTEL, III, 873) Cyborea had been known as the whore of Tyre before she married Herod the Great. As the wife-consort of Simon Magus she was called the Lost Sheep of the House of Israel. (Barnstone, OB, 607 and Pe' trement. ASG, 80-85) A unifying part of this testimony is the repeated phrase, "it is written". In the Torah, this tag is attached to or quoted from the Sirach family. (Roth, EJ, X. 762)

Another Samaritan allusion is the word 'hear', the tag in the Torah that refers to Samaritan Micah.

ELS for Joseph Caiaphas (of Haifa) begins within Isaiah 52:5 as well as the beginning of ELS for 'whip, demon, devil, alas, woe, the whip of destruction', 'exalted in his name', Salome, seed, and 'weep bitterly.' (Rambsel, HNJ, 18, 19, 21, 28, 34, 45,46) Since 'adversary' is the description of the devil, the words 'up', 'down', 'exalted' and 'cast out' give further unity to the testimony. When Korah protested and Aaron allowed the worship of a golden calf, he was swallowed up. His children became temple slaves or doorkeepers. The Psalms of Korah are 42, 44-48, 84-85 and 87-88. Having the heritage of Korah, the Dositheans were proud to be doorkeepers. (cf. Psalm of Korah 84:10)

The overall theme is "up-down", and Satan is an adversary. Helen Blavatsky notes numersous ways of comparing Krishna, the second person of the Hindu Trinity and Jesus Christ, the second person of the Christian Trinity. (Blavatsky, IU, II, 173) Examination of the testimony of Joseph Caiaphas, uncle to Judas Iscariot, seems to relate to the written works of (or about) Krishna and to the Psalms of Korah. The Kenites (Cainites?) were traveling metalworkers who may have been in India at times. Cain was sent to the Land of Nod. Amongst scholars only Von Bohlen identifies Nod with India, and the Hebrew name Hind is similar in sound to Hindu. (McClintock, CBTEL, 13) Korah was the epitome of Hebrew skepticism. By the tenth century c.e., Cainites honored Judas Iscariot as their 'founder'.

The Altar of Burnt Offering in the Temple at Jerusalem with the bull being a symbol of earthiness. On Holy Days the blood flowed freely. In astrology the river of blood is associated with Aries, not Taurus (the bull). (Hall, STAA, 645)

PART ONE: STATIONS OF THE CROSS

This is a dual biography for Satan and Jesus. Names for Satan unify Part One, but the idea behind the devil is 'adversary'. If the Sadducees could not accept spiritual manifestation such as angels, Mary's virginity and the possibility of life after death, how could they accept Satan? Annas was a Sadducee and father-in-law of Joseph Caiaphas (Haifa). Since men from Haifa had a speech impediment, they were not allowed to become priests.

SUBJECTS (Luke 4:1-13, Satan, cast up, it is written, Psalm 91:11-12, Psalm of Korah 46:10) Chorazin was two miles from Capernaum. At Tell Hum, a ruinous depressed space a half mile long and a quarter mile wide may have been called Chorazin. (Peloubet, PBD, 109) The name Caiaphas means 'depression'. Korah criticized Aaron and Moses, so Moses sent him to a place where he was swallowed up. Then his family including women protested that his inheritance should come to them. (Numbers 27:3) After the Jews returned from exile, the Samaritans were still rejected by the priests. Samaritans accused other Jews of not following the written word. (Deuteronomy 28) The Samaritans worshiped on Mount Ebal and Mount Gerizim.

Korah had accused Moses of hypocrisy. Even after Aaron's sin of idolatry, Moses allowed Aaron to remain in charge of worship and sacrifice. Korah reminded Moses that while Moses was up on the mountain, Aaron had allowed the making of a new idol. The ground swallowed up Korah, but not all his tribe. (Numbers 16: 26:9, 27:3) Korahites descended from Korah continued as doorkeepers and choir members in both Samaria and Jerusalem.

Krishna was said to be coming to cause the accursed (Satan) to fly for refuge to the deepest hell. (Blavatsky, IU, II, 556)

FAMILY (Luke 1:39-56, down, exalted, seed, Micah 7:20, Isaiah 2:2, Psalm of Korah 42:4) The Virgin Mary sang the Magnificat which was first sung by Hannah as worship. (I Samuel 2:1-10) By gospel times, it was also known as a battlehymn. (Bromiley, ISBE, III, 220)

Felix (Antonius Julianus) of Samaria was father to Joseph Caiaphas and Simon Magus. (Schneemelcher, NTA, II, 512) Caiaphas had risen to a high position in Jerusalem by marrying the daughter of High Priest Annas. (Jeremias, JTJ, 194-195) In time Felix would be appointed Procurator of Samaria with the help of Jonathan and Felix's three wives. First there was Rachel the Samaritan, second the granddaughter of Anthony and Cleopatra, and third fourteen-year-old Drusilla (daughter of Joshua ben Gamla) Felix's fall began when Jonathan accused him of laziness, so Felix manipulated Jonathan's death. (Schurer, HJP. I. 2. 174-178) Felix had a brother named Pallas in Rome who was a favorite of Claudius. (Ibid.)

Krishna was also prophesied to be the son of a virgin. (Blavatsky, IU, II, 556)

GENEALOGY (Luke 20:27-38, up, seed to brothers, Micah 4:7, Isaiah 6:9, Psalm of Korah 49:7, Daniel 7:14) A question came up about the true husband of Cyborea, the mother or stepmother of Judas Iscariot. The Sadducees who deny that there is any resurrection asked Jesus about Levirite marriage, probably phrasing it to apply to Judith. (Schurer, HJP, II.3.32-35 and Genesis 38:8) Jesus replies that there is no marriage in heaven. Levirite marriage is not an issue there. The question of lineage applies to living, not to the dead.

Cyborea was known as the Lost Sheep of the House of Israel. Krishna was born of a royal family, but the shepherds protected him and kept his secrets. (Blavatsky, IU, II, 537) The shepherds came to Bethlehem to see Jesus, but they did not know who his father was.

SERMON (Luke 4:1-13, Satan, up, written, Psalm of Korah 47:3) Satan argues with Jesus using the 'written' words of God. Jesus said he was being tested. Now Judas Iscariot had Isaiah 53, Psalm 22 and Zechariah as written words. Perhaps he had faith that Jesus would be saved as Isaac was. Isaac's father Abraham tried a blood sacrifice, but it was not needed when God provided his own sacrifice, a ram in the bushes. (Genesis 22:7)

Krishna crushes the head of a serpent with his heel. (Blavatsky, IU, II, 446) In gospel times, serpents were worshiped by the Hivites in Israel. Perhaps Hivites and Dositheans influenced each other.

MARVEL (Luke 8:26-37, devil, down, Psalm 106:30-40 related to Phineas, not Korah, Psalm of Korah 46:5, Isaiah 17:11) Aland notes that 8:28=4:34. The Tribe of Gad (fortune) was fierce and warlike. In gospel times Gadara the city was deserted with fallen Greek columns and broken pavement. These reminded mankind that wealth and learning can be destroyed by war and natural disastors like earthquakes.

Jesus healed Fortunatus, the brother of King Gundaphorus of India. He was an outcast at Gadara. After he was healed, Thomas went with him to India. Fortunatus also went to Rome where he dishonored a female corpse. (Schneemelcher, NTA, II, 197-201) After that, he died by snakebite. John said, "Devil, thou hast thy son."

Krishna announced that he was to reconcile all creatures. (Blavatsky, IU, II, 556)

FAME (Luke 13:10-19, Satan, cast down, seed, Psalm of Korah 84:2, Isaiah 1:3) Jesus healed a woman who could no longer stand up straight. A great discussion was going on about the proper position for each required Jewish prayer. At least one prayer was to be said standing up straight. (re Shammai in Charlesworth, H & J, 431) She could not stand up straight until Jesus healed her. Dositheus led worship in Samaria on Mount Gerizim. He questioned the Sabbath practices in Israel. Jesus taught on Sabbath days.

Leviticus was the Samaritan authority on cleanliness. For example, Leviticus 5:1 says that one must confess before worship even for having heard cursing, blasphemy or witnessing evil. Then he may present his sin offering and his burnt offering.

The people of Haifa did not pronounce nor hear the breathmarks of other Jews. For example, "Profane not the Holy Name' became "Praise not the Holy Name." (Vilnay, SL, III, 5) Joseph Caiaphas (of Haifa) was in charge of sacrifice in worship at Jerusalem. He and his brothers-in-law declared lambs brought in as unclean. Then they sold them lambs they had raised or confiscated which they now declared perfect or clean . (Edersheim, LTJM, I, 371-372) Jesus made persons and things clean. Ophites were a sect having to do with metallurgy. They worshiped Sophia, the Jewish form of the Hindu female Nari. Since Nari could not stoop down, she sent the world her emissary Sophia-Akamoth. (Blavatsky, IU, II, 174) Their hope of salvation was to become androgenous.

PROPHECY (Luke 10:17-20, Satan, written, Psalm of Korah 84:10, Isaiah 27:1) It is said that once a voice came from heaven to Dositheus: " You can have one or the other, but not both—either the Book or the Sword. If you choose the Book, you must renounce the Sword. Should your choice be the Sword, the Book will perish." (Ausubel, BJK, 39) In Haifa, the words book and sword were homonyms. Cain meant lance or nest, the symbols of war and peace.

Jesus called seventy disciples after he called the twelve. Joseph Caiaphas or his brother Simon Magus (father of Judas Iscariot) could have followed out of curiosity for a time. Satan was seen to come out of the heavens. Jesus said it would be more important if their names were written (in the Book) in heaven.

LAST WEEK (Luke 22:31-32, Satan, cast, wheat=seed, Isaiah 40:29, Psalm of Korah 88:14) Either Simon Magus or Simon bar Jonah could have been given this word by Jesus. Joseph Caiaphas was brother to Simon. Simon Magus went to Rome after the Ascension of Jesus. He made life miserable for Peter (Simon bar Jonah), for he claimed to be the risen Christ. (Schneemelcher, NTA, II, 511-516)

Krishna forgave the hunter whose betrayal led to Krishna's being nailed upon a tree with an arrow. (Blavatsky, IU, II, 545-546) Jesus seems to offer forgiveness to both Simon's.

DEATH (LUKE 22:1-6, Satan, up, betray, contra Isaiah 50:10, Psalm of Korah 49:15,17) One reason for the annual feasts was to ask God's blessing upon the people for another year. Judas Iscariot is torn between being a gatekeeper for Jesus and a gatekeeper for his family including Joseph Caiaphas. When King Gundaphorus and the other two Wise Men came to see the infant Jesus, they left money. It had been placed in the Temple at Jerusalem. Joseph gave 30 pieces of it to Judas to betray Jesus, but the messenger kept back one for himself. (Paffenroth, J, 79)

At Passover Jews recalled that blood placed on the doors had prevented the angel of death (Satan) from killing their sons in Egypt. (Exodus 12:12) Samaritans worshiped at the Rock of Salvation 2000 cubits high on Mt. Ebal in Samaria. The grave of Enoch (or Seth) is supposedly there. Christians believe that the blood of Jesus was a sufficient sacrifice for their sins. No further blood sacrifice is needed, for worship is a sacrifice of one's life out of appreciation.

As all humans, Jesus in the flesh was to die eventually. The fulfillment of prophecy in Isaiah 53 and Psalm 22 (not a psalm for Korah) was proof for the Jews he was the Messiah of Deuteronomy 18:18.

According to Hindu belief, Brahma is both the sacrificer and the victim through his son Krishna. Brahma came to die on earth for the world's salvation. (Blavatsky, IU, II, 558)

A. D. (Luke 24:5, down) According to the Gospel of Nicodemus, Annas and Caiaphas said the guards had been bribed with money to take the body of Jesus out of the tomb. Other priests said to blame the disciples. Then Caiaphas asked how it could be that Jesus was alive and waiting in Galilee. (Schneemelcher, NTA, 516)

The Hindu response to miracles and divine mysteries is found in the Vyasa Maya: Worship of divinities, under the allegories of which is hidden respect for natural laws, drives away truth… (Blavatsky, IU, II, 242)

PART TWO: THE LORD 'S PRAYER

If Joseph Caiaphas, eyewitness, prayed the Lord's Prayer, this is what he might say.In the sense of the question, "Will a man rob God?" (Malachi 3:8), an overliteral interpretation would call all of mankind thieves. Thief is the unifying word in this section of testimony.

OUR (Luke 23:32-38, written, thief, cast lots, Isaiah 53:12, Psalm 84:10) The descendants of Korah were gatekeepers. When the Holy Family was on its way to Egypt to escape the Slaughter of the Innocents, they met thieves. The thieves asked for the gold that the Wise Men had brought to the infant. Then after hearing their story, they returned it to Mary and Joseph. Titus and Dumachus (Dismas and Gestas) were their names, and at least one of them was crucified the same day that Jesus was. (Hone, LBB&FBE, 47)

FATHER (Luke 18:9-14, cast up, extortion=steal, exalt, Isaiah 45:1, Psalm of Korah 84:10) Note that Luke 18:13=23:48. Felix Antonius Julius was a Samaritan who might have been descended from Korah. Both Thallus and Pallas were authors and they could have been brothers to Felix. Thallus had a brother Pallas who was the beloved of Tiberius and so did Felix. At least they all had the same critical attitude toward Jesus. Felix (happy, blessed) was father to Joseph Caiaphas. One may be sure that Simon Magus in Rome traded on the family name when in Rome.

NAME (Luke 3:2-6, written, high up, Psalm of Korah 85:6, Isaiah 40:3-5) "The Infancy of Jesus" by Joseph Caiaphas might have been used by Mohammad when he wrote the Koran. It contains stories not found in conventional gospels. (Hone, LBB&FBE, 38-59) When he was High Priest, he heard the words of John the Baptist quoting from Isaiah, "Prepare ye the way of the Lord." and "Repent for the Kingdom is at hand." (Isaiah 40:3-5) He had a daughter named Sarah who might have gone to Egypt with Mary Magdalene after the Ascension. When Mary reached France, she had a girl servant named Sarah with her. (Haskins, MM, 222)

KINGDOM (Luke 3:19-20, shut up=cast into, Isaiah 53:8, Psalm of Korah 49:20)

Herod Antipas was married to the Queen of Edom, and they had two sons. Their marriage was approved by the Roman Senate giving it the validity of a treaty. Herod went to Rome where he met his divorced sister-in-law Herodias. They returned as lovers. Herod and Herodias lived together openly in Jerusalem, so his wife returned to her father Aretas IV in Edom. Border war began. In 37 c.e., Tiberius ordered Herod and Aretas to Rome for trial. Two Roman possessions could not war against each other. Aretas IV could not be found.

According to Caiaphas, Mary and Joseph were traveling along the border. Out of fear of the authorities they went to the haunts of thieves. As they approached, the thieves heard a great noise and were frightened away. (Hone, LBB&FBE, 42)

EARTH (Luke 8:4-15, devil, takes away=steals, Psalm of Korah 44:2) The Word of God is likened to the devil taking away the word out of their hearts lest they believe. (Genesis 3:1) Jesus explains that spreading the Word of God is part chance but dependent upon the receiver. Some words that are homonyms suggest the receivers. Some seed was taken by the birds of the air (Arabians and Assyrians). Some fell upon the rock (Petra or Tyre). Without water (baptism), the newborn plants perished. Simon ben Boethus was a descendant of Cantheras (akantha=thorn), but he crowded out the words of Jesus with other words.

BREAD (Luke 12:32-48, thief, down, alms, Psalm 127:1 (shamar sounds like Samaritan) Aland would note that Luke 12:37=17:7-8. Caiaphas emphasizes caution lest one offend the authority. Jesus is praising those whose intent is to please God, their true master.

To Mandaeans, the written word of God was called Treasure. (Mead, GJB, 86) Judas Iscariot said that the ointment used on Jesus should have been sold instead. (Luke 7:46 and John 12:6) Such practicality was typical of Hindu worship.

EVIL (Luke 19:45-48, thief, cast down, written, Isaiah 56:7, Jeremiah 7:11) Aland notes that Luke 19:47=21:37, 22:53 and Luke 19:47-48= Luke 20:29, 22:2. Annas and Caiaphas forbid the use of faced coins within the Temple. Since such coins were rare antiques, the priests made a business of exchanging faced money for faceless money for those who came to Jerusalem to worship. Then they retrieved the same coins from the collection so they could sell them again. (Edersheim, LTJM, 371-372) Jesus observed this practice and said the temple had become a den of thieves.

FORGIVE (Luke 22:47-53, come, cut off=cast off) Caiaphas and his family were involved in asking Judas to kill Jesus. Perhaps they reminded him that God provided an alternate sacrifice that spared the life of Isaac. Caiaphas's brother Simon Magus, father of Judas, announced in Rome that he was the risen Messiah. He stole from at least one of those who came to hear him preach (Eubula in Schurer, HJP, II, 302) Simon Peter forced him to leave Rome.

AS WE FORGIVE (Luke 19:45-48, cast out, thief, hear, written, Psalm of Korah 46:10) Aland notes that Luke 19:47= 21:37, 22:53 and Luke 19:47-48=20:19, 22:2. Jesus accuses the sons of Annas of money changing. They ordered that faced coins could not be used in worship. They almost had a monopoly on ancient faceless coins, sold them for a profit, collected back them in worship and sold them again. They kept the profit. (Edersheim, LTJM, I, 371-372) Although they cited the prohibition of idols, it was a sin to misinterpret the intent of the Law.

AMEN (Luke 14:34-35, cast out, dung, Malachi 2:3, Lamentations 4:5) Aland notes that Luke 14:35=8:8. Jesus used several word plays. Salt (praise) is fit to be cast out as dung (shouted) when it is not making a difference in life (has lost its savor). Jesus warns them to learn the difference between the power of light and the power of darkness. Jesus asks why the authorities had not stopped him when he preached openly. He knew the answer. As a thief comes suddenly when he is unexpected so shall Jesus.

PART THREE: THE TEN COMMANDMENTS

The family of Annas said they were Sadducees. Joseph Caiaphas married a daughter of Annas. Sadducees accepted Pharisees as necessary, but they delighted in hearing woes against the Pharisees.

ONE GOD

(Luke 24:25-30, written, fall down, Isaiah 30:10, Exodus 20:3) Aland notes that Luke 24:25-27=24:44 and Luke 24:30=22:19. The Temples of Samaria and of Jerusalem were challenged by an Alexandrian translation of scripture called Seventy. Samaritans accused Israel of reinterpreting and redefining Law. Israel blamed Alexandria.

IDOLS

(Luke 7:24-30, written, look up, Malachi 3:1, Isaiah 3:2, Exodus 20:4) John the Baptist paved the way for the ministry of Jesus. Even though he was the greatest of prophets, he was not the Messiah.

HOLY NAME

(Luke 24:44-49, written, up, darkness, Isaiah 55:4, Exodus 20:7) Jesus had fulfilled many of the scriptures before he said this: Isaiah 53, Psalms 22, Zechariah 9:9, and Isaiah 7:14. In the name of God, Jesus promises power from on high at Pentecost.

SABBATH

(Luke 4:14-30, written, up, prophet, Genesis 3:15, Deuteronomy 30:3, Isaiah 61:1-2, Exodus 20:8) Aland notes that Luke 4:22=3:23, but Caiaphas does not report 3:23. One would wonder why since Cantheras had a son named Eli who had been High Priest long before Boethus returned from Alexandria. Jesus was preaching at Nazareth when he said he was fulfilling scripture.

PARENTS

(Luke 16:1-9, written, fall down, light (not darkness), Isaiah 30:9, Exodus 20:12) Felix was said to be a prodigous writer. He however did not keep up with his accounts.

The Anti-Roman Party was composed of religious and political fanatics. They plundered the homes of prominent citizens. Jonathan the High Priest urged Felix to pay more attention to duty, for he had recommended his appointment. In return, Felix urged his own enemies the Sicaii to assassinate Jonathan. (Schurer, HJP, I. 2. 178, 181)

KILL

(Luke 18:31-34, written, up, Isaiah 53, Psalm 22, Exodus 20:13) Jesus prophesied his own death and resurrection after three days.

ADULTERY

(Luke 3:6-18, cast, wheat=seed, Isaiah 52:10, Exodus 20:14) This was originally attached to 3:19-20 which deals directly with the issue of adultery. John the Baptist warned the people that the Messiah was coming.

Because of Eve, women were often blamed for adultery just because they were women. Beauty made a woman suspect. Flaunting it was sin. Both Judas Iscariot and Mary Magdalene had red hair. (Klassen, JBFJ, 4) She often went naked. She told Tiberius about Jesus a year before the crucifixion. (James, ANT, 148)

STEAL

(Luke 20:17-26, fall down, written=superscription, Exodus 20:15) Aland notes that Luke 20:19=19:47-48, 22:2 and Luke 20:20=11:54. Concerning honor as expressed by images on coins, Jesus said to render unto Caesar what is Caesar's and unto God what is God's.

LIE

(Luke 5:17-26, up, down, 'written law against blasphemy', Isaiah 63:8, Exodus 20:16) Ptolemy, a kinsman of Nicodemus, was said to be huge. Jesus heals him. If Ptolemy is possibly Thallus, it raises questions about Nicodemus and Felix. Some thought, once a slave, one no longer had rights.

COVET

(Luke 23:32-38, over=up, cast, written, Isaiah 53:12, Exodus 20:17, Psalm of Korah 84:10, Genesis 4:4, 8)   Abel's gift of sacrifice was accepted. When Cain's was not accepted, he killed Abel, his brother. Two thieves were crucified with Jesus, one of them had attempted to rob the Holy Family on its way to Egypt. Lots were cast to receive Jesus's clothes. Above his head written in three languages were these words, "This is the King of the Jews."

BIBLIOGRAPHY

Aland, Kurt, et al., eds, The Greek New Testament. Un ited Bible Societies (New York:1975)

Ausubel, Nathan. The Book of Jewish Knowledge. Crown Publishers Inc. (New York:1964)

Barnstone, Willis, ed. The Other Bible. Harper & Row (San Francisco:1984)

Bible Data Bank. A Concordance to the Apocrypha. Wm. B. Eerdmans Publishing Company (Grand Rapids, Michigan:1983)

Blaiklock, E. M. and R. K. Harrison, eds. The New International Dictionary of Biblical Archaeology. Regency Reference Library. Zondervan (Grand Rapids:1983)

Blavatsky, Helen. Isis Unveiled. 2 vols. Pb. Theosophical Publishing (Wheaton, Illinois:1972)

Bromiley, Geoffrey W., gen. ed. The International Bible Encyclopedia. 4 vols. William B. Eerdmans Publishing Company (Grand Rapids,Michigan:1988)

Charlesworth, James H. and Loren L., eds. Hillel and Jesus. Fortress Press (Minneapolis:1997)

Edersheim, Alfred. The Life and Times of Jesus the Messiah. Wm. B. Eerdmans Publishing Company (Grand Rapids, Michigan:1976)

Encyclopedia Judaica. Macmillan Publishing Company (New York:1972)

Hall, Manly P. The Secret Teachings of All Ages. Pb. Penquin (New York:2003)

Ferguson, Everett, ed. Encyclopedia of Early Christianity. Garland Publishing Company (New York:1990)

Harrison, R. K., ed. The New Unger's Bible Dictionary. Moody Press (Chicago:1988)

Haskins, Susan. Mary Magdalen. Pb. Harcourt, Brace and Company (New York:1994)

Hastings, James. Dictionary of the Bible. 5 vols. Charles Scribner's Sons (New York:1909)

Hengel, Martin. The Zealots. T & T Clark (Edinburgh:1989)

Hone, William. Lost Books of the Bible and Forgotten Books of Eden. Crown Publishers (New York:1979)

James, Montague Rhodes, tr. The Apocryphal New Testament. Clarendon Press (Oxford:1963)

Jeremias, Joachim. Jerusalem in the Time of Jesus. Fortress Press (Philadelphia:1969)

Josephus. Complete Works. Kregel Publications (Grand Rapids:1983 edition)

Keller, Werner. The Bible as History. Pb. Bantam Books (New York:1976)

Klassen, William. Judas, Betrayer or Friend of Jesus. Fortress Press (Minneapolis:1996)

Kraeling, Emil G. The Disciples. Rand McNally and Company (USA:1966)

Lightfoot, John. Commentary on the New Testament from the Talmud and Hebraica. 4 vols. Hendickson Publishers (USA:1995)

McBirnie, William Steuart. The Search for the Twelve Apostles. Tyndale House Publishers (Wheaton, Illinois:1997)

McClintock, John an d James Strong. Cyclopedia of Biblical, Theological and Ecclesiastical Literature. 12 vols. Baker Book House (Grand Rapids, Michigan:1981)

Mead, G. R. S. Fragments of a Faith Forgotten. University Books (New Hyde Park,New York:1960)

Paffenroth, Kim. Images of the Lost Disciple. Westminster JohnKnox Press (Louisville:2001)

Peloubet, F. N. Peloubet's Bible Dictionary. Universal (Philadelphia:1947)

Pe'trement, Simone. A Separate God, the Origin and Teachings of Gnosticism. HarperSanFrancisco (New York:1984)

Pritchard, James B. Ancient Near Eastern Texts Princeton University Press (Princeton:1969)

Rambsel, Yacov. His Name Is Jesus. Pb. Word Publishing (Nashville:1999)

Roth, Carl. Enclyclopedia Judaica. Macmillan and Company (New York:1972)

Schneemelcher, Wilhelm,ed. New Testament Apocrypha. 2 vols. James Clarke and Company (Westminster:1992 edition)

Schurer, Emil. A History of the Jewish People. 5 books in 3 vols. Hendrickson (Peabody, Massachusetts:1994)

Unger, Merrill F. ed. Unger's Bible Dictionary. Moody Press (Chicago:1966)

Vilnay, Zev. The Sacred Land. 3 vols. Jewish Publication Society (Philadelphia:1973)

Wilson, Ian. The Bible Is History. Regency Publishing Company (Washington, D.C.:1999)

VI. JAIRUS (ARISTARCHUS)-JESUS-SOLOMON (JEDIDIAH)

In Equidistant Letter Sequencing, Isaiah 52:9 is the beginning point for counting out the letters of 'light'. (Rambsel, HNJ, 29) The name Jairus means 'he enlightens'. Kabbalists use a Book of Light, although its origin is in doubt. (McClintock, CBTEL, II, 2-3) ELS for Ezekiel 1:1 is also light. Other ELS words beginning at Isaiah 52:9 are Jesse (gift, wealthy) and 'together.' (Rambsel, HNJ, 25) Jairus's mother was Imma Shalom whose name is the feminine form of the name 'Solomon'. Jairus's father was Eleazar ben Hyrcanus (Lazarus, a former High Priest brother to Joezer) and his stepfather was Simon of Cyrene. Solomon's servants (Nethinim) sounds like Nathan (gift), and the word give is often repeated in this testimony. (cf. I Kings 9:20-21) Solomon built and dedicated the Temple at Jerusalem. Elkesaites were charismatics, in gospel times probably using Lake Mareotis as a retreat. Their inspiration was an Egyptian play called Exogogue produced by Therapeutae. Moses and Miriam led a dance reel. Then the dancers went into seclusion to study the psalms for weeks. Abstinence and celibacy were not required. (Wigoder, EJ, 79) Elkesaites were usually wealthy faith healers who opposed slavery. Since Jesse (gift, wealthy) is associated with Isaiah 52:9, the probable allusion is to Revelation 7:4-8 at Gad (fortune),

At the dedication of the temple by Solomon, the shekinah glory (light) filled

the temple along with 120 trumpeteers and 4000 musicians. The light was so great that the ritual of the priests was suspended for a time. (Rambsel, HNJ, 240)

Once Jesus said, 'I am the Light of the World.' At his birth, light filled the sky in that the glory shone around. On the Mount of Transfiguration, there was shining. At his crucifixion there were several hours of darkness. At Pentecost tongues of fire were described. The Aurora Borealis and St. Elmo's fire occur within an electromagnetic system when dust particles collide moved by solar winds. Among the Jews the Sabbath was ushered in when a fire on a mountain could be seen out of the darkness. The date of Passover was determined by the moon.

PART ONE: STATIONS OF THE CROSS

These are notes for a dual biography about Jesus and Solomon The key or clue word is 'wise'. The wisdom of Solomon is expressed in the Song of Solomon, Book of Proverbs and Ecclesiastes. Part one has a Carrington triad for the word 'astonished'. The significance of the frequent use of 'give' and 'all' in this testimony may be an allusion to communal living.

SUBJECTS (Luke 11:31-36, wise, full=all, idea of visit, Deuteronomy 1:17, I Kings 10:1-10, Proverbs 16;16) Sheba is probably Saba on the southwest coast of the Arabian peninsula (modern Yemen, Bromiley, ISBE, IV,9) Since the Holy Family is sometimes called Barsabas, this is interesting. However Ethiopians claim that Menelik I, the Queen's son by Solomon, gives them a claim superior to that of the Jews to be God's chosen people. Solomon tricked the Queen of Sheba by forcing her to take a vow not to steal anything. Then she was fed salty food until she 'stole' some water. (Bromiley, ISBE, IV, 10) She got even by having Solomon give the Ark of the Covenant to her son.

At Paneas (Caesarea Philippi) a statue to honor Jesus was placed. Either it was done because what Jesus did for the daughter of Jairus or for Bernice. (Maier, ECH, 264-265) Pan the god of shepherds was honored there by the smashing of lamps to release the light.

FAMILY (Luke 7:30-35, wisdom, all, Psalm 30:11, 24:8-10, Genesis 3:6, Numbers 12:6, Proverbs 19:8, 16:16) Solomon was thought to be the wisest of all men, but in the end he acted foolishly. He failed the test of time advocated by Simon ben Gamaliel, a brother to Imma Shalom (a form of the name Solomon).

Elkesaites recognized multiple marriages. Imma Shalom from Bathyra (Araq el-Emir) was either married many times or her husband used many names: By Eleazar ben Hyrcanus, she had Jairus (Aristarchus). By Simon of Cyrene she had Rufus and Alexander. By Simon of Arimathea, she had Domitilla (Titus's mistress), Saul (Paul), and Joseph of Arimathea (Obodas II).

GENEALOGY (Luke 10:21-24, wise, all, give, glory, Psalm 27:13, 96:7) The Book of the Hidden Power might have been Isaiah II because of its hidden equidistant lettering system. Elxai, supposed founder of the Elkesaites said the book fell from heaven. It taught that the Christ had been born many times. When under duress, believers could renounce their beliefs. It recommended frequent bathing. It contained a saying that reads the same right to left and left to right in Hebrew; I am witness over you on the great day of judgment. In gospel times, Elkesaites could be found in Iturea, the territory of Herod Philip. If they became Christian, they had bread and salt for communion instead of bread and wine. (McClintock, CBTEL, III, 165)

SERMON (Luke 12:16-35, rich, all, give, glory, What shall I do?, I Kings 10:4-7, Psalm 147:9, 96:8) Aland notes that Luke 12:22=22:29, Luke 12:24=12:7 and Luke 12:32=18:22. Jesus says that those who can not add a cubit to their own stature, should listen. Solomon in all his glory was not dressed as well as the lilies. Hiram of Tyre had added lilies to the tops of columns in the Temple at Jerusalem. Jesus advises Jews to sell what they have. All they want shall be given to them after they give alms to help the poor. (cf Acts 5:1)

Elkesaites wore red for Holy occasions and white for daily life. (Ferguson, EEC, 296) Jesus asks his followers to have their lamps burning. To worship Pan, lamps were smashed. Miners were given a daily allowance of oil. When it ran out, they could surface; that is, quit work.

MARVEL (Luke 2:41-52, wisdom, astonished, all, idea of together, Exodus 12:24-27, I Kings 3:7,11, Proverbs 25:6, 3:4, Psalm 8:5) The child Solomon was about to be king, but he said that he did not even know how to go out and come in. He asked God for the gift of understanding. The child Jesus stood in the temple demonstrating his understanding. However, when his parents missed him, they thought he did not know how to go in or go out of Jerusalem. This was all the more dramatic because Judas of Galilee, a relative of Jairus, led that uprising during Passover when Jesus was twelve.

Tradition says that Jair (Aristarchus) became bishop of the church at Apamea. (Peloubet, PBD, 45) Near Apamea at Palmyra, the ruins of a temple of similar measurements and design to that of Solomon still stands.. (near Tarsus, Roberts, SBJ, 340-345) It was said that Hiram built a duplicate, so this might be the one he built. The third known temple of the same design was at Alexandria. The difference was that in Jerusalem the lighting was in the form of a giant grapevine with hanging oil lamps and gold bunches of grapes, but Alexandria had a hanging chandelier. (Josephus, 269, 280, 425) The temple at Palmyra has a fountain which may symbolize the Lion of Judah. (Lapp in Perdue, ABI, 165-184). Judas Maccabee was 'like a lion'. (Schurer, HJP, 1. 1. 213) Not one of these temples is still used as a temple in modern times. Ezekiel 40-44 has developed the idea of the body being the temple. Jesus said the Kingdom of God is within 'you'. The ancient evangelist argued that Hindus thought certain miracles proved their god's divinity. If Jesus performed the same miracles, shouldn't they at least listen?

FAME (Luke 2:8-20, visit of the shepherds (wise men), idea of together, all, Isaiah 40:9, Psalm 57:5,11) Aland notes that Luke 2:14=19:38,Luke 2:19=2:51 and Luke 2:17= 2:10-12. I Kings 17:17, 3:16) Aland notes that Luke 7:12=8:42. Solomon became famous for his decision to give the surviving infant to the mother who would give it up rather than to let it die.

The shepherds told what they had seen and heard. When Herod Antipas heard from them or the Magi, he pretended he too wished to worship the infant. Instead he ordered the slaughter of infants under the age of two years. Pan (mentioned above) was the god of the herdsmen. (Patrick, CBGM, 67)

PROPHECY (Luke 16:1-12, rich, wise, light, give, What shall I do?, everyone=all, Psalm 73:6, 149:5) Aland notes that Luke 16:10-12=19:17-26. According to the Testament of Solomon (written in the first century), Solomon had a ring that had curative powers, and those who kissed his ring were healed. According to legend, Solomon used the ring to charm the 'demons' into building the Temple for him. (Charlesworth, OTP, I.962)

Solomon tried to pay Hiram of Tyre with giving him some Jewish cities. The residents were to become slaves. Slavery was an abomination to the Elkesaites, an attitude appropriate for Solomon's Servants.

Jesus comments that one must be faithful in one's own in order to expect that others will be faithful. Jair (probably an ancestor to Jairus) was the eighth judge of Israel. He had thirty sons who rode thirty ass colts to judge thirty cities. (Judges 10:4) The son of Jairus, Eleazar ben Ari, would die at Masada for his faith in 73 c.e. (Schurer, HJP, I.2.252)

LAST WEEK (Luke 21:8-33, all, wise, glory, I Maccabees, 3:45,51, Psalm 79:1, 96:3) Aland notes that Luke 21:12=12:11 and Luke 21:18=12:7. Jairus was called on to testify that Jesus had healed his daughter on the Sabbath. Bernice who had touched the hem of his garment offered to testify, but it was denied because she was a woman. Usually women of royal birth were allowed to testify. Reluctantly (Luke 21:14) Jairus testified to the truth along with his brother Alexander. (Acts of Pilate in Barnstone, OB, 362, 366) Aristarchus (his new name) became in time a fellow prisoner with Paul. (Acts 19:29, 20:4, 27:2) Daily Elkesaites prayed to be a witness for God. They believed Mother Sophia was daughter of All (the overall word clue to this section) and Jesus was her son. Elkesaites influenced Mani later on. They used astronomy to set times for religious rites like baptism.

DEATH (Luke 12:22-26, glory, all, astonished, together, Proverbs 14:29, I Kings ll, Psalm 24:10) Jesus wept at Dominus flevit, (Jesus wept, John 11:35) an overlook near and above the Garden of Gethsemane.

(Duffield, HBL, 110) It is said that Jairus is buried there, for a tomb has been found with his name inscribed amongst others. The names of Jairus, Martha, Mary, Salome and Simon bar Jonah are marked on Christian ossuaries there. (Finegan, LFAP, 333) In 37 c.e., Jairus could not have known he would be buried there.

God had a covenant with Solomon which Solomon broke. The name Solomon seems to refer to the sun. Kabbalists broke lamps at Panias (Caesarea Philippi) to release the light hidden from man ever since Eve sinned in the Garden of Eden. (based on Crossan, EJ,101) Statues were erected at Panias to honor Jesus, but it is not known whether it was for the daughter of Jairus or for Bernice.

From time to time, the Throne of Solomon was decorated with patches of cloth. Arabs hope that the person who once owned the garment will be cured. A legend says that Solomon made a staff from a carob plant. When he knew he was dying, he sat on his throne propped up with the staff. Worms ate the staff and he fell helpless in regard to the powers that once served him. (Vilnay, LOJ, I, 44-45)

AFTER THE DEATH (Luke 12:54-57, sky, Isaiah 55:6, Psalm 102:27, sun =sol) While Egyptians worshiped the sun, Jews worshiped the Creator of the Sun. Christians had the star which led the wise men to the infant Jesus. At Pentecost, however, it is the wind that is mentioned and not a blinding light as they might have expected.

PART TWO THE LORD'S PRAYER

If Jairus prayed the Lord's Prayer, this might be what he would say. Jair was a well-known name because of a judge named Jair had thirty sons who rode thirty horses to judge the people of Israel. (Judges 10:3) In gospel times, the stepfather of Jair (Simon of Cyrene) was the weaver carried the cross part of the way for Jesus. Jesus had restored Jairus's birth father Eleazar ben Hyrcanus (Lazarus) to life. This section refers to clothing as 'robes'.

OUR (Luke 23:5-12, together, robe, 'peace', all, Psalm 8:5, Proverbs 1:10-16) Aland notes that Luke 23:7=3:1 and Luke 23:8=9:9.

Like Solomon, the Elkesaites did not object to serial multiple wives. They admired wealth, fame and noble birth. (Charlesworth, H&J,180) Like Hillel, they considered the Book of Ecclesiastes as sacred. (Moore, J. I. 242) They required seven witnesses and kept the Sabbath day holy. They blended Judaism, 'Christianity', magic and astrology. They wore red robes on holy days like the Sabbath and white daily. They prayed daily to become witnesses for Jehovah. (Ferguson, EEC, 491)

At Cesarea, Herod Agrippa wore a magnificent shining robe. It was so magnificent he was called a god. Within a few days he was dead. (Josephus, 412) Rome had confiscated all Jewish ceremonial robes, but lent them back for occasions. Herod Antipas who invited Jesus to visit dressed him in a royal robe. How ironic it would be if Herod Agrippa and Jesus wore the same robe.

Solomon may have known the key to Qabbalah (equidistant letter sequencing?) for the Talmud says that he did. (Hall, STAA, 576) Isaiah had lived about three hundred years after Solomon, but it should be noted that ELS occurs within the Pentateuch as well as in Isaiah. (Rambsel, HNJ, in passim.) Shiloh had fallen before David became King.

FATHER (Luke 16:19-31, all, rose (arise), Exodus 4:15, Psalm 73:12) Simon of Cyrene is believed to have been a weaver, one of the seventy sent out by Jesus. A beam looks much like the crosspiece of a cross. II Kings 6:2, Psalm 104:3) Simon was likely the son of Jason of Cyrene who authored Wisdom bar Sira (Ecclesiasticus). The work was about Solomon and Judaism. (Hastings, DOB, IV, 541-542) Not formed before 100 c.e., the proto-Elkesaites believed in multiple marriages: Imma Shalom was first married to Eleazar ben Hyrcanus, and Jair was their son. Then she married Simon of Cyrene and Rufus and Alexander were their sons.(Mark 15:21) She may have gone to Cyrene to study medicine, for there was an outstanding medical school there. Then she married Simon of Arimathea and their children were Domitilla (Titus's mistress), Joseph of Arimathea, and Saul (Paul). Simon Asira was her husband also, but that might have been just another name for Simon of Arimathea.

When Jesus heard that Eleazar (father of Jairus, Lazarus) was dead, he went to the tomb, called to him and brought him out. Eleazar was a son of a priestly family called Boethus, but the Chanina family also had many priests. (Jeremias, JTJ, 194-195) Jesus comments that even the resurrection of Lazarus will not make believers in and of itself.

NAME (Luke 8:40-56, all, arise, give, astonished, hem of a robe, Psalm 57:8) As Aristarchus, Jairus would be a fellow prisoner with his half-brother Saul. (Acts 19:29) Elkesaites were a faith-healing Jewish-Christian sect which may have developed from the synagogue at Jerusalem for Solomon's Servants and their descendants. Solomon's study house where he wrote was also a mint, and it was called al-Aksa. (Vilnay, LOJ, 37-38) After the Ascension, Jairus was sent to Apamea (Therma) with the name Aristarchus (cf Luke 8:41) Aristarchus was made a Christian bishop there. (Peloubet, PBD, 45). The Book of Hidden Power did not go to Rome from Apamea until the Second Century. (Ferguson, EEC, 296)

Apamea had a culture which had once worshiped Pan. Pan's principal activity was sex and interest in the fertility of sheep. He was the god of herdsmen. (Patrick, CBGM, 67) Even Jews called their religious leaders shepherds. (cf Psalm 23)

In 47 b.c. Herod had killed Hezekiah (Iexai, brother of Elxai who founded the Elkesaites). Jair had a daughter and three sons: Eleazar who killed himself at Masada, and Judas and Simon who fought in defense of the Temple. (Hengel, Z, 332)

KINGDOM (Luke 9:27-36, robe, glory, accomplish=achieve all, Psalm 78:14, 96:7, Proverbs 11:30, Daniel 4:12) Aland notes that Luke 9:31=9:22, 13:33) Solomon gave Hiram of Tyre twenty cities including Helcias, hometown of Nehemiah. (Gordon, BANE, 212) Hiram refused them. Solomon's Servants were citizens of Helot (Helcias?) before Solomon made them cutters of wood and citizens of Canaan. They became dedicated slaves to serve the Temple of God which was being designed in part by Hiram of Tyre. Hiram designed the lily tops of its columns. (I Kings 5:17-18) The ancient library at Gadara was said to contain the library of Nehemiah. It included Solomon's Book of Cures condemned by Hezekiah as he condemned Enoch's Book of Cures. He thought faith healing to be superior to medical methods. (Schurer, HJP, 1. 2. 155) In addition to medicine, the Book of Hidden Power (which was kept secret) included astronomy, mathematics and 'magic=chemistry and physics'. By the time of Jesus, Gadara was a deserted university town having been ravaged by war and earthquakes. Eerily beautiful broken columns and unkempt but blooming gardens hid the outcasts of human society. (Blaiklock, DBA, 201)

> Jesus went to the Mount of Transfiguration where he was seen in shining robes.A voice from heaven repeated that Jesus was the beloved son of God. Elkesaites thought he was one of many 'sons' born over the centuries.

EARTH (Luke 7:24-29, robe, all, Malachi 3:1, Psalm 29:2, 34:16) Aland notes that Luke 7:26=1:76, Luke 7:28=1:15, and Luke 7:29=3:7,12) Jewish priests went barefoot, but they usually wore beautiful robes. John the Baptist did not wear 'manufactured cloth'.

for the Messiah. Elkesaites called him the Righteous One, and at Qumran the Righteous Teacher was a pivotal leader. "Repent, for the Kingdom of God is at hand."

BREAD (Luke 15:11-32, robe, all, Exodus 28:4, Tobit 11:9, Proverbs 9:12) Joseph of Arimathea (Obodas II), a stepbrother to Jairus, married the sister of Herod the Great. Because she was Queen of Edom, he became Governor of Edom. Joseph then left on long voyages. When he returned home, his father welcomed him but his brother Sylleus did not. His father put the best robe on him. (Lawlor, NHP, 91-101) His brother would not come in to share bread with him.

EVIL (Luke 23:26-38, robe, anyone=all, forgive as a form of giving, offer=give, Psalm 21:8a LXX) Simon of Cyrene was a weaver and a possible revolutionary when married to Imma Shalom, the mother of Jairus. A seamless robe has no part that is missing and no part that does not belong. In contrast the infant Jesus was wrapped in linen discarded as wrapping for the Torah, and he was buried in similar linen.

Because Jesus's robe was seamless, the soldiers cast lots to see which of them would receive it. Receive is a code-word for Kabbalists, an overall term that includes Elkesaites. Jason of Cyrene wrote Ecclesiasticus (Wisdom bar Sira) about Solomon. (Hastings, DOB, IV, 541-542) Al-Aksa was the name given to the mint Solomon used. (Vilnay, LOJ, 37-38)

FORGIVE US (Luke 20:45-47, robe, all, Proverbs 15:8, Psalm 62:7, Exodus 28:4, Proverbs 25:6-7) The charismatic Therapeutae enjoyed their religion. It is not surprising that they liked drama and showmanship; i.e., the best seats.

Elkesaites wore red robes on holy occasions and white on other times. Jesus notes that appearances can be deceiving. A long robe suggests dignity, but appearance and popularity do not impress God. Priests were quarreling about the proper length of morning and evening prayers. Jesus asked for heart-felt prayers of any length.

The widowed mother of Mariamne the Hasmonaean suffered long and constantly wrote letters to Rome asking for justice. Herod the Great had married and then killed her daughter the Queen of Edom. He had not returned her property to her family according to the Edomite inheritance laws in which descent of title is matriarchal. Herod had his sister Alexandra Salome first marry their uncle and then their nephew Joseph of Arimathea to hold the property unlawfully.(Josephus, 324) After the defeat of Cleopatra, Herod was given Gadara. (Josephus, 325)

AS WE FORGIVE (Luke 12:35-41, give, all, gird, I Kings 18:46, II Kings 4:29,9:1, Proverbs 31:17, Psalm 62:7) Aland notes that Luke 12:37=17:7-8. Elkesaites did not lack enthusiasm, but other aspects of readiness may have escaped them. Jair means 'he enlightens'. The parable of the virgins and their lamps does not appear in Luke, but it may reveal the intent of this passage. (Matthew 25:1-13) Worshipers of Pan would throw their burning lamps and break them to release the light.

AMEN (Luke 5:36-39, no one implies all, patch of fabric=remnant, cf Leviticus 13:45, Psalm 130:6, 29:2) A new patch of fabric puts a strain on old cloth. Likewise the teachings of Jesus put a strain on the social fabric already in place. Patches of cloth were attached to the area known as the Throne of Solomon. Pan was asked to heal the one to whom the garment had once belonged. Some Arabians still offer patches for the blessing of healing.

PART THREE THE TEN COMMANDMENTS

Glory is the unifying word in Part Three. Elkesaites had retreats lasting seventy days with much studying and writing of psalms. Then they had a celebration, the reenactment of Moses crossing the Red Sea. They would dance a reel all night with feet slip-sliding as if on sand and hands clapping. Then they would go back to isolation in separate places for seventy days. Psalm 27:1 may have inspired the editor (author) of the Gospel of Luke. Jairus means 'he enlightens' and Jesus said that he is the Light of the World. In Egypt Therapeutae were similar, but probably included worship of the sun god Re. The Queen of Sheba had taken the Ark containing the Ten Commandments to Egypt with her. Perhaps she also took the Psalms of David.

ONE GOD

(Luke 7:11-18, visit, glorify, God, all, arise,, Exodus 20:3, Isaiah 42:6, 49:6, 46:13, 8:14, 40:1,49:13, 40:5, 52:10) Aland notes that Luke 2:25=22:51,2:38, The ancients said that the Temple at Jerusalem was built so that it shed its light upon the world. Solomon built its windows wide outside and narrow inside to increase the light. (Vilnay, LOJ, 82-83)

Jesus restored Maternus to life. This son of Leah studied in Rome with Peter. Then he built and dedicated a church to the Virgin Mary beyond the Alps.

(McBirnie, STA, 60-61)

IDOLATRY

(Luke 17:10-19, glorify God, give, arise, all) Aland notes that Luke 17:19=18:42 and Luke 17:13=18:38. Eliezer ben Hyrcanus was removed from his academy for heresy. (Ausubel, BJK, 150) Legend says that the heresy was that he was a secret Christian. (Eisenman, J, 218) At Paneas

(Caesarea Philippi), a statue was erected to Jesus either by Bernice or the daughter of Jairus to honor Jesus.(Maier, ECH,264-265)

Jesus healed ten men of leprosy. Nine went to the Temple to give thanks. The Samaritan was not welcome at the Temple, so he thanked Jesus.

HOLY NAME

(Luke 18:35-43,glorify God, give, all, Exodus 20:7, Psalm 3:3, 50:23) Aland notes that Luke 18:42=17:19, 8:48. Rabbi Phineas ben Jair would say, "If thou seek wisdom as silver, that is, if you seek the things of Law as hidden treasures…" (Lightfoot, CNT, III. 157)

The blind man who may have once been Herod the Great's physician was healed with a holy name. Jairus's testimony was that Jesus had healed on the Sabbath. Jesus gave Baba ben Buta back his eyesight on the Sabbath. Herod the Great had blinded him after ordering his sons killed before his eyes. (Edersheim, LTJM, I, 120, 126)

PARENTS

(Luke 2:25-35, glory, all, peace, Psalm 85:9, 50:23) Simon ben Boethus became High Priest in Jerusalem although his training was at On in Egypt. He had twin sons who were High Priests before him- Joezer (Thomas) and Eleazar (Thomas). Simon ben Boethus was Jairus's grandfather.

KILL

(Luke 19:26-40, glory, give, all, II Kings 9:13, Psalm 118:26, 102:15) Aland notes that Luke 19:26=8:18, 19:32. Perhaps some of Solomon's Servants (Nethinim) were called 'the given ones'. (Orr, ISBE, V, 2025b-2026) They had the job of caring for the balsam groves. They had been started by clippings the Queen of Sheba brought to Solomon. In gospel times the laborers tried to usurp the land. The owner wrote to Agrippa and Bernice asking for help. (Josephus, 3)

ADULTERY

(Luke 3:15-20, give, all, Exodus 20;14, Proverbs 20:27) John the
Baptist was considered to be the Messiah that all hoped for. He said he
was not worthy to untie the shoes of the Messiah. Only non –Jewish
slaves had to untie shoes. (Marshall, COL, 146)

The practice of adultery leads to trouble as surely as placing a lit
candle under a hay-filled mattress leads to trouble.

STEAL

(Luke 4:1-13, all, give, glory, Exodus 20:15, Proverbs 22:16) Moses
specified that Jews must use the same measure for buying and selling.
Herod the Great had given the balsam groves in Arabia to Mark
Antony who gave them to Cleopatra. The Governor of Edom was
to sharecrop and send her her share by Herod the Great. He told
the farmers to report short. He hoped that Cleopatra would think
Herod the Great was skimming. (Josephus, 319) Eliezer ben Hycanus
(second century so not the father of Jair) called for continued 'eye
for an eye', but Rabbi Ishmael recommended financial repayment for
injury. (Ausubel, BJK, 423)

The devil tempts Jesus to take power from those who misuse it.
Jesus turns to scripture and resists temptation.

LIE

(Luke 5:17-26, glorify God, arise, all, Psalm 31:5, 38:11, 88:8)
Aland notes that Luke 5:20=7:48 and Luke 5:21=7:49. Ironically the
Elkesaites prayed daily that they might witness for Jehovah. The Jews
accused Jesus of blasphemy when he said that the sins of Ptolemy (may
have been Nicholas of Damascus or his brother) were forgiven. To Jair's
credit, he did not lie but trusted Jesus. When he was asked under oath,
Jairus said that Jesus had healed his daughter on the Sabbath.

COVET

(Luke 23:46-49, commend=give, glorify God, Psalm 31:5, 88:8, 38:11)
Jews and Samaritans had a long history of covetousness. In gospel
times this rivalry was expressed in the priesthood of each. Perhaps he
alludes to the Book of Hidden Power.

The four priestly families did not cooperate. They tolerated each
other. Herod the Great had killed so many Levites they stayed together
for safety. They wanted to get rid of Jesus. Even so, the Roman Longinus
recognized Jesus as a righteous man.

PART FOUR BIBLIOGRAPHY

Aland, Kurt et al, eds The Greek New Testament. American Bible Society (New York:1975)

Ausubel, Nathan. The Book of Jewish Knowledge. Crown Publishing (New York:1964)

Barnstone, Willis, ed. The Other Bible. Harper & Row (San Francisco:1971)

Blaiklock,Edward M. et al. The New International Dictionary of Biblical Archaeology. Regency Reference Library (Grand Rapids, Michigan:1983)

Bromiley, Geoffrey W. The International Standard Bible Encyclopedia. 5 vols. William B. Eerdmans Company (Grand Rapids, Michigan:1982)

Carrington, Philip. The Primitive Christian Calendar. University Press (Cambridge:1952)

Charlesworth, James and Loren L. John. Hillel and Jesus. Fortress Press (Minneapolis:1997)

Charlesworth. James, ed. The Old Testament Pseudepigrapha. Doubleday & Company (Garden City,New York:1983)

Crossan, John Dominic and Jonathan L. Reed. Excavating Jesus.Pb. HarperSanFrancisco (San Francisco:2001)

Duffield, Guy P. Handbook of the Bible Lands. Pb. Regal (Glendale, California:1973)

Edersheim, Alfred. Life and Times of Jesus the Messiah. Wm. B. Eerdmans (Grand Rapids, Michigan:1971)

Eisenman, Robert. James the Brother of Jesus. Viking Press (New York:1996)

Ferguson, Everett, et al. eds. Encyclopedia of Early Christianity. Garland (New York:1990)

Finegan, Jack. Light from the Ancient Past. Oxford University Press (London:1959)

Gordon, Cyrus H. and Gary A. Rendsburg. The Bible and the Ancient Near East. W. W. Norton and Company (New York:1997).

Hall, Manly P. The Secret Teachings of All Ages. Pb. Penquin (New York:2003)

Harrison, R. K.,ed. The New Unger's Bible Dictionary. Moody Press (Chicago:1988)

Hastings, James ed. Dictionary of the Bible. 5 vols. Charles Scribner's Sons (New York:1909)

Hengel , Martin. The Zealots. Tr by David Smith. T. and T. Clark (Edinburgh:1989)

Jeremias, Joachim. Jerusalem in the Time of Jesus. Pb. Fortress Press (Philadelphia:1967)

Josephus, Complete Works. Tr by William Whiston. Kregel (Grand Rapids, Michigan:1985)

Lapp, Nancy L., "Araq el Emir" in Perdue, Leo G. et al. eds. Archeological Excavations and Biblical Interpretation. John Knox Press (Atlanta, Georgia:1987)

Lawlor, John Irving. The Nabataeans in Historical Perspective. Pb. Baker Book House (Grand Rapids, Michigan:1974)

Lightfoot, John. A Commentary on the New Testament from the Talmud and Hebraica. 4 vols. Hendrickson (USA:1979)

Maier, Paul. Eusebius, the Church History. Kregel (Grand Rapids, Michigan:1999)

Marshall, I. Howard. The Gospel of Luke. William B.Eerdmans Company (Grand Rapids, Michigan:1978)

McBirnie, William Steuart. The Search for the Twelve Apostles. Pb. Tyndale (Wheaton,Illinois:1977)

McClintock, John and James Strong. Cyclopedia of Biblical, Theological and Ecclesiastical Literature. 12 vols. Baker Book House (Grand Rapids, Michigan:1981)

Moore, George Foot. Judaism. 2 vols. Hendrickson (Peabody, Massachusetts:1960)

Orr, James, gen. ed. The International Standard Bible Encyclopedia. 5 vols. Wm. B. Eerdmans Company (Grand Rapids, Michigan:1939)

Patrick, Richard. The Colour Book of Greek Mythology. Octopus Books (New York:1972)

Peloubet, F. N. Peloubet's Bible Dictionary. Universal Book and Bible House (Philadelphia:1947)

Rambsel, Yacov. His Name Is Jesus. Pb. Word Publishing (Nashville:1999)

Roberts, Paul William. In Search of the Birth of Jesus. Riverhead Books (New York; 1995)

Schurer, Emil. A History of the Jewish People in the Time of Christ. 5 vols. Hendrickson (Peabody, Massachusetts:1994)

Vilnay, Zev. The Sacred Land. 3 vols. The Jewish Publication Society of America (Philadelphia:1973)

Wigoder, Geoffrey, ed. Et al. The Encyclopedia of Judaism. Macmillan Publishing Company (New York:1989)

VII. NICODEMUS (BONAI BEN GORION)-JESUS-JOHN THE BAPTIST

Isaiah 52:7 is the beginning of the Equidistant Letter Sequencing of the name Lord God (Joel), Moriah, water, lamb, shalom and 'his signature'. (Rambsel, HNJ, 31 ,39, 46) Thousands of years earlier in Mari, the revealer of divine truths and will was called the Apeli (the Answerer). (Bromiley, ISBE, III, 991) In Mari correspondence, irrigation is mentioned (Bromiley, ISBE, III, 246). Bunni ben Gorion (Nicodemas) was an Irrigator (Lightfoot, III, CNT, 262), a job more important at Petra and Qumran than elsewhere. N icodemas and Apollos who was with Paul knew only of John's teaching. (I Corinthians 3:6) Nicodemas was seeking the divine secret of life when he went to visit Jesus at night. Another famous night Journey was that of Mohammed.

Repentance as preached by John was drowning in the sanctified waters of the Jordan rather than washing away sin. (cf Ezekiel 36:25-26) The John Book has inspired a religious group called the Mandaens in Mesopotamia. As Joel emphasized the Day of the Lord, so does John. Joel (means Lord God or Lord Lord) used the phrase 'I am' in his book of prophecy. The testimony of Nicodemas uses the word 'answer' frequently and suggests teachings from a divine oracle. He called Jesus 'a teacher come from God'. (John 3:2) To the Roman Senate Nicodemus is saying, 'If you believed this about them (your gods), why not believe this about Jesus? At least listen and compare.' Sabianism seems connected with Buddha and Yemen. (Blavatsky, IU, II, 290-291 and Picknett, TR, 333-334)

Only the Masoretic Version of Isaiah contains the ELS found by Yacov Rambsel.

Job 37:9 and 38:32 contain the word 'mazzarot', a word that defies translation. Perhaps it meant predestination. It is assumed to refer to fate, astronomy and the doctrine of predestination. (Bromiley, ISBE, I, 347) Predestination is assumed by astrology and may have inspired the Mohammedan doctrine. (McClintock, I, 499)

PART ONE STATIONS OF THE CROSS

These are notes for a dual biography about Jesus the Divine and John the Baptist. Perhaps the best known idea about Nicodemus is that he came secretly at night to see Jesus. The clue phrase for Part One is 'tell no one'. At the trial of Nicodemus (or Nicholas of Damascus), the defense was put in terms of Exodus 23:7, "The Naki (innocent) slay thou not." The judgment was framed in terms of Psalm 10:8, "In covert places doth he put to death the Naki." (Mead, JCT, 72) The phrase, 'tell no one' refers to the word 'covert'.

SUBJECTS (Luke 20:1-8, did not tell, teach, answer, heaven) Aland notes that Luke 20:4=3:3, 16. When asked to name his authority, Jesus in turn answered by asking his questioners the source of John's authority. In gospel times, Roman emperors had begun to claim divine authority. They each hinted that they were the reincarnation of one of the original twelve in the Roman Pantheon. Jesus had called twelve followers. If the twelve represented the Zodiac (Darlison, GTZ, in passim.), Christianity was illegal to the Romans. If the twelve represent the tribes of Israel, Christianity is Judaism and legal.

FAMILY (Luke 2:8-20, did not tell, Numbers 6:34, Josephus 55, Isaiah 40:11, heavenly host, Gospel of Nicodemas 6:17) Aland notes that Luke 2:27=2:10-12 and vice versa. The Queen of Heaven was a title used for Isis, an Egyptian goddess. (Picknett, TR,292-293) The Mandaeans would use astrological symbols and called the divine the Good Shepherd. (Mead, GJB, 81-86) The heavenly host was fit for a new type of queen, the Virgin Mary. Jesus and John were born six months apart, making the solstice revelant. Jesus was associated with the day and John with the night. An astrologer might say Jesus was born on September 15 under the sign of Virgo, the virgin. (Seymour, BC, 130)

Those with a scientific orientation would attribute the shining in the sky to a magnetic pole attracting solar wind particles to crash into gas particles. (Seymour, BC, 137) One example of this effect would be the lights at the North Pole. The Magi might have been able to predict the time and place of solar winds by the movement of the planets.

GENEALOGY (Luke 1:5-38, could not tell, answer, Lord God, I am, day, angel) Aland notes that Luke 1:13=1:59-60 and Luke 1:30-31=3:6. Isaiah 7:14 prophesied that the Messiah would be born of a virgin. Many Jewish girls prayed that they would be worthy to bear the Messiah. Even so, Mary is quoted as asking the equivalent of 'What shall I do?" (Luke 1:34)

Elizabeth was descended from Aaron, and Mary descended from David of the Tribe of Benjamin. When Jews met at Shiloh for pilgrimages, they allowed the Tribe of Benjamin to date-rape-marry those of other tribes and perhaps even pagan hangers-on. (Judges 21:19-21) Their numbers had been affected by deaths due to war and natural disastor.

At Tyre, the former home of Nicholaus of Damascus, a meteorite named Ka-mut-f was worshiped as the Theban god Amun. (Bauval, OM, 203) A son killed his father in order to mate with his mother as a form of proto-cloning. The point was to cheat death.

SERMON (Luke 3:1-22, water, fruit, What shall I do?, Holy Ghost) In the Gospel of Nicodemas 19:1 are these words, "Then Jesus stretched forth his hand, and said, come to me, all ye my saints... who were condemned by the tree of forbidden fruit..." (Hone, LBB. 86) For political reasons Nicodemus could have attended the sermons of John, but not those of Jesus. The sermon of John asks three times, 'What shall we do?'

The Mandaeans may have saved John and Elizabeth when Zechariah died, or John may have become a Mandaean in another way. They envisioned the night sky as a light ship with the name of the Great

Light at its helm. (Mead, GJB, 75) When John baptizes Jesus, a voice from the heavens speaks.

MARVEL (Luke 8:40-56, tell no one, answer, spirit) Aland notes that Luke 8:48=7:50 and Luke 8:56=5:14. The Hindu God Krishna healed a young girl. He asks 'Why do you weep?' and 'Do you not see that she is just sleeping?' He said to her,'Rise and walk.' God's healing power is universal rather than false. (Blavatsky, IU, II, 241) Jair, the father of the young girl, will later on be asked to testify that Jesus healed on the Sabbath, contrary to Jewish Law. Bernice was healed on the same day but she was not allowed to testify because she was a woman. (Barnstone, OB, 362)

The Magi may have brought this story of divinity to the Holy Land. Perhaps Nicodemus recognized that Jesus had already done the same thing.

FAME (Luke 5:10-16, tell no man, testimony) Aland notes that Luke 5:14=8:56. The John Book often uses the words 'fishers of men'. (Mead, GJB, 14) Aesculapius was said to have brought sight to the blind and to have raised the dead as signs of divine power. (Picknett, TR, 269) Isaiah 61:1-2 describes what the Messiah will do. Jesus healed but he told no one he was the Messiah. He went into the desert to pray.

Luke uses the word for 'to take alive' which is descriptive of net-fishing and evangelism. (Marshall, L, 205)

PROPHECY (Luke 9:7-22, tell no one, answer, water, I am, day, Exodus 3:14, Josephus 365, risen prophet, Gospel of Nicodemus 3:4) Aland notes that Luke 9:7-8=9:18 and Luke 9:18=9:7-8. Belief in reincarnation is known to most Christians in that many thought that John the Baptist was the reincarnation of Elijah. Some of John's followers thought that since the constellation Orion went below the horizon when Elijah died and reappeared when John was born, so John was the reincarnation of Elijah. Most Jews believed that God would send Elijah to help them in time of trouble. (Picknett, TR, 270) When the angel prophesied John's birth, he quotes Malachi 4:5: Elijah would return before the (judgment) Day of the Lord.

Some Jews thought the Messiah would be Nehemiah or a son of Joseph. Peter answers that Jesus is the Christ of God. Jesus said to tell no one.

LAST WEEK (Luke 23:6-12, did not tell, answer, day, Isaiah 53:7, miracle, Gospel of Nicodemus 11:1, 12:6) Aland notes that Luke 23:8=9:9. Zohar, the Book of Radiance, describes the arrangement for the Virgin Mary to marry Joseph. (Barnstone, OB, 707-722) Perhaps the name of the city of Zoar has its origin in Zohar.

Herod Antipas knew he had had John beheaded, but it intrigued him that Jesus could be the reincarnation of John the Baptist. Jesus was like the lamb in Isaiah 53:7, 'He was oppressed, and he was afflicted, but he opened not his mouth: he is brought as a lamb before slaughter, so he opened not his mouth." This seems ironic for the fulfillment of Isaiah 40:9-11 which is about the victorious shepherd. Numbers 24:17 states, "I shall see him, but not now. I shall behold him, but not nigh. There shall come a Star out of Jacob..."

DEATH (Luke 22:66-71, would not tell, Exodus 3:14, revelation, Isaiah 65:12, Gospel of Nicodemus 3:10) God was asked his name in the Torah and he replied 'I Am.' Jesus is asked before the Sanhedrin if he is the Christ. The answer is 'Ye say that I am.' It could mean, 'You say. I am.' Jesus rose from a rock tomb as did Mithra, the Persian God of Light. (Harrison, NUBD, 877 and Picknett, TR, 269) After John's death, some Mandaeans affirmed John as the King of Light and called Jesus a false prophet who had led the people astray. (Picknett, TR, 349)

Using astronomy, there was a prediction that the Messiah would come the year that Nicodemus approached Jesus at night. It was the year of the crucifixion, not the birth. Jesus as Messiah had come after five thousand and a half years as predicted. (Hone, LBB, 90)

AFTER THE DEATH (Luke 12:1-12, secrets told, teach, Deuteronomy 32:4, Isaiah 32:6, 3:9, an gels, Gospel of Nicodemus chapter X) Aland notes that Luke 12:2=8:17, Luke 12:7=21:18,24 and Luke 12:11=21:12. The journey to the underworld and the path of death has inspired many versions. (Bierlein, PM, 200-236) In the Gospel of Nicodemus Jesus goes into hell to save those inside. He leaves three including Herod the Great who killed the infants. Herod had been inspired by the astrological beliefs of the Pharoah who killed the baby boys in the time of Moses. Then the appearing of Jupiter and Saturn as one had been interpreted as a threat to the Pharoahs. The story of Eleazar (Lazarus) is noticeably not included in the Gospel of Nicodemas but it is in Luke 16:19-31.

If Nicodemus prayed the Lord's Prayer, this is what he might say. The word 'water' has its ELS beginning in Isaiah 52:7 as does the name Moriah. (Rambsel, HNJ, 46) Mt. Moriah was the time and place of sacrifice. Carrington triads in this part are 'knock' and 'dig'. Nicodemus was also known as Bonai ben Gurion, the digger of wells. (Lightfoot, CNT, III, 262) The word 'dig' was used not only in the agricultural sense but also to mean making an effort to understand scripture.

OUR (Luke 6:42-48, dig, idea of answer, (command) water, Exodus 33:22, cf Josephus, 245, Isaiah 32:2) . Nicholaus of Damascus was asked by Marc Antony and Cleopatra to live at Petra. They wanted him to teach their children (which they called the Sun and the Moon). The relationship between Nicholaus and Nicodemus could have been family with Ptolemy as a brother to one of them. (Hastings, DOB, III, 543)

Petra (rock) was the capital of Nabatea where Aretas IV was Governor. Tyre (rock) the former home of Nicodemus was once an island. Nabatea was at border war with Herod Antipas. During the trial of Pontius Pilate, Aretas was absent, but Herod Antipas was present. Nicodemus was on the side of Aretas IV and spoke for him. Herod Antipas was exiled to France.

One Bunni (ben=son) was a Levite in the time of Nehemiah 9:4. When the mother and brothers of Jesus came to see him, Jesus answered, 'My mother and my brethren are those which hear the Word of God and do it."

Jesus demonstrates his power to command the winds and water.

FATHER (Luke 10:13-14, Tyre, Exodus 33:22, Isaiah 32:2) Nicholaus of Damascus was from Tyre, the son of Mennius of Tyre (or Tyrus of Mayence). Nicodemus was somehow related to that family. Mennius was killed by one of his sons who believed in Ka-mut-ef, a religion from Thebes. (Doresse, SBEG, 93). A man 'clones' himself by killing his father and mating with his mother to produce his 'twin'. Nicholaus and a brother Ptolemy came to Samaria/Petra afterward. (cf Hastings, DOB, III, 544, Josephus 285 and Finegan, A, 282)

NAME (Luke 11:5-13, answer, knock, Leviticus 19:23, Holy Spirit, Gospel of Nicodemas 5:11) Son (Bunni) is the clue word. Also Demas (giving) is an abbreviated form of Nicodemas (Nakdimon). The name Bonai ben Gurion may suggest the phrase 'a man of the world'. (Lightfoot, CNT, III, 262) He had the ability of the Patriarch Joseph to dig the grain storage tanks in the desert. They increased the time grain could be stored. For charity he chose to help face to face. An exception was grain that he sent to the Temple at Jerusalem when it was under siege about 70 c.e. He was a nephew of Ptolemy that Jesus healed. (Luke 5:17-26, Josephus, 471) Joseph, the father of Jesus, was known for giving bread to the poor. Nicodemas left carpets at his door so the poor could stay warm. When asked if he were a believer, he answered that he chose to take his lot with Jesus. When Nicodemus was put on trial, the charge was Exodus 4:23, but his defence was Exodus 4:22. (Dalman, JCT, 72)

Nicodemus said, "We see that you are a teacher from God." (John 3:2)

KINGDOM (Luke 13:6-9, answer, (water), fig, dig, fruit, wrath of God) Fruit sometimes required irrigation. The gardener in the parable gives the trees three years to produce fruit. Time was important to Nicodemas. He reasoned that Jesus was the Messiah because 5,000 years and a half had passed since a prophecy said he would come (return) at that time. (Hone, LBB, Gospel of Nicodemas, Chapter 22) He thought 'Jesus' had come to earth before. As the kingdom was discussed, Jesus told Nicodemus that those who see the Kingdom of God must be born again. (John 3: 3)

Nicodemus saw that there was not enough water at a feast in Jerusalem. He asked a man of great wealth to lend him twelve wells of water. If it had not rained by a certain day, they would be delivered. On the stated day, Nicodemus gave a speech and lifted his arms to pray. It began to rain so the seller and Nicodemus debated about when it began to rain. The sun came out, and he was given the name Nicodemus because the sun shone for him. (Lightfoot, CNT, III, 262)

EARTH (Luke 7:37-47, answer, tears (water), tell no one, Exodus 20:8, Isaiah 26:19, forgive sin, Gospel of Nicodemus 1:4,2:17) Aland notes that Luke 7:48-49=5:20-21. Like Attis and Adonis, Jesus was attractive to women. (Picknett, TR, 269) Perhaps the woman is Mariamne, once married to Herod the Great, who had returned to live with her father Simon ben Boethus. Babylonian women were forced to serve Venus as a prostitute at least once in their lifetimes. (Harrison, NUBD, 537) In effect she served God the day she anointed Jesus as king.

Because Nicodemus became a Christian, his family lost its great wealth. His daughter whose former bed cost twelve deniers was seen picking up barleycorns from cow dung to feed herself. (Lightfoot, CNT, III, 263)

BREAD (Luke 13:10-16, Day, water, teach, ox, ass, miracle, Gospel of Nicodemus 5:25, 2:17) Aland notes that Luke 13:15=14:5. The Sanhedrin was debating about the proper position for prayer. A certain woman could not stand the recommended way. Jesus healed her so that she could stand up straight. (Charlesworth, H&J, 431-432)

The beast could drink water on its own accord on the Sabbath, but its owner must not carry water to it. (Lightfoot, CNT, 142) People should come to faith in baptism on their own accord.

EVIL (Luke 16:19-31, water, miracle, Gospel of Nicodemus chapters 15-18 and cf 12:23) Descriptions of hell are appropriate if one is writing about the Day of the Lord. Whether wealth was desirable was debated. Abraham's wealth was considered a sign of God's blessing. "He shall be as a tree planted by rivers of waters. " John the Baptist and the Rechabites renounced wealth as a means by which men mistreated the poor. The importance of water to the thirsty is noted. (Lightfoot, CNT, III, 166-167) As stated above, Nicodemus did something about it when he realized the people were thirsty.

FORGIVE US (Luke 5:17-26, answer, dig into roof, Leviticus 24:16) The friends of Nicodemus (or Ptolemy) realize that Jesus could help him. Because of the crowd, they dig a hole in the roof and lower him into the presence of Jesus. Jesus forgives his sins, but the Pharisees say only God can forgive sin. They accuse Jesus of blasphemy. He heals the man, but he has not cured Nicodemus of his timidity. (Bromiley, ISBE, I, 183)

AS WE (Luke 16:1-13, dig, What shall I do?) Although it was not his to give, Herod the Great ceded some balsam groves in Petra to Marc Antony who gave them to Cleopatra. The Governor of Edom tenant-farmed these plants given to Solomon by the Queen of Sheba. The first year he sent the full share for Herod to give it to Cleopatra, but after that he shorted and delayed sending her share. He wanted Herod to be blamed for the shortage so she would deal with him directly. (Josephus, 319) Nicodemus was his adviser.

Later at Petra (Rock or Tyre) , Aretas IV was Governor (like a king). They were having border wars because Herod Antipas was husband to the daughter of Aretas IV. Even though they had two sons, Antipas was living openly with Herodias, his brother Philip's ex-wife. She had caused John the Baptist to be beheaded. The daughter of Aretas IV Shaqailath escaped to Petra. Nicodemus was on their side, but Rome favored peace at any cost. (Josephus, 382) Tiberius died before the trial. Nevertheless, the Roman Senate sent Herod Antipas and Herodias to France.

By trying to please everybody, Nicodemus lost all he had.

AMEN (Luke 21:12-33, answer, fig tree, teach, day, fruit, Lord Lord, Isaiah 4:8) Aland notes Luke 21:12=12:11 and Luke 12:18,24=12:7. Tiberius, Emperor of Rome, had gone to school in Rome with Pilate, Antipas and Aretas IV. Tiberius loved Nicholaus dates (may have been figs). He ordered the travelers coming from Israel to bring them to him. Jesus speaks of a fig tree as the symbol of Israel. It has not born fruit for God, its owner. The gardener will work with it a while longer, but if it does not produce fruit, it will be cut down.

A grave said to be containing Stephen who was helped by the Good Samaritan, Gamaliel and Nicodemus has been found. (Orr, ISBE, IV, 2142) One might wonder if they died at the same time because they had become Christians.

PART THREE: THE TEN COMMANDMENTS

The Roman Senate had to decide whether or not Christianity was just another sect of Judaism. If it were, Pilate had offended in that Judaism was a religion recognized by the Roman Senate as legal. Tiberius sought to disband monotheistic religion, but he accepted Judaism as necessary for peace. (Schurer, HJP, 302) This religious charge would supplement the charge of breaking the Pax Romana.

The Herod in this section is Herod Antipas, the enemy of Aretas IV. At the end of the year 37 c.e. he and Herodias were exiled to Gaul. (Harrison, NUBD, 559) Perhaps the testimony of Nicodemus played a part in the decision, but expulsion would have been the decision of the Roman Senate, not of Tiberius. Tiberius died just before the party of eyewitnesses for the trials of Herod Antipas and Pontius Pilate arrived.

The name Edom and the word for behold (idou) have similar sounds.

ONE GOD

(Luke 10:25-37, answer, Lord God, behold, heaven (eternal life) The questioner wanted to know about eternal life. Jesus first tells him to obey the Ten Commandments. Then he tells the story of the Good Samaritan. Perhaps he was the tetrarch Herod Philip who assisted exiles from the warring territories of his brothers. Herodias deeply resented John the Baptist's preaching. He said the Messiah would not come so long as Antipas sinned openly living with her. John was beheaded, breaking the pax Romana in 34 c.e. Tiberius had since that warned Pilate, Aretas and Antipas were not to break Pax Romana again.

IDOLS

(Luke 4:1-13, answer, Lord God, Jesus beheld the kingdoms, angels) Aland notes that Luke 4:3,9=22:70. Men are tempted to use magic, force or status to meet their unfulfilled needs. The devil promises Jesus good if he will compromise on obedience to the scripture. Jesus refuses.

HOLY NAME

(Luke 13:1-9, blood, answer, behold) Pilate had taken money from the Temple at Jerusalem to repair the city's water system. Some saw this use of God's money (Corban) as a sin. Then an overhead arch fell on the place where sick people waited for water from the spring of the virgin to come rushing down. Instead the nearly repaired arch fell and crushed them. Some saw this as God's wrath over the money. (Josephus, 380, 479)

SABBATH

(Luke 14:2-6, answer, day, behold, I am, ox, ass, Psalm 118:26, Isaiah 1:3, miracle) Aland notes that Luke 14:5=13:15. Isaiah says that the ox (cf bous=Boethus) knows its owner and the ass (cf onus=On) its crib, but the people of Israel do not know their god. The Boethus lineage of priests was from the Temple at On.

At Qumran it was a sin to defecate on the Sabbath, so when several holy days were in a row, some got sick of 'dropsy'. Jesus healed such a one.

PARENTS

(Luke 1:46-79, answer, day, Lord God, behold, miracle (John's birth), Gospel of Nicodemus 16:19) Aland notes that Luke 1:59-60=1:13. When the angel told Zechariah of John's impending birth, Zechariah could not speak. When he did, he said his son's name is John (gift of God).

KILL

(Luke 11:39-51, blood, answer, behold) Wars with Greeks, Syrians and Samaritans were so numerous that this seems not to relate to one event. Nicholaus of Damascus was sent by Augustus to advise Herod the Great and his sons. (Josephus, 351) Marc Antony and Cleopatra wanted him to tutor the Sun and the Moon (their children) at Petra. He assists Edom (Nabatea) in its struggles against the Herods. He advised another Herod to restore Jewish monuments at Hebron. Judas Maccabee went out against the Edomites, "besieged and destroyed Hebron." (Schurer, HJP, I, 1, 121)

ADULTERY

(Luke 20:27-38, answer, Lord God, Judges 21:16, angels) The Tribe of Benjamin lost many men and women in battle. Benjaminites were given the right to date-rape-marry women from other tribes who came to the feasts at Shiloh. Obviously this did not lead to clear lineage. Jesus said marriage is for the living. Although adultery was the announced objection to Antipas, he had sinned worse when he allowed John to be beheaded. It was done in part to protect his acts of adultery.

STEAL

(Luke 20:21-26, answer, I am, watch=behold, teach) Jesus was asked about coins with images on them. The sons of Annas were charging worshipers to exchange them for ancient faceless coins. They would not allow 'images' within the temple. Then they sold them again and kept the profit for themselves. (Edersheim, LTJM, 371-372) Jesus said to render unto Caesar what is Caesar's and unto God what is God's.

LIE

(Luke 5:17-26, answer, behold, Exodus 20:3, miracle) Some thought that only God could forgive sin. When Jesus said that the man's sins were forgiven, Ptolemy's sins were forgiven, the people called Jesus a blasphemer because they said only God can forgive sin.

COVET

(Luke 12:12-21, fruit, What shall I do?, cf Gospel of Nicodemus 5:10-11) Jews were allowed to store two and a half years' supply of grain. All else belonged to the widow, the orphan and the stranger. If he stored more, it would be a sin. (Lightfoot, CNT, III, 261-262)

PART FOUR BIBLIOGRAPHY

Aland, Kurt, et al. eds. The Greek New Testament. United Bible Societies. American Bible Society (New York:1975)

Atwell, Joseph. The Roman Origin of Christianity. Pb. (2001)

Barnstone, Willis, ed. The Other Bible. Pb. HarperSanFrancisco (San Francisco:1984)

Bauval, Robert and Adrian Gilbert. The Orion Mystery. Doubleday Canada Limited (Toronto:1994)

Bierlein, J. F. Parallel Myths. Pb. Ballantine Publishing Group (New York: 1993)

Blavatsky, Helen P. Isis Unveiled. Pb. 2 vols. Theosophical Publishing House

(Wheaton,Illinois:1972)

Bromiley, Geoffrey W. The International Bible Encyclopedia. 4 vols. William B. Eerdmans (Grand Rapids, Michigan: 1979)

Carrington, Philip. The Primitive Christian Calendar. University Press

(Cambridge:1952)

Charlesworth, James H. and Loren Johns, eds. Hillel and Jesus. Fortress Press (Minneapolis: 1984)

Dalman, Gustaf, et al. Jesus Christ in the Talmud, Midrash, Zohar and the Liturgy of the Temple. Deighton, Bell and Company (New York:1893)

Darlison, Bill. The Gospel & the Zodiac. Duckworth Overlook (New York:2007)

Doresse, Jean. The Secret Books of the Egyptian Gnostics. MJF Books (New York:1986)

Edersheim, Alfred. The Life and Times of Jesus the Messiah. 2 vols Wm. B. Eerdmans (Grand Rapids, Michigan:1976)

Finegan, Jack. Light from the Ancient Past. Princeton (Princeton:1959)

Harrison, R. K. New Unger's Bible Dictionary. Moody Press (Chicago:1988)

Hastings, James, ed. Dictionary of the Bible. 5 vols. Charles Scribner's Sons (Edinburgh:1908)

Hone, William. Lost Books of the Bible. Crown Publishers (Cleveland,Ohio:1979)

Jeremias, Joachim. Jerusalem in the Time of Jesus. Pb. Fortress Press (Philadelphia:1975)

Josephus. Complete Works. Translated by William Whiston. Kregel (Grand Rapids, Michigan:1981)

Lightfoot, John. A Commentary on the New Testament from the Talmud and Hebraica. 4 vols. Hendrickson Publishers (USA:1995)

McClintock, John and James Strong. Cyclopedia of Biblical, Theological and Ecclesiastical Literature. 12 vols. Baker Book House (Grand Rapids, Michigan:1981)

Mead, G. R. S. The Gnostic John the Baptizer. John M. Watkins (London:1924)

Picknett, Lynn and Clive Prince. The Templar Revelation. Pb. Simon and Schuster (New York:1997)

Rambsel, Yacov. His Name Is Jesus. Word Publishing (Nashville, Tennesee:1999)

Schurer, Emil. A History of the Jewish People. Hendrickson (Peabody, Massachusetts:1994)

VIII. ZACCHAEUS (MATTHIAS)-NOAH -JESUS

The name Matthias is found to begin at Isaiah 53:5 in Equidistant Letter sequencing. Also stemming out from Isaiah 53:5 are other ELS for 'enter into our salvation ', 'life for the grace of Noah', 'wise', 'wine' and, ' for our transgressions'. (Rambsel, HNJ, 25, 36. 43, 46, 74) Publicans like Matthias (Zacchaeus) obeyed civil law based on the Noahic Covenant. Whether Noah was one man in a single generation or one of many in the lineage prior to Enoch, the Covenant had seven terms. God told mankind to choose between two ways. (Genesis 30:15-20) Zacchaeus was probably one of the seventy, for he was chosen to replace his nephew Judas Iscariot after the Crucifixion. He wrote a book called Traditions. Perhaps Matthew 15:6 refers to it. Enoch had written Similitudes (comparisons using the words like or as). Using 'Son of Man' and 'Kingdom of God', Enoch describes God as Creator of all time. In His own time God decides what is good and what is evil. (Ferguson, EEC, 299) Hellenism counted time as circular repeating itself as stars do, but Christians thought time was more like the unrolling of a single scroll until the end of the universe. (Doresse, SBEG, 111)

Noah and his family were saved from the sea. Many religions report a god coming out of the sea; for example, the Mayas and Quetzalcoatl.

PART ONE: STATIONS OF THE CROSS

These are notes for a dual biography of Noah and Jesus. Alllusions to time and to the number 'two' unify Part One of the testimony of Zacchaeus. The Book of Jubilees deals with the relation ship between astronomy and time. In the Egyptian book Pistis-Sophia, Jesus demonstrates that he is the master of time. He changed the movement of the spheres so canceling the power of the astrologers. (Doresse, SBEG, 68) One may even suspect that Zacchaeus-Matthias may have been called Secundus at a later time. (Acts 20:4) On the other hand, Thomas or Agrippa II may have been Secundus.

SUBJECTS (Luke 6:38-40, as, shall be=at some time, master and student=two, Genesis 6:9) Having the same (like) measure was an example of the behavior expected from Jews and from Gentiles living in the land. (Charlesworth, OTP, I, 171) Actually publicans were allowed to follow Noahic Law instead of Mosaic Law. God called Noah perfect, and Zacchaeus is quoted as saying a disciple shall be perfect as (like) his master. (Hastings, DOB, Extra, 437, in his book called Traditions.)

FAMILY (Luke 2:8-24, day, night, enter, two, Genesis 9:12, Ezekiel 1:28) Aland notes that Luke 2:9=24:5, 2:14=19:38 and 2:19=2:51. Zaccheus was son of High Priest Annas, but he served as priest under the aegis of his father-in-law Simon ben Boethus, an Egyptian. (Jeremias, JTJ, 155, 194-5) Originally the Chanina (Annas) family were singers. Angels and demons are an integral part of the Book of Enoch. Angels singing in the sky emphasize God as the Creator of all. God placed a rainbow in the sky to seal his promise to Noah. God allows one-tenth of the demons to remain after the flood to tempt mankind. (Hastings, DOB, III, 557 in Jubilees)

The Egyptian lunistellar calendar was very old. A year was divided into flood, plant-and-harvest and low water. (Finegan, LFAP, 564) By 2937-2821 b.c., it was the standard civilian calendar, but around 2500 b.c, it was abandoned. An Apamenian garrison existed in Egypt, so the use may have been taken to the Mount Ararat-Apamea area from Egypt. (Finegan, LFAP, 565-566, 409) Noah's Ark is said to have ended its trip at Mount Ararat, and Noah was worshiped or honored at Apamea. (Peloubet, PBD, 455) The Book of Noah may not have been written until a time between 50 b.c. and 80 c.e. (Hastings, DOB, III,

557) Interest still existed in Noah in gospel times although Jews like Marcion in Alexandria, Egypt, protested.

GENEALOGY (Luke 3:21-23, years, enter (open), Genesis 8:6-9) Aland notes that Luke 17:33=9:24. Noah needed a sign that the waters had receded so that the people could leave the ark. He sent out a dove and a raven. When John the Baptist baptizes Jesus, the voice of a dove is a sign that the Messiah has come. The Annas (Chanina) family was descended from Zakir, the first Aramaic king of North Syria. (Chan means 'grace' and one ELS for Isaiah 53:5 is 'for the grace of Noah'.)

Zacchaeus was a son to the High Priest Annas, but he was also a tax collector. His short stature made him 'disabled'. His father and brothers, even brother-in-law, were all priests of the Chanina family before him. The family ran the 'Booths of Annas' on the Mount of Olives, selling wine and oil. For profit they sold their own 'perfect' animals for sacrifice, and they exchanged coins to eliminate images on the offerings. (Edersheim, LTJM, 371-372)

SERMON (Luke 17:22-36, days, Son of M an, two, Genesis 7:11,7) Aland notes that Luke 17:21=17:23, 21:8, Luke 17:25=9:22, 18:32-33, Luke 17:27=21:34 and Luke 17:33=9:24. The word 'drank' suggests wine, and Noah gets drunk after he leaves the ark. Matthias had written a book called Traditions, which of course means 'looking back'. (McBirnie, STA, 243) Some have suggested that Matthias wrote or inspired the Book of Hebrews. Its writer hoped to stop new Christians from returning to Qumran.

Enoch uses the phrases Son of Man and Kingdom of God, and this testimony does, too. The two men in one bed could have been Jesus and Judas Iscariot, nephew of Matthias. Judas left the Last Supper to betray Jesus who was left. The two women who were grinding spices may have been Mary Magdalene and the wife of Matthias. Mary Magdalene left to tell the Good News. Perhaps Matthias was one of the two men at Bethany, the other being Jesus.

MARVEL (Luke 9:10-26, day, Son of Man, two, Genesis 9:20) Aland notes that Luke 9:24=17:33 and Luke 9:26=12:9. God had a plan for Noah and his family to survive after the Flood. Noah took the animals on board two by two so they could reproduce later. Jesus took five loaves and two fish to feed the five thousand. There were four (two by two) priestly families that dominated the priesthood in the time of Jesus.

FAME (Luke 10:1-12, day, Kingdom of God, enter, Genesis 7:2) Enoch uses the phrases 'Kingdom of God' and 'Son of Man'. Jesus sends the seventy disciples out two by two. When it was time to replace Judas Iscariot as one of the twelve, two men, his uncle Matthias and Joseph Justus, were considered. They had been members of the seventy. Matthias was chosen by lot.

Acccording to the Egyptian Book of Norea, Norea was the wife of Noah. Because she did not want to enter the Ark, she set fire to it three times. (Doresse, SBEG, 163)

PROPHECY (Luke 14:12-24, time, enter (come in), two (second), II Enoch, 179,) Noah had three sons. Although the messenger (Jesus?) calls three men, each has a religious reason not to come to the banquet. However. reason reveals their reluctance is not on religious grounds. The first says he has bought land, but the only land he was allowed to buy had been in his family for generations. He already knew it. The second said he had bought five yoke of oxen which he needed to prove. To prove was to work together, but even the strongest of men could only prove three. The third said he had married a wife. Jewish men were exempt from battle until an heir was born, but going to a banquet would not endanger his lineage. The master (God?) told the messenger (Jesus?) to invite others to come in (enter salvation). Those he invited first (some of the Jews?) would not be allowed to enter, but the Gentiles (even some publicans) were invited.

LAST WEEK (Luke 19:28-44, time, enter, two, Genesis 9:20-23, Zechariah 9:9, Psalm 118;26) Aland notes that Luke 19:32=22:13 and Luke 19:38=2:14. The scene as described is a coronation. Zechariah prophesied the Christ as follows: Rejoice greatly, O daughter of Zion; shout, o Daughter of Jerusalem; behold, thy King cometh to thee. He is just and having salvation; lowly and riding upon an ass, and upon a colt the foal of an ass. 'Thy day' seems to relate to Deuteronomy 5:29, Psalm 95:7 and Hebrews 3:13.

When Noah got drunk and was naked, his sons threw garments over his body. When Jesus made his triumphal entry, people threw their garments upon his path.

DEATH (Luke 24:1-8, morning, enter, two, Genesis 9:29) Aland notes that Luke 24:5=2:9. By Zacchaeus reporting what Jesus said about death rather than reporting on the death of Jesus, one may assume that he was not an eyewitness. His father, brothers, brother-in-law and nephew were the instigators of the crucifixion. Since he was chosen to replace Judas Iscariot, one can assume he was not party to the plot.

Noah (at least one Noah) reached the age of 950 years.

AFTER THE DEATH (Luke 24:13-35, day, enter (went), two, Genesis 9:6-32) Aland notes that Luke 24:30=22:19. The family of Seth included Enoch and they walked with God. The family of Annas claimed to be descended from Seth.

After the Resurrection, Jesus walked on the road to Emmaus with two men. The name Cleopas can mean 'son of a famous father'. Later on in Rome, Matthias Zacchaeus (son of High Priest Annas) was asked to negotiate peace between his brother-in-law Simon Magus (son of Felix Procurator-to-be of Samaria) and Simon Peter, the apostle. (Schneemelcher, NTA, II, 514) Peter had said he wanted Matthias Zacchaeus to replace his nephew Judas Iscariot. Jesus had stayed and rested in his house. (The name Noah means rest or comfort. Schneemelcher, NTA, II, 517)

PART II: THE LORD'S PRAYER

If Zacchaeus were to pray, this is what he might say. The unifying word in Part Two is '"wine"'.

OUR (Luke 7:29-35, equinox, Son of Man, like, 'two', wine, Exodus 32:19, Isaiah 65:13, Psalm 30:11, Hebrews 13:15) Aland notes that Luke 7:29-30=3:7. The proposed wedding of Herod Antipas and Herodias was a matter of shame. The death of Lazarus became a matter of rejoicing when Jesus raised him from the dead. When John the Baptist was alive, he was considered too strict, but when Jesus ate with sinners (like Zacchaeus=Matthias), he was too lax. To offer praise for both would be more pleasing.

Legend says that John the Baptist was conceived during the winter equinox and born in the spring. Once Matthias's mother sold her hairlace so that he could have the proper ceremonial wine. (Lightfoot, CNT, 190-191) When he died, he left a great quantity of wine to his sons including Johanan ben Zakki. (McBirnie, STA, 198)

FATHER (Luke 3:2-11, Annas, generation, likewise, salvation, two, Genesis 14:8, Isaiah 61:6, Psalm 23:1, Hebrews 5:10, 7:1) Aland notes that Luke 3:7=7:29-30 and style of Luke 3:6=19:9. Enoch writes about Melchisedek. Christ was the High Priest according to the Order of Melchisedek. Annas claimed the heritage of Seth, the good son of Adam and Eve. (Peloubet, PBD, 35) In Samaria the three stones called the Steles of Seth were known to be a site of ancient worship. The Syrians called their priests shepherds.

Annas was high priest (6-15 c.e.) and so were his five sons, one son-in-law (Caiaphas) and one grandson (Matthias). (Jeremias, JTJ, 94) Zacchaeus (Matthias) was a son and the grandson was Matthew, the son of Theophilus ben Annas. Matthew's wife, Mary, Joshua ben Gamla's wife Martha, Eleazar (Lazarus) and high priest Joazar were the children of high priest Simon ben Boethus. (Jeremias, JTJ, 154-155) His daughter Mariamne ben Boethus was desired by Herod the Great. To improve the family's status, he made them High Priests. Matthias chose to be considered a son of his father-in-law Boethus instead of becoming High Priest by his birth father Annas. Joseph Caiaphas was brother-in-law to Matthias because he married his sister.

NAME (Luke 19:1-10, today, Son of Man, salvation, enter). Aland notes that Luke 19:10=15:4, 6, 9 and Luke 19:7=5:30. The idea is similar in Luke 19:9 and 3:6. Zacchaeus climbs up into a tree to see Jesus passing by. Jesus invites him to share a meal, and Zacchaeus becomes a believer. He repents and promises to restore anything he took wrongfully. Sheep were to be restored fourfold. Tax collectors bid on a location and could charge as they wished. If unemployed by the priests, Levites were often hired by Rome because they could read and write. Those who favored the Noahic Covenant said that metallurgy, the use of blood and reading-and-writing caused the downfall before the Flood. (Hastings, DOB, III, 556) Matthias said he would restore fourfold anything he had taken by false accusation .

KINGDOM (Luke 13: 18-19, 'time'. Kingdom of God, like, Ezekiel 17:23, 31:6, 'two') Aland notes the similarity of style. II Enoch is called Similitudes. Cannibals were known to exist near Sinope (near homonym for mustard seed). Andrew or Thaddeus is credited with saving Matthias from the cannibals near Sinope. (McBirnie, STA, 243) The name Sinope is a near homonym to 'mustard seed'. Modian (Measures) may be a clue to understanding the second similitude. Moses had taught that men should have only one measure for buying and selling. This second comparison may allude to killing or sparing lives. The Maccabees built a tower at Modein which had a shelf. Rather than bury their numerous dead, they placed their dead upon the shelf for birds to carry them to heaven. Leaven was a symbol of evil which only God can judge in the Kingdom of God. The death of Jesus and his resurrection are keys to the kingdom.

EARTH (Luke 10:1-12, day, two by two, Kingdom of God) One can wonder about the seventy. Going out as lambs amongst wolves would mean the need to rely on the shepherd. The allusion to Sodom may refer to its destruction. That is to be matched by a future destruction as devastating as Noah's Flood. In the meantime Jesus says to eat and drink whatever is offered to them. Matthias was chosen out of this group. (Acts 1:21-22)

BREAD (Luke 22:14-20, hour, Kingdom of God, cup=wine, likewise, broke into two) Aland notes that Luke 22:19=24:30. The wine represents the blood of Jesus. The original Noahic Covenant forbids the shedding of blood. It was later amended so that butchers could drain blood from animals used for food. (Genesis 9:4-5) Jehovah's Witnesses and others still forbid the use of blood in transfusions.

There is a hint of the Nazirite Vow which when fulfilled precedes God's blessing.

EVIL (Luke 16:13-18, until time, Kingdom of God, two) Divorce is the evil. Israel was ashamed when Herod Antipas wanted to divorce his wife to marry his brother's ex-wife. They would have asked the priests for an opinion.

Enoch II talks about the two ways and the Elect One. Jesus is teaching that the heart must choose one way, but that way fulfills the promise of the old way. For example, Matthias did not choose to remain as High Priest in Jerusalem. He went to Armenia as an evangelist.

The idea that a man shall be like his master is a quotation from the Book of Traditions which Matthias wrote. (Hastings, DOB, Extra, 437) Justification for resusing the quote in this testimony is the number two.

FORGIVE US (Luke 5:30-39, straightway=time, wine) The creation of new wine in Cana was wine better than the old. (John 2:10) Matthias had difficulty choosing whether his dominant faith was Judaism or Christianity. (cf Jeremias, JTJ, 194) Matthew must have been nephew to Matthias which makes Theophilus Matthew's father. Matthias ben Annas (Zacchaeus) was offered the position of High Priest in 41 c.e. and in 65 but he declined. He had been overlooked earlier because of his stature which was considered a deformity. His nephew as Matthias, son of Theophilus, became High Priest in 65-67 c. e. (Jeremias, JTJ, 378)

In Alexandria the Cantheras family had manufactured bottles. One bottle has the shape of a head with very small handles that resembled ears.

AS WE (Luke 21:34-38, time, wine, Genesis 14:16, Isaiah 5:11, cf Psalm 104:15) Aland notes that Luke 21:34=17:27 and Luke 21:37=19:47. As in the days of Noah and Lot, the people had turned to pleasures, including wine, and they had forgotten God.

Even so, Jesus went to Solomon's Porch almost every morning to teach. At night he went to the Mount of Olives. The Chanina (Annas) family certainly knew of his presence, but they did not object lest the people defend him.

AMEN (Luke 10:25-37, morrow, wine, two, Genesis 18, Isaiah 29:22, Psalm 104:15)9:20, Isaiah 61:3, Psalm 1:3, Hebrews 13:9) Certainly there were many robberies. One occurred when Stephanus, a servant of the emperor, was carrying furniture. (Schurer, HJP, I.2.172) Jesus told the story of the Good Samaritan who promises to 'return'. The Good Samaritan used oil and wine to cleanse the victim's wounds.

Once Zacchaeus was threatened by cannibals near Sinope. Andrew saved him, and their king wanted to kill their enemies. Zacchaeus and Andrew pled for their lives for they wanted to save them. Then Zacchaeus was sent there a second time. He healed the wife and son of King Bulphamus. They became Christians which angered the king. The king had Zacchaeus burned in the courtyard of his palace. (Kraeling, TD, 228-229) His body was placed in an iron coffin in the sea. The next morning the church could see his sinking iron coffin with a shining cross above it. (Kraeling, TD, 228-229)

PART THREE: THE TEN COMMANDMENTS

The writings of Matthias are called the Book of Traditions. Luke 16:13 and Luke 6:40 are quotations from that book. (Hastings, DOB, Extra, 437) Isaiah 53:5 is the starting point for the ELS for 'enter into our salvation'. To seek and save the lost is the theme of Part Three.

ONE GOD

(Luke 9:49-56, time, Son of Man, seek to save, second village) James and John ask Jesus to burn a Samaritan village. He refuses for he came to save men, not destroy either Jews or Samaritans. Zacchaeus was destined to die in a fire.

IDOLS

(Luke 15:11-32, days, Son of Man, seek, likewise, two) As tax collector, Zacchaeus was privy to the Treasury of the Temple at Jerusalem. Joseph of Arimathea was its Treasurer because he was husband of the Queen of Edom (Nabatea). He neglected his duties at the Temple shamefully for many years. (Lawlor, HNP, 91-101)

HOLY NAME

(Luke 18:1-8, end, Son of Man, seek vengeance) Aland notes that Luke 18:8=11:7,8. Perhaps the Anna in the temple thought that the Chanina family had been slighted when Herod the Great imported an

117

Egyptian High Priest, Simon ben Boethus. Matthias did not object and married one of Simon's daughters. Eventually Felix of Samaria settled the complaint described herein.

SABBATH

(Luke 6:1-5, days, Son of Man, seek to eat, second) The Noahic Covenant insisted on observance of the Sabbath. By gospel times additional Sabbaths had been added. Jews were not supposed to defecate on the Sabbath. Several Sabbaths in a row led to physical problems.

PARENTS

(Luke 2:41-52, days, seek (sought), Son, three) Aland notes that Luke 2:51=2:19. Joseph of Nazareth hired Matthias to be a teacher of Jesus. After several lessons, Jesus asked him who Beta (evil) is. When he did not answer, the lessons were discontinued. (Schneemelcher, NTA, I, 445) During the Passover when Jesus was twelve, the Zealots attacked. In the confusion, Jesus's parents did not know where he was. He said he was about his father's business. The priest's business, the Bazaars of Annas, was not the business to which Jesus referred.

KILL

(Luke 12:1-12, hour, Son of Man, don't seek words, two) Aland notes that Luke 12:2=8:17, Luke 12:7=21:18, Luke 12:9=9:26 and Luke 12:11=21:12. Enoch gives a description of torment or hell. Jesus warns that men should fear the one who can cast them into hell.

ADULTERY

(Luke 7:36-50, two, enter, time) The woman who anointed Jesus for his baptism was a sinner, probably adultery. The words about forgiveness of sin are similar to those in Luke 5:17-26. If one is blasphemy, they both are.

STEAL

(Luke 12:35-40, hour, Son of Man, seek to be ready) As a tax collector Matthias handled money every day. Matthias would bid on a Roman tax contract. If he won the bid, he could charge whatever amount he chose. God had given the priests authority to handle the Temple funds. The Chanina family set up money-changing tables, for they refused to let coins with images inside the Temple. Scarcity of the old coins gave them a monopoly, and the offering returned the old coins to their care. They kept the profits. (Edersheim, LTJM, 371-372)

LIE

(Luke 5:17-26, today, Son of Man, seek to know) Jesus is accused of blasphemy. In the process of healing, he said that the man's sins were forgiven. Onlookers objected saying his words were blasphemy, for only God could forgive sin.

COVET

(Luke 22:47-53, daily, Son of Man, did not seek) Aland notes that Luke 22:49=22:36. Noah was said to have saved the Book of Enoch on the Ark. Certain religious persons felt threatened by its popularity. Enoch walked with God. In the Book of Hebrews, "By faith Enoch was taken up so that he should not see death…" (Hebrews 11:5) In contrast Jesus did die, was resurrected and then was taken up. Numerous people were covetous, but none more than Simon Magus, brother-in-law to Zacchaeus. He claimed in Rome to be the risen crucified Messiah. Zacchaeus was asked to make peace between Simon and Peter, a leader of Christians in Rome. (Schneemelcher, NTA, II, 514-516)

PART FOUR BIBLIOGRAPHY

Aland, Kurt et al. trs. The Greek New Testament. American Bible Society (New York:1975)

Bromiley, Geoffrey W. The International Standard Bible Encyclopedia. 4 vols. Eerdmans (Grand Rapids, Michigan:1986)

Charlesworth, James and Loren Johns, eds. Old Testament Pseudpigrapha. 2 vols. Doubleday and Company (Garden City, New York:1985)

Doresse, Jean. The Secret Books of the Egyptian Gnostics. MJF Books (New York:1986)

Edersheim, Alfred. The Life and Times of Jesus the Messiah. Eerdmans (Grand Rapids, Michigan:1976)

Ferguson, Everett, ed. Encyclopedia of Early Christianity. Garland Publishing Company (New York:1990)

Finegan, Jack. Light from the Ancient Past. Princeton University Press (Princeton, New Jersey:1959)

Hastings, James, ed. A Dictionary of the Bible. 5 vols. Charles scribner's sons (Edinburgh:1908)

Jeremias, Joachim. Jerusalem in the Time of Jesus. Pb. Fortress Press (Philadelphia:1975)

Kraeling, Emil. The Disciples. Rand Mc Nally (n.a.:1966)

Lawlor, John Irving. The Nabateans in Historical Perspective. Pb. Baker Book House Grand Rapids, Michigan:1974)

Lightfoot, John. A commentary on the New Testament from the Talmud and Hebraica. 4 vols. Hendrickson(USA:1979)

McBirnie, William Steuart. The Search for the Twelve Apostles. Pb. Tyndale House Publishers (Wheaton, Illinois:1973)

Peloubet, F. N . Peloubet's Bible Dictionary. Universal Book and Bible House (Philadelphia:1947)

Rambsel, Yacov. His Name is Jesus. Word Publishing (Nashville:1999)

Schneemelcher, William, ed. New Testament Apocrypha. 2 vols. Revised. John Knox Press (Westminster:1992)

Schurer, Emil. A History of the Jewish People in the Time of Christ. 5 vols. Hendrickson (Peabody, Massachusetts:1994)

IX. JOSHUA BEN GAMLA-JESUS-MOSES

Joshua and Moses were teachers. Equidistant Letter Sequencing existed before Luke wrote or edited the Gospel of Luke. Yacov Rambsel found Equidistant Letter Sequencing for Yeshua (Joshua), at Isaiah 53:10. Other words and phrases stemming in ELS from that same verse include, Mary, John, Moses, my prince, Beri (Barabbas), teacher of righteousness, cross, Passover and bride (Joshua's wife, Martha ben Boethus). (Rambsel, HNJ, 44, 28, 29, 37, 67, 20) The testimony about Pontius Pilate in Rome in 37 c.e. hinged on whether or not Christianity and Judaism were the same. Then all testimonies about Jesus and his disciples were divided up and sorted as they related to the five books of the Pentateuch. Since Matthew's book was arranged according to the Pentateuch within the Ezra cycle, parts of Luke were rearranged for easier comparison to Judaism. Thus synoptic gospels reflect upon the Pentateuch rather than upon each other. Scripture was the authority that the Jews believed.

Each part of three parts is subdivided into ten parts to correlate with ten fingers (Hall, STAA, 356. 361), then labeled with a caption showing how that subpart is related to the other nine. The first citation is a reference within the Gospel of Luke. It is followed by words or phrases that tie the passage to ELS or to triads as found by Philip Carrington. Perhaps the frequent use of the word pass is meant to refer to Passover, (Rambsel, HNJ, 20) The second citation is a reference to the Old Testament to support the theory that Christianity and Judaism are being compared. Other references are echoes either forward or backward in time. Last of all, Aland's stitchworts are given to show internal unity of the three parts. Also numbers and ordinals are used within this testimony to tie it to Moses who wrote the Book of Numbers.

Hebrew theology developed into three understandings-the literal law, the intent of the law and the soul of the law. The last was called Kabalah, the soul of the law. (Hall, STAA, 356) At Bathyra (Araq el-Emir) all three were taught. Kabalah refers to letters which are probably the same ELS found in Isaiah 52-54.

PART ONE: STATIONS OF THE CROSS

These are notes to be used to write a dual biography of Jesus and Moses. Each chreia in this section contains a number and the name Moses except Luke 4:1-13 which quotes Moses and Luke 18:31-34 which refers to the prophets. The key word Moses is spelled out in ELS beginning at Isaiah 53:10. The phrase 'my prince' is also spelled out from Isaiah 53:10, and it could refer to the life of Moses in Egypt. (Rambsel, HNJ, 28) The lesser rulers in Edom were called princes, so the sons of Simon ben Gamaliel might have been called princes.

SUBJECTS (Luke 24:25-32, Moses, one, pass, Exodus 19:25, Isaiah 53, Psalm 22) Aland notes that Luke 24:27=18:31 and 24:44. Bathyra (Araq el-emir, Tyrus) was the academy built on the deserted estate of John Hyrcanus. (Josephus, 256) Herod promised five hundred Babylonians taxfree status forever if they built a military academy there to protect his border. On their own they also established a religious academy with such teachers as Hillel and Gamaliel who taught Paul. (Lapp, in Perdue, ABI, 165-184)

FAMILY (Luke 2:2-14, Moses, two, Exodus 13:2,12, Isaiah 6:3, Psalm 145:7) In Jerusalem, there was a circumcision party. Circumcision meant that Jesus was a party to the Mosaic Covenant. He was subject to its terms. It was the duty of Joshua (a form of the name Jesus) to reinstate the law for the generation born in the wilderness. He did so at the Jordan River. (Harrison, NUBD, 238)

GENEALOGY (Luke 20:27-38, Moses, seven, Exodus 2:5, Isaiah 26:19, Psalm 17:15) James the Less was head of the Circumcision Party. He was descended from his Mother Escha a Levite, but Jesus was not a Levite. Moses had declared that only Levites could be priests and they could not own land. Then it was amended that only descendants of Aaron could be priests. Upon ascending into power, Herod the Great had thousands of the descendants of Aaron killed, thus creating a shortage. Behind the Sadducee's question was the existence of one Melchisedek recognized as a priest by Abraham, but without lineage. (Harrison, NUBD, 832) Since Moses recognized Melchisedek as a priest, perhaps Jesus could be recognized as a priest.

SERMON (Luke 4:1-13, Moses, forty, Exodus 4, Isaiah 63:9, Psalm 91:11,12) Aland notes that Luke 4:3,9=22:70. Moses and the people were tempted and tested forty years in the wilderness. Jesus was tempted and tested forty days. In the wilderness. hunger was a temptation common to both. The Chaldeans had taken the Ark, the tables of stone, the holy anointing oil and the jar of manna hidden by Josiah. The Messiah was expected to restore these. (Harrison, NUBD, 813) Jesus was tempted to turn the stones into bread.

MARVEL (Luke 9:28-31, Moses, eight, pass, Exodus 34:29, Isaiah 42:1, Psalm 2:7) Neither Moses nor Elijah died earthly deaths, for they were translated into the heavens. Jesus, who is soon to die but be resurrected, will also be translated into the heavens. Moses' face was shining after an encounter with God, and Jesus's face was shining on the mountain with the shekinah glory, Such shining was an expression of the divine presence of God, especially shining above the mercy seat between the wings of the cheribim . (Harrison NUBD, 1175-1176)

FAME (Luke 5:12-16, Moses, multitude, pass, Nos. 12:10,15, Isaiah 8:20, Psalm 93:5) Aland notes that Luke 5:14=8:56. Moses casts Miriam outside the camp for leprosy, but she is healed and returns. Jesus was confronted with a man who wanted to be healed of leprosy. He healed him and sent him away to a priest who could declare him clean. Then he could reenter the society. Jesus's fame spread, but Jesus went into the wilderness to pray.

PROPHECY (Luke 18:31-34, idea of Moses, twelve, idea of pass in the word accomplished, Deuteronomy 3:28, Isaiah 53:10, Psalm

22) Aland notes that Luke 18:31=24:27. Not only did Moses prophesy, but the prophets had told of a Messiah (Son of Man). Jesus would be mocked, spit on and die. He would rise again on the third day. The disciples could not understand how this prophecy could be. The verse Isaiah 53:10 seems to be the same prophecy. That verse is the beginning point of ELS for Yeshua (Joshua).

LAST WEEK (Luke 9:32-36, Moses, three, pass, Exodus 34:29, Isaiah 42:1, Psalm 2:7) Aland notes that Luke 9:35=3:22. Peter was so overcome upon the Mount of Transfiguration that he wished to worship all three. They represented the Prophet, Priest and King, but Peter would learn that the Trinity to be worshiped was Father, Son and Holy Ghost. That is, Moses was not to be worshiped.

DEATH (Luke 16:19-31, Moses, five, pass, Deuteronomy 34:5, Isaiah 25:8, Psalm 73:12) Jesus is crucified, and the story of Lazarus in hell sheds light on the resurrection. God had said that those who already had Moses and the prophets needed to believe in resurrection. Even if they saw Moses and Elijah rise and not die, the people chose not to believe God had plans for the afterlife. To Jesus, heaven and hell were more than just words.

AFTER THE DEATH (Luke 24:41-47, Moses, fulfilled may be idea of passed, third, Exodus 19:25, Isaiah 53, Psalm 118:29) Aland notes that Luke 24:44=18:31, 24:27. Perhaps the message of Moses was just for the Jews. At least they thought so at the time. Jesus, however, after the Resurrection announces that salvation is for all nations. He said he came not to cancel the law, but to fulfill the law. (cf Spong, LTG, in passim.)

PART TWO: THE LORD'S PRAYER

If Joshua ben Gamla were to pray, this is what he might say. Yeshua (a form of the name Joshua) is to be found beginning at Isaiah 53:10. (Rambsel, HNJ, 44) ELS for the words cross and Passover can also be found originating at Isaiah 53:10. (Rambsel, HNJ, 20) In Part Two, the words cross , law and behold are each used as Carrington triads. The name Gamaliel comes from Gamla (camel) and is a near homonym to the word reward which is used three times. The Book of

Revelation lists the tribe Isaachar (God has rewarded me) as ninth in order. (7:4-8) Passover is used once as a key word, but as above the word pass is used..

Information about the eyewitness is organized by words taken from the Lord's Prayer.

OUR (Luke 6:22-23, reward=gamla, company=number, Exodus 32:14, Isaiah 7:15, Psalm 137:8) Aland notes that Luke 6:23=11:47. Gamla was the name of a mountain whose top ridge was shaped like a camel's back. The path up the mountain called a

Siq was so narrow that two camels could not go up at the same time. Flat-roofed houses lined the path. When Romans attacked Gamla, they decided to ascend by getting up on the roofs. Their weight and that of their war equipment caused the houses to fall like dominoes, and they were then easily defeated. (Josephus, 522, 523)

FATHER (Luke 6:35, reward, none, Lev 25:35-36, Isaiah 1:23, Psalm 58:11) Gamaliel the son of Pedahzur was chief of his tribe when Moses marched into the wilderness. (Nos. 10:23) In the first century Simon Gamaliel was the grandson of the great Hillel. He required that all sides be heard before the Sanhedrin voted. He was fond of asking whether or not a law would benefit all the people. (Charlesworth, H&J, in passim) He said that all, even the heathens should be greeted with the words 'Peace be unto you'. Among his legal decisions were (1)Heathen have the right to glean, (2) widows have the right to be protected from their children (Hastings,DOB, II, 106), (3) A widow needed only one witness to affirm that her husband was dead, (4) former husbands could not annul a divorce, and (5) Holy days on leap years must be observed by a strict interpretation of time. (important to credit) (Hastings, DOB, II, 106)

NAME (Luke 18:18-25, reward, idea of ten, Exodus 20:13-16, Isaiah 58:2, Psalm 119:143) Aland notes that Luke 18:18=10:25. Joshua ben Gamla was obviously named for Joshua, Moses' righthand man. Joshua ben Gamla favored universal male education so that all males could read the Torah. He studied a work called Mekilta or Measures.(Ausubel, BJK, 451) Moses had said that the same measure should be used whether buying or selling. Joshua ben Gamla married

Martha, the wealthy widow of Judas of Galilee, the daughter of High Priest Simon ben Boethus. She bribed the authorities to make Joshua a high priest about 63-65 c.e. (Jeremias, JTJ, 156 and Hengel, Z, 211fn) In Acts 27;17, the word 'boetheia' is translated 'measures'. (Bromiley, ISBE,III, 295)

In Egyptian religion Gamaliel was the name of one of three messengers about the man of truth and light. (Doresse, SBEG, 83)

KINGDOM (Luke 22:14-18, twelve, Passover, Exodus 12:12, Isaiah 32:1, Psalm 103:19) Jesus said that if he were an earthly king his disciples would fight. Pacifist Joshua ben Gamla organized the Peace Party, hoping to negotiate more favorable terms with Rome. His twin brother Judas of Galilee died about 6 c.e. Judas had founded the Fourth Philosophy or Zealots. (Hengel , Z 330) Their brother Beribi (Barabbas) was released from a death sentence by Pontius Pilate. Barabbas thought he was burning a temporarily deserted village called Hippos. Inside were looters, women and children, who died in the fire. He was tried and found guilty of murder. He was released at a Passover rather than Jesus.

EARTH (Luke 9:22-27, cross, third, Exodus 20:3, Isaiah 46:5, Psalm 43:10) Aland notes that Luke 23=14:27, 14:24=17:33, 14:26=12:9. Joshua's father Simon spoke out against a death penalty without a trial and an overnight cool-off time. (Acts 5:34-39) He said, 'If it be of God, ye cannot overthrow it; lest haply ye be found even to fight against God.' By 37 c.e. war existed between Herod Antipas and Aretas IV. Joshua ben Gamla was called to Rome along with R. Akiba and R. Eleazar b. Asariah to testify. (Schurer, HJP, II. 1. 370) Because he was already in Rome, he became a witness in the trial of Pontius Pilate.

BREAD (Luke 10:38-42, one, pass, Numbers 11:14, 17, Isaiah 41:6, Psalm 27:4) Martha was the wife of Joshua ben Gamla. Lazarus, whom Jesus restored to life was her brother. Her sister Mary was present when Jesus was visiting. Mary listened, but Martha complained. Simon ben Boethus had married a daughter of Herod the Great named Mary, so the double vocative may just mean Mary daughter of Mary. One thinks of food for thought. Joshua favored universal male education, not female. Jesus seems to think that females who seek to learn should be encouraged.

EVIL (Luke 11:46-47, law, one, Numbers 11:14, Isaiah 13:1, Psalm 55:22) Aland notes that Luke 11:47=6:23. During Joshua's time, Hebron had been restored. Much of the work was slave or volunteer labor. Once Joshua the patriarch had taken Hebron (Joshua 10:36-37, 12:10) and Caleb retook it. (Joshua 14:14) Hebron was known as the City of Four-Adam, Abraham, Isaac and Jacob. One can only wonder if the inspiration for the name Fourth Philosophy is not related to the City of Hebron (Kiriath-Arba, Peloubet, PBD,246) While wondering, recall that some thought Iscariot might refer to Kiriath. .

FORGIVE US (Luke 14:25-30, cross, law, Genesis 11, Isaiah 5:2, Psalm 61:3) John Hyrcanus desired to retire and started to build a retirement home. Its cost exceeded his funds. He commited suicide, and the estate was deserted. Then Herod the Great gave it to Babylonians in return for guarding his border. It was called Bathyra, Araq el-Emir. The tower was called the Castle of the Slave. Its sanctuary appears to have the remains of a statue fountain on the altar. Perhaps it was a symbol of the Lion of Judah or even of the Golden Calf. (Lapp, in Perdue, ABI, 165-184) Among the best teachers of scripture were Simon ben Gamaliel and Hillel. It is rumored that Simon Gamaliel, not Joshua, was a follower of Jesus.

In Acts 5:39, he warned the authorities that the rebels might be of God. "If it be of God, ye can not overthrow it; lest ye be found even to fight against God."

AS WE FORGIVE (Luke 23:13-26, cross, one , Exodus 32:2, Isaiah 53:12, Psalm 22:7-8) Pilate asked the people whether he should spare Jesus or Barabbas. In the shouting it was impossible to say whether the shouts for Bar Abba (Son of God=Jesus) or for Beribi (son of Gamaliel) were louder. Joshua had to forgive his father if a bribe had been offered to Pilate to save his brother. An ancient Syriac manuscript calls Barabbas, Jesus Son of Abba. (Internet, Champions of Truth, 9)

AMEN (Luke 17:1-4, seven, forgive, pass in trespass, idea of law, Leviticus 4:20, Isaiah 57:15, Psalm 130:4) Both Judas of Galilee and Barabbas were Joshua ben Gamla's brothers. They were very different in their views. The allusion to a millstone may have its basis in a story of the time. One Samuel said that it was a tradition for a man to marry before applying himself to a study of the Law. Another responded 'Why should he start his study with a millstone about his neck?' (Lightfoot, CNT, III, 177)

PART THREE: THE TEN COMMANDMENTS

The teaching at Bathyra depended on Babylonian understanding of the Law, but the Boethusians depended on Alexandrian understanding. Bathyra (Araq el-Emir) was the site of authority for the Babylonian interpretaion of scripture, for both Hillel and his grandson Simon Gamaliel were there. The skill of the Babylonian interpretation was held with such high respect that Gamaliel and his sons sat as President of the Sanhedrin for seven times. (Bromiley, ISBE, II, 393-394)

Hillel was especially known for his version of the Golden Rule later taught by Jesus. At Bathyra, no vote was taken until all sides had been heard. Then those present were asked to vote using the standard, 'Will this change benefit all the people?' (For more, Charlesworth, H&J, in passim) The key phrase in Part Three is ' all the people.'

ONE GOD

(Luke 9:10-17, all the people, Exodus 16:14, (Nehemiah 9:20), Psalm 78:24)

Moses called on God, and manna came from heaven. Jesus took a few loaves of bread and a few fish to feed five thousand.

IDOLS

(Luke 21:34-38, all the people, Exodus 20:4, Isaiah 66:3, Psalm 96:5) Jesus understood there would be temptations, and the disciples needed to be aware. One question was whether or not the Messiah had to be a priest. Indeed, one objection to the custom of choosing high priests was involved. Moses had limited the priesthood to the descendants of

Aaron. Then Aaron worshiped a golden calf. For some, Moses should have eliminated Aaron for that reason alone. Moses like Jesus forgave.

HOLY NAME

(Luke 18:35-43, all the people, Exodus 20:7, Isaiah 6:9, Psalm 69:23) Jesus healed Bartimaeus who called him the Son of David. All the people praised Jesus. An angel had told the Virgin Mary that her son would sit on the throne of David.

SABBATH

(Luke 13:10-17, all the people, Exodus 20:8, Isaiah 1:3, cf Psalm 22:10) Hillel and others pondered over the correct posture for morning, evening ...prayer. (Charlesworth, H&J, 427-459) The woman that Jesus 'straightened up' had been bent over too much to pray in the 'legal' posture. Moreover, if Martha had chosen to, she could have protested about the exclusion of women from worship.

PARENTS

(Luke 3:27-33, all the people, Exodus 20:12, Isaiah 42:1, Psalm 2:7)

Simon ben Boethus says that Jesus is the Redeemer for all people. At the time, many thought of a God as belonging to a specific nationality..

KILL

(Luke 23:46-49, all his acquaintance=all the people, Exodus 20:13, Isaiah 10:2, Psalm 38:11) Jesus was declared a righteous man by a Roman named Longinus. Longinus may have been a relative of Rufus Pudens, brother-in-law to Seneca the Elder.

ADULTERY

(Luke 8:40-56, all the people, Exodus 20:14, Isaiah 37:22, Psalm 144:12) Bernice (Veronika) touched the hem of Jesus's garment. She was the eldest daughter of Herod Agrippa I. When her fiancée Marcus died, she was married to her uncle Herod of Chalcis. When he died, she lived with her brother (and was accused of incest with him). Then she had a brief marriage to Polemon before becoming mistress to Titus. (Harrison, NUBD, 564) Bernice, not the daughter of Jairus, was considered an adultress.

STEAL

(Luke 19:41-48, all the people, Exodus 20:15, Isaiah 56:7, Psalm 66:19-20)

The question was whether or not a man would rob God? Moses had forbidden the Levites to own land, so the Temple was to supposed support Levite families in their cities. Corruption caused much of the money to stay in Jerusalem. Jesus said in the Temple, 'It is written, "My house is a house of prayer, but you have made it a den of thieves."'

LIE

(Luke 24:18-20, all the people, Exodus 20:16, Isaiah 32:1, Psalm 10:16)

Obviously Jesus was only pretending not to know what had happened.

He wanted to hear what the two men were saying. They said he was mighty in word and deed before God and all the people.

COVET

(Luke 7:24-29, all the people, Exodus 20:17, Isaiah 61:1-2, Psalm 27:11)
Certain Jews wanted to compare Jesus and John to the disadvantage of both. Some were even saying that John the Baptist was the Son of God. Pointedly, Jesus says that John was born of woman. Of course he was, too, but Jesus did not have an earthly father. Many thought that Primal Adam before the Fall and his son Seth were superior to all men because they were not born after sex (fornication)..

PART FOUR BIBLIOGRAPHY

Aland, Kurt et al.,eds. The Greek New Testament. American Bible Society (New York:1975)

Ausubel, Nathan. The Book of Jewish Knowledge. Crown (New York:1964)

Bromiley, Geoffrey W., ed. The International Bible Encyclopedia. Eerdmans (Grand Rapids, Michigan:1988)

Carrington, Philip. The Primitive Christian Calendar. University Press (Cambridge:1952)

Champions of Truth, program on the Internet, p, 9.

Charlesworth, James, and Loren L. Johns, eds. Hillel and Jesus. Fortress Press (Minneapolis:1997)

Doresse, Jean. The Secret Books of the Ancient Egyptians. MJF Books (New York:1986)

Hall, Manly P. The Secret Teachings of All Ages. Pb. Penquin (New York:2003)

Harrison, R. K.,ed. New Unger's Bible Dictionary. Moody Press (Chicago:1957)

Hastings, James, ed. A Dictionary of the Bible. 5 vols. Charles Scribner's Sons (New York:1909)

Hengel, Martin. The Zealots. T & T Clark (Edinburgh:1989tr)

Jeremias, Joachim. Jerusalem in the Time of Jesus. Pb. Fortress Press (Philadelphia:1967)

Josephus. Complete works. Tr. By William Whiston. Kregel (Grand Rapids, Michigan:1985)

Lapp, Nancy L. "Araq el-Emir" in Perdue, Leo G. et al.,eds. Archaeology and Biblical Interpretation. John Knox (Atlanta:1987) , pp.165-184.

Lightfoot, John . A Commentary on the New Testament from the Talmud and Hebraica. 4 vols. Hendrickson (USA:1995)

Peloubet, F. N. Peloubet's Bible Dictionary. Universal Book and Bible House (Philadelphia:1947)

Rambsel, Yacov. His Name Is Jesus. Word Publishing (Nashville:1999)

Schurer, Emil. A History of the Jewish People. 5 vols. Hendrickson (Peabody, Massachusetts:1994)

Spong, John Shelby. Liberating the Gospels. HarperSanFrancisco (San Francisco:1996)

X. JAMES BEN ZEBEDEE-JACOB-JESUS

The editor of the Gospel of Luke knew of the Equidistant Letter Sequencing. He associated the beginning of the name James (Jacob) with Isaiah 52:2 (Rambsel, HNJ, 44), and that verse marks the beginning of ELS for Jerusalem and for 'the heart of my treasured people.' 'My face' in ELS begins at Exodus 33:20. (Rambsel, HNJ, 139)

The word for face and the name Peniel, the place of Jacob's religious experience, are homonyms. The overall key words are place names including Jerusalem.

Shining is a literal translation of Zohar and of Phabes (Fabatus). the family name of James of Zebedee. Mandaeans believed in a lightship captained by a Fisher. (Mead, GJB, 42f) Zachariah and Zebedee were descended from Barak (thunder) who saved Israel. (Judges 4:5-6, Matthew 23:35, Mark 3:17)

This testimony is in three parts. The first is a ten-point enconmia that compares the Patriarch Jacob and Jesus. As with the other parts, each reference to Luke is followed by a reference to the Pentateuch. The point to be made was whether or not Christianity and Judaism were the same religion. Key words follow which are taken from ELS in relation to Jacob or triads as defined by Philip

Carrington. The key word in Part One is Jacob. The second part is about the eyewitness; in this case, James ben Zebedee. The name

James is a form of the name Jacob. This information is organized by a sequence of words taken from the Lord's Prayer. The key word is face as Peniel means the face of God. The third part is a comparison of the teachings of Moses in the Ten Commandments with what James said that Jesus taught.

The key sentence is 'What shall we do?' It appears James still thought in terms of John the Baptist's teaching. (Szekely, GE, 129)

PART ONE: STATIONS OF THE CROSS

These are notes for a dual biography about Jacob the Patriarch and Jesus. The key words are Jacob, shining and sky. Shining is a literal translation of Phabes.

Zechariah, Zebedee, and Escha (mother of James the Just) were members of the Phabes (Fabatus, Phiabi) family. The Mandaeans were once called Nazoreans. (Mead, GJB, 29) From them John the Baptist was aware of the Light-ship of the Fisher. (Mead, GJB, 75-81) James and John, the sons of Zebedee, were disciples of John the Baptist before they were called by Jesus to become fishers of men.

SUBJECTS (Luke 1:31-33, sky, shining, Jacob, Jerusalem implied by throne, Gen 16:11, Revelation 22:16, cf James 5:12) The conjunction of the planets Jupiter, Mars and Saturn in Pisces occurred in 7 b.c. This led wise man and astronomers to journey to Bethlehem. (Bromiley, ISBE, I, 344) At least one interpreter says that the wise men went to Beit Lahm in Gadara first. They may have been seeking the altar Jacob built after seeing the ladder to heaven there. Egyptians called pyramid steps a ladder to heaven. Beit Lahm had warm springs with twelve openings, each designated to heal a different disease. (McClintock, CBTEL, III, 706-797) To climb the seven steps which represent the astrological influence of the seven steps meant to free the spirit. (Hall, STAA, 538)

The stone of remembrance that Jacob set up as an altar at Peniel was used many years as part of the English Coronation Ceremony. (Cahill, HISC, 137) For Christians the stone of remembrance would be the stone in the Garden of Getsemane. James was there.

FAMILY (Luke 2:8-14, sky, shining, compares to Jacob's experience,, Bethlehem, Genesis 28:10, Revelation 3:4, cf James 1:17) Fabatus was a steward for Herod the Great. Sylleus accused him of plotting against Herod. (Josephus,464) Fabatus (Phabes=shining) was father of Zechariah (the father of John the Baptist), of Zebedee (the father of James and John), and of Escha (the mother of James called the brother of Jesus.) Thinking Fabatus had had his ancestor killed, Herod the Great had him killed. (Josephus, 464) In gospel times Herod Agrippa I had his 'cousin' James the Less (Escha=Least) killed in 44 c.e. (Actually Heodian incest makes a term of relation almost impossible.)

Jacob the Patriarch cheated his brother Esau of his birthright. (Genesis 25:33) Then in time Jacob's uncle Laban cheated Jacob by replacing Jacob's bride with her sister Leah. (Genesis 29:31) When Leah stopped bearing children, Jacob became father to Gad (Legion, Troop) by her handmaid Zilpah. (Genesis 30:11)

GENEALOGY (Luke 20:27-38, Jacob, Hebron= home of Judith, Deuteronomy 25:5, Revelation 3:1, I Kings 17) Since both Elizabeth and Zechariah were descendants of Aaron, John the Baptist was descended from Aaron as well. Moses had set aside the Levites to serve God, but later he said that only the descendants of Aaron could be priests. Elizabeth was a descendant of Aaron (Luke 1:5) and Zechariah of the course of Phiabi (instead of Abia cf Matthew 1:7) Herod the Great created an artificially small supply of Aaronic descendants through mass murder. Even so, one Jesus son of Phiabi had been high priest from 35 to 22 B.C. Ishmael ben Phiabi was high priest from 15-16 c.e. (Jeremias, JTJ, 377)

> Jesus answered those who questioned lineage that there is no marriage in heaven. Judith a wife of Esau was not accepted by Isaac and Rebecca. (Genesis 26:34-35)

SERMON (Luke 13:22-30, Jacob, Jerusalem, Genesis 48,49, Revelation 16:10, James 1:12) God had promised Jacob what he had given to Abraham, as far as he could see in all four directions. Jesus says the first shall be last and the last shall be first. Perhaps Jesus meant that Herod Agrippa the First would have less reward than James, the son of Escha (Last, least) Perhaps Agrippa just thought that was what

Jesus meant, so this led to his having his cousin James ben Zebedee beheaded. (Acts 12:2)

MARVEL (Luke 7:11-18, Jacob's wife Leah, Judea, Genesis 30:11, Revelation 3:1, I Kings 17:17, 1:27) Aland notes that Luke 7:12,13=8:42,52, and Luke 7:14=8:54. The widow's name was Leah, the name of one of Jacob's wives. Her son being buried was Maternus. He became a disciple under Peter in Rome. He built a church dedicated to honor the Virgin Mary. (McBirnie, STA, 60-61) When the Apostles' Creed was formed, James the son of Zebedee was linked with "and in Jesus Christ, His only Son, Our Lord." (Hone, LBB, 91)

FAME (Luke 8:26-39, Legion was a son of Jacob, Gadara, Genesis 30:11, Revelation 1:18, James 2:17) Aland notes that Luke 8:28=4:33-34. The man Jesus healed said that his name was Legion, which was the name of one son of Zilpah whom Leah named Troop (Legion, Fortunatus). Later he was found to be the brother of King Gondophares of India. The King had been one of the Wise Men who came to Bethlehem to see the infant Jesus. Legion (Fortunatus) later became a secretary to Herod Agrippa in Rome. (Schneemelcher, NTA, II, 199-201) He accompanied Thomas to India where he died of snakebite. (Barnstone, OB, 470)

PROPHECY (Luke 1:76-80, sky, face, Exodus 13:21, Revelation 14:14, James 1:5) John the Baptist was to go before Jesus as Isaiah had prophesied. (Isaiah 40:3-5) Jews and Mandaeans thought that dawn and dusk were significant spiritually. For a short time the dayspring could be seen as a crescent. The constellation Orion had 'disappeared under the horizon ' when Elijah left, but it reappeared when John the Baptist was born. (Gilbert, M, 215) Another source states without explanation that they are children of thunder because James is called Levi (the priestly household) and John Judah (the royal household, McBirnie, STA, 61-62, 102)

Hermogenes dared James the son of Zebedee to debate with servant, Philetus. Philetus returned saying he lost. Angry Hermogenes ordered that James and Philetus be bound in fetters. They were but angels freed them. James sent Philetus back to Hermogenes and ordered that he return with him bound. When they returned, James said Jesus had told him to return good for evil. Hermogenes became a good and faithful disciple and preacher from that day. (McBirnie, STA, 92)

LAST WEEK (Luke 9:28-36, sky, shining, Jerusalem, face, mountain, Exodus 24:15, Revelation 4:5, cf James 5:7) James was present when Jesus went up to the Mount of Transfiguration to pray. Jacob had struggled at Peniel (homonym for face) where he saw the face of God. (Genesis 32:30) His name was changed to Israel. The shekinah glory denotes the presence of God. Luke reports that the face of Jesus was shining on the Mount of Transfiguration. (It implies the face of God.)

James fell on his face when the Virgin Mary appeared to him after the Resurrection. To honor her, he built a church on that spot in Jerusalem called Our Lady of the Pillar. (McBirnie, STA, 91, 99) The design was similar to the church Maternus built beyond the Alps. (McBirnie, STA, 60-61)

DEATH (Luke 23:27-30, mountains, Jerusalem, Exodus 23:26, Revelation 6:16,17, cf James 5:3) Rachel, wife of Jacob, died in childbirth when Benjamin (Fortunate) was born. (Genesis 35:18-20) Jacob set up a pillar in her memory. The Mount of Transfiguration may have been Sirion where thunder and lightning were very severe. It was said that one could hear Rachel crying for her children. Being barren was a problem to Sarah and Rebecca. Joakim and Anna had no children before the Virgin Mary. (cf 'Infancy Gospel of James' in Barnstone, OB, 385) After a tragedy, some say, 'It might have been better if I had never been born.' Surely that occurred to Jesus on the cross, but the truth was that the cross which was evil became a means for good.

AFTER THE DEATH (Luke 24:1-18, face, shining, James, Jerusalem, Exodus 20:10, Revelation 1:16,18, James 2:1) Jesus had asked James and John if they could drink of

the cup he did. (Mark 10:35-40) Their mother was present when the women found that Jesus had arisen from the tomb. James may have been the other disciple. (John 20:8) This other disciple saw and believed.

PART TWO: THE LORD'S PRAYER

The theme of Part Two may be the blessing found in Numbers 6:24-25, "The Lord bless and keep thee: the Lord make his face to shine upon thee, and give thee peace." . According to ELS, the beginning of the spelling out of the words face and Jerusalem begin at Isaiah 52:2 as does the name James. Jacob the patriarch had his experience at Peniel which means 'face'. Their clue words are fiery end, treasure in heaven and white. Christian Mandaeans may have chosen to call themselves Essenes. (cf Szekely, GE, in passim.)

OUR (Luke 7:24-29, face, Genesis 27:43, Revelation 21:2, James 1:12, cf Mark 3:17)

The Christians of Saint John (Mendaeans) had a zodiac which corresponded to the stars and the months of the year. (cf Darlison, GZ, 33) The more pious bathed daily, but all were baptized at least once a year. James and John followed John the Baptist for a time before they followed Jesus. In time others accused them of assimilating older pagan religions like the worship of stars. Their churches were built East to West so they faced the dawn and dusk. (McClintock, CBTEL, VI, 80-83)

The Book of Revelations strangely lists the order of some tribes in Revelation 7:4-8. Levi is eighth in order. Although the connection is not clear, Levi (my husband shall be joined to me) was what Zebedee called James.

FATHER (Luke 5:10-16, face, go to Jerusalem) The name Zebedee (gift of Jehovah) could be related to 'worship in Edom.' Zeboim was one of the five cities of the Plain destroyed by fire from heaven. (Genesis 19:17-29, Deuteronomy 29:23, Hosea 11:8) Mandaeans in the John-Book relied heavily on the Fisher of Souls Saga in relation to their concept of Good and Evil. (Mead, GJB, 71-80) Good seems to be equated with justice in the John-Book, but of course Jesus taught the Beatitudes in which even injustice can become a means of being blessed.

NAME (Luke 22:24-30, Israel, Genesis 3:1, Revelation 3:21, 19:9, James 1:9) James ben Zebedee was called Levi after his father's father. (McBirnie, STA, 101) Usually the older brother like Esau was given the birthright, but Jacob became the progenitor of the Jews. The way was regrettable. James and John the sons of Zebedee were conscious of status. Before James the brother of Jesus became Bishop of Jerusalem, James the son of Zebedee may have been Jerusalem's Christian leader. (Eisenman, JBJ, 95) Their mother had once asked Jesus if one could sit on his right hand and one on his left. (Mark 10:35v.) Jesus said he could not grant that. James would die at the hands of his 'cousin' before 44 c.e., but John would be the last of the original twelve disciples to die.

Jesus asked James and John if they could drink from the same cup he did. (Matthew 20:20-28) He is aware that status or greatness matters to them. Jacob's name was changed to Israel. (Genesis 32:28) When Jesus says that all this had happened for the sake of James, he may have actually said 'for the sake of Israel'.

KINGDOM (Luke 21:34-38, face, Mount of Olives,) James was very much into religion which becomes visible as it is lived. For some time Jesus preached on the porch of Solomon's Temple. Eusebius relates a story that the judge who gave the order for James's execution became a Christian because of James's testimony. They were then executed together. (Kraeling, TD, 124-125)

The Rechabites who called themselves the beloved ones had been promised that they would always have a man to stand before the throne of God. (Jeremiah 35:19) John may have been called Beloved for two reasons.

EARTH (Luke 12:54-59, face, sky, compare Jacob and Esau, court=Sanhedrin Jerusalem, Deuteronomy 18:15, Revelation 22:9, James 2:14-16) Jesus was aware that many sins had been commited because of hunger. Esau became the tool of Jacob because he was hungry. Ambition, like hunger, can motivate sin. Families like the Herodians were split by religious belief and practice. James as said above would be killed by a relative.

BREAD (Luke 8:40-56, (fell on his face, James present, Capernaum, Exodus 15:26, Revelation 13:3, James 5:16) Aland notes that Luke 8:42=7:12, 8:52=7:13 and 8:54=7:14. Although the teaching is about the daughter of Jair who is told to eat, a woman touched the garment of Jesus. She was Bernice (Veronica), mother of Herod Agrippa I and daughter of Salome who danced when John was beheaded. (Harrison,

NUBD, 557) Philates above touched the garment of James and was healed. (McBirnie, STA, 92) Incidentally, John the Baptist would not touch unleavened bread, even at Passover. (Mead, GJB, 113)

EVIL Luke 11:32-36, shining, Nineveh, Genesis 1:3, Revelation 22:5, James 4:11) Essenes and Mandaeans thought that good and evil were in the world. The good is represented by light that is trapped within the body. Jesus said that the kingdom was within the body. All are urged to let their light shine that God may see their good works. (Matthew 5:16)

FORGIVE US (Luke 9:46-56, face, Jerusalem, Genesis 33:19, Revelation 22:17, James 1:13,14) Aland notes that Luke 9:46=22:24. Jesus, James and John are at Jacob's Well in Samaria. (John 4:5) First there is a word play on the name of the founder of the Mendaeans, Mannichaeus= Greek Chaeus and Latin fundo (poor, scatter). (Barnstone, OB,678) Then Jesus teaches the sons of Zebedee that his spirit is not to win by violence, but by salvation. His love reaches out to the Samaritans regardless of their genealogy.

At Jacob's Well (Nablus) the road divides. One arm goes to and the other from Jerusalem. (Bromiley, ISBE, II, 955) ELS appears only in the Masoretic text. Darlison says that the word for Zodiac is mazzaroth (divided and separated). (Darlison, GZ, 33)

AS WE FORGIVE (Luke 22:63-65, face, Jerusalem, Genesis 25:33, Revelation 21:8, James 1:4) Being perfect was one of the steps in following Manichaeism. Jesus was being tested to see if he were an omniscient God. Ironically the symbol of justice in a constellation shows that justice is blindfolded. The Patriarch Jacob had taken advantage of his father's blindness, but then his Uncle Laban got him blind drunk. Because of that blindness, Jacob was married to Leah although he wanted Rebecca.

AMEN (Luke 17:11-19, face, Jerusalem, Leviticus 14:4, Revelation 21:8, James 4:17) The priests at Jerusalem were strict about entrance into the Temple. Samaritans had to offer gifts outside because they had intermarried with Gentiles while other Jews were in exile. The

Samaritan, possibly Allogenes, started to go to the Temple. Then he realized Jesus had healed him. He knelt before Jesus.

PART THREE.: THE TEN COMMANDMENTS

The town Zoar (Pritchard, TAB, 33, index) was near to the site of Zeboim, and it was sometimes called Es-safi. Possibly Elizabeth escaped to Zeboim with the infant John the Baptist because Zebedee, Zachariah's brother, was there. Essenes from that area claimed Elijah, John the Baptist, John the Beloved and Jesus as healers and teachers. (Szekely, GE, 129) Their Book of Righteousnes repeatedly uses the question, 'What shall I do? (Szekely, GE, 79) In another place, Joseph of Nazareth asks about his pregnant wife Mary, 'What shall I do?' (Protoevangelium in Barnstone, OB, 390)

ONE GOD

(Luke 4:31-37, What shall I do?, Exodus 20:3, James 4:12) Essenes and Mandaeans agreed on frequent bathing and baptism. Aland notes that Luke 4:33-34=8:28. Jesus did not object to frequent bathing. He objected to its substitution of ritual for whole-hearted devotion. The Treasure said that those who refuse to see the light will fall into The Great End Sea for their final washing. (Mead, GJB. 88)

IDOLS

(Luke 12:16-23, What shall I do?, Exodus 20:4, James 4:15) Herod Agrippa was fair in many ways, but he liked luxury. He might have been the Good Samaritan. The accumulation of things is tempting, but greed should always be seen for what it is.

The Treasure said that those who pray to idols will not ascend to Life's House. (Mead, GJB, 92)

HOLY NAME

(Luke 18:35-43, What shall I do? Exodus 20:7) Bava ben Buta was Herod the Great's physician. Then Herod the Great ordered that his sons be killed before his eyes and then Bava be immediately blinded. The sons escaped with the help of Joseph of Arimathea who was married at the time to Alexandra Salome, Herod's sister. When she decided to divorce Joseph in 8 c,e,, she revealed the deception to Herod Antipas and the sons were killed. (Edersheim, LTJM, 120, 370, 372) The Treasure says the Lightship of the Great Fisher bears lamps whose wicks shift not. (Mead, GJB, 75)

SABBATH

(Luke 18:18-24, What shall I do? Exodus 20:8) One cannot earn eternal life, but the rich young ruler may have thought it the next step. Among the Mandaeans one could reach a stage called 'being perfect'. Jesus said his followers are to be perfect even as his father in heaven is perfect. (Matthew 5:48) Herod Agrippa who would kill James was called perfect. Noah was righteous and perfect in his generation (Genesis 6:9) At Qumran, some were called Men of Holiness and some Men of Perfect Holiness. (Eisenman, JBJ, 246) The Treasure asks those who are perfect to instruct one another. (Mead, GJB, 89)

PARENTS

(Luke 1:34, idea of What shall I do? Exodus 20:12) James and others were aware of confusion about the Virgin Birth. Indeed some thought Panthera , a Roman soldier, was the birth father of Jesus with Miryai his mother. The Treasure said a Mary (Miryai) was betrothed to John the Baptist, but she was raped by Panthera (Pandira). Her fiancée left her, and her son Jesus once commented 'What have I to do with thee? (cf John 2;4) (cf. Mead, GJB, 62-67) When those around rebuked Jesus of Nazareth for his rudeness to his mother, he declared her innocence, but not her virginity at his birth. (Blavatsky, IU, 386 fn) James of Zebedee believed in the virginity of the mother of Jesus of Nazareth. The Infancy Gospel of Jesus states that James' mother Salome tested her virginity at the time of Jesus's birth and believed. (Barnstone, OB, 390)

KILL

(Luke 3:14-16, What shall I do? Exodus 20:13) James may have been present when this passage was part of John the Baptist's sermon. Then when he became a follower of Jesus, he would have asked him about it. (Szekely, GE, 79) John the Baptist did not forbid his followers from being soldiers. He described their role almost as police or peacekeepers (using minimal violence). Since many soldiers looted to increase their means, John urged them to be content with their wages. The Treasure said of the wicked and liars that they would be cast into a blazing fire. (Mead, GJB. 98)

ADULTERY

(Luke 15:3-7, idea of What shall I do? Exodus 20:14) Cyborea, mother of Judas Iscariot was called the Lost Sheep of the House of Israel. Instead of meaning that Jesus and Cyborea had physical contact, he may have converted her. Trachelos suggests that he put 'a yoke' on her. (Kohlenberger, EVED, 777)

The Treasure warned against commiting adultery lest they never mount up to Light. (Mead, GJB, 92)

STEAL

(Luke 3:9-13, What shall I do? Exodus 20:15) Aland notes that Luke 3:12=7:29, James visited the twelve tribes in diaspora urging them to send firstfruits directly to the church (temple) instead of sending them to Herod. (McBirnie, STA, 90) The Treasure does not mention stealing, perhaps because Edom's raids on Israel's crops were so frequent. Instead it warns borrowers not to get into excessive debt. (Mead, GJB, 92)

LIE

(Luke 16:1-8, What shall I do? Exodus 20:16) Edomite women had the right to inherit. When Zechariah was killed, Elizabeth's property was not returned for many years. Indeed Felix returned it after 44 c.e., but James would die before that. The Treasure warns against moving boundary stones. (Mead, GJB. 92)

COVET

(Luke 12:13-15, What do you want me to do? Exodus 20:17) Note the same problem in Luke 22:24-27. Sybling rivalry existed between Cain and Abel as well as Jacob and Esau. James and John were the sons of Zebedee and each coveted what the other had. Jesus refused to arbitrate, but he urged them and others to seek spiritual rather than material treasures. The King of the Nazoreans makes his investment, but not in gold or silver, possessions, envy or even food. (Mead, GJB, 87)

BIBLIOGRAPHY

Aland, Kurt, ed et al, The Greek New Testament. United Bible societies (New York:1975)

Barnstone, Willis, ed. The Other Bible. Pb. HarperSanFrancisco (New York:1984)

Blavatsky, Helen P. Isis Unveiled. Pb. 2 vols. Theosophical Publishing House (Wheaton, Illinois:1972)

Bromiley, Geoffrey W. The International Standard Bible Encyclopedia. William B. Eerdmans (Grand Rapids, Michigan:1988)

Cahill, Thomas. How the Irish Saved Civilization. Pb. Nan A. Talese. Doubleday (New York:1955)

Carrington, Philip. The Primitive Christian Calendar. Cambridge University Press (Cambridge:1952)

Darlison, Bill. The Gospel & the Zodiac. Duckworth Overlook (New York:2007)

Edersheim, Alfred. The Life and Times of Jesus the Messiah. 2 vols. Eerdmans (Grand Rapids, Michigan:1976)

Eisenman, Robert. James the Brother of Jesus. Viking Press (New York:1996)

Gilbert, Adrian. Signs in the Sky. Bantam Press (New York:1988)

Hall, Manly P. The Secret Teachings of All Ages. Pb. Penquin (New York:2003)

Harrison, R. K., ed. The New Unger's Bible Dictionary. Moody Press (Chicago:1957)

Hone, William. Lost Books of the Bible. Bell Publishing (New York:1979)

Jeremias, Joachim. Jerusalem in the Time of Jesus. Pb. Fortress Press (Philadelphia:1967)

Josephus. Complete Works. Tr. William Whiston. Kregel Publications (Grand Rapids:1981),

Kohlenberger, John R,,ed. The Expanded Vine's Expository Dictionary of New Testament Words. Bethany House Publishers (Minneapolis, Minnesota:1949)

Kraeling, Emil G. The Disciples. Rand McNally and Company (USA:1966)

McBirnie, William Steuart. The Search for the Twelve Apostles. Pb. Tyndale House Publishers (Wheaton, Illinois: 1977)

McClintock, John and James Strong. Cyclopedia of Biblical, Theological and Ecclesiastical Literature. 12 vols. Baker Book House (Grand Rapids, Michigan:1981)

Mead, G. R. S. The Gnostic John the Baptizer. John M. Watkin s (London:1924)

Pritchard, James B.,ed. The Times Atlas of the Bible. Crescent Books (New York:1996)

Rambsel, Yacov. His Name is Jesus. Pb. Word Publishing (Nashville:1999)

Schneemelcher, Wilhelm. New Testament Apocrypha. 2 vols. James Clarke (Westminster:1992)

Szekely, Edmond Bordeaux. The Gospel of the Essenes. Pb. The C.W. Daniel Co Ltd. (Hillman Printers of Great Britain:1976)

BABYLONIAN ZADOKITES

HILLEL

xxxxxxxxxxxxxxxxxxxxxxxxxxx

SIMON BEN GAMALIEL   IMMA SHALOM

xxxxxxxxxxxxxxxxxxxxxxxxx   xxxxxxxxxxxxxxxxxxxxxxxxxx

x	x	x	
JOSHUA BEN	JUDAS OF	BARABBAS	md. (1) ELEAZAR BEN HYRCANUS
GAMLA	GALILEE		father of JAIRUS (ARISTARCHUS)
md. MARY	md MARY		(2) SIMON OF CYRENE
DAUGHTER	OF CLEOPAS		father of RUFUS AND ALEXANDER
OF BOETHUS			(3) SIMON OF ARIMATHEA

Father of SAUL, DOMITILLA (wife
of TITUS) and OBODAS II (Joseph
of Arimathea, Philogenes)

CHANINA OR ANNAS FAMILY

SETH (maybe Dositheos, Chanina ben Dosa)

x

ANNAS (H.P. 6-15 C.E.)

xxxxxxxxxxxxxxxxxxxxxxxxxxxxxxxxxxxxxxxxxxxxxxxxxxx

x	x	x	x	x	
ELEAZAR.	JONATHAN	THEOPHILUS	ZACCHAEUS	DAUGHTER md.	
LAZARUS	H. P. 37 C.E.	H.P. 37-40	(MATTHIAS)	JOSEPH CAIAPHAS	
H.P. 16-17 C.E		md. MARY		H.P. 18-37 C.E.	
		(MAGDALENE?)		x	
		x x			
		JAMES MATTHEW		SARAH	

MD. WIDOW
MARY OF CLEOPAS

x

JUDAS THADDEUS

XI. PONTIUS PILATE-JOHN THE BAPTIST-JESUS

Isaiah 53:11 is the beginning verse in the Equidistant Letter Sequencing for the name John, Caesar, Messiah, Mary and 'exceedingly high, Yeshua is my strong powerful name.' (Rambsel, HNJ, 15, 17, 18, 44, 45) The editor or author of the Gospel of Luke used clues based on Isaiah's readymade system. For example, in addition to the names, the idea of authority was used to be a clue in Part One and power in Part Three of this report. Pontius Pilate was not an eyewitness in the usual sense, but his report to the Roman Senate in 37 c.e. was at his own trial. The issue was whether or not Christianity was the same religion as Judaism. If it was, his fault was in treating it as superstition and allowing Jesus to be crucified.

His old schoolchum Tiberius Caesar had warned him at the time of John the Baptist's death that he was to keep the peace or be removed. Another ELS for Caesar at Isaiah 53:11 is 'wicked Caesar to perish', and a second ELS at different numerical intervals is 'for my people trouble'. (Rambsel, HNJ, 15) Although it is not obvious in English translations, a verb is used in "I bring you good news" is repeated at Luke 2:10, 3:18, 4:18, 43, 7:22, 8:1, 9:6, 16:16, and 20:1.(cf Isaiah 41:27 and Marshall, L, 61)

Stoics believed nature was the substance of the world. God was mixed in. Meekness was the most admirable trait. Pilate was not especially religious, but he knew about stoicism. To him, wisdom brought one to old age, not to eternal life. (Hall, STAA, 23)

PART ONE: STATIONS OF THE CROSS

In Part One, notes for a dual biography of Jesus and John the Baptist are given. In Part One, John and 'authority' are the clue words as well as 'good news'.

SUBJECTS (Luke 20:1-8, John, authority, good news, what, Genesis 12:1-3, Isaiah3:2) During the early days of Christianity, many thought that John the Baptist (Yahya ben Phabes) was the Messiah. Pontius Pilate as an eyewitness at his own trial knew that Tiberius Caesar had agreed to overlook the beheading of John the Baptist. He would face an order to commit suicide if he broke pax Romana again. Looking back, John's 'grandfather' Fabatus (Phabes, Phiabi) had been involved in the death and beheading of the father of Herod the Great. (Josephus, 359, 464)

FAMILY (Luke 1:5-80, I Samuel 2:1-10, John, authority, what, Luke 15:12-32, mighty, merry, what, perish, II Samuel 16:6, Genesis 25:22 LXX, Isaiah 11:1, cf Acts of Pilate 1:1,2) Mandaeans thought that Jesus was conceived at spring equinox and born at winter solstice. John was conceived at winter equinox and born at summer solstice. (cf Gilbert, M, 229) Mandaeans often lived in Edom. During gospel times Joseph of Arimathea (Obodas II) was Governor of Edom.

GENEALOGY (Luke 1:5-25, 3:21-38, John, 'Whereby shall I know this?"=what, Genesis 22:2, Isaiah 42:1, Acts of Pilate 13:13) Aland notes that Luke 3:23=4:22 and 3:22=9:35. Christians believe that the dove spoke to Jesus saying he was the Son of God. Mandaeans would have thought that the dove spoke to John. John's message seems focused on outward behavior and Jesus's on spirit, but each sought to bring Israel to God.

Content of prophecy for John the Baptist can be found at Isaiah 40:3-5. For Jesus the co ntent of prophecy can be found at Isaiah 61:1-

2. ELS has to do with letters, not content. As an official of Rome, Pilate had access to genealogical charts used to determine property rights.

SERMON (Luke 3:7-18, 4:16-22, John, source of authority missing, mighty, good news, What shall I do?,Genesis 12:1-3, Isaiah 52:10, 61:1-2) Aland notes that Luke 4:22=3:23, Luke 3:16=3:3, and Luke 3:12=7:29. John the Baptist was concerned that the people were indifferent to God. He spoke out about the corruption in high places. (Isaiah 40:3-4) Jesus announced that the prophecy of Isaiah was in the process of fulfillment through him by healing. Instead of joy, the people accused him of blasphemy. Pilate would have been made aware of the scene at Nazareth. He would have known that some thought John was the Messiah, but others thought Jesus was.

MARVEL (Luke 7:19-23, 9:35-45, mighty, John, authority, good news, what, Exodus 30:7, Isaiah 7:14) Aland notes that Luke 9:35=3:22. Luke 9:44=18:32, and Luke 9:45=18:32.=1:45. John's disciples come to Jesus to ask him if he is the Messiah. Jesus paraphrases Isaiah 61:1-2 and asked them to report to John that Isaiah's prophecy is being fulfilled.

Luke 1:15 describes a Nazirite vow. John is to have the power and might of Elijah. Elsewhere it is said that Jesus is to have the throne of David. (Luke 1:32)

FAME (Luke 9:18-21, 4:31-44, 10:10-20, Kingdom of God,mighty, merry, John, authority, good news, what, Deuteronomy 24:16, Isaiah 30:7, Acts of Pilate 10:6) Aland notes that Luke 9:19=9:7. John had most likely died before Jesus asked 'Whom do the people say that I am?' Peter answers the Christ of God. Jesus asks him to tell no one. However, as Jesus walks by a synagogue on a Sabbath, a demonic spirit with a loud voice recognized Jesus. Jesus healed the man affected by the spirit. Fame spread about the great things Jesus had done.

PROPHECY (Luke 5:32-35, 7:24-29, 19:28-40, King , mighty, John, authority, why, Exodus 23:20, Isaiah 35:5, Acts of Pilate 12:11) Aland notes that Luke 7:26-1:76, Luke 7:28=1:15, Luke 7:29=3:7,12 and Luke 19:22=22:13. The people noticed that the disciples of John kept strict dietary laws, but those who followed Jesus did not. Jesus does not condemn fasting as a form of worship, but indicates that fasting and mourning are of the same spirit.

LAST WEEK (Luke 3:18-20, 11:1-4, 16:1-8, What shall I do?, John, good news, Genesis 12:1-3, Isaiah 26:19, cf Acts of Pilate 1:14-17)) Aland notes that Luke 3:19=9:7-8. In the last days of John, he spoke out against Herod Antipas and Herodias. Herod Antipas was married to the Queen of Edom (Nabatea) and had two sons. Their union was made by a treaty agreed upon by the Roman Senate. Herodias was the deposed

Herod Philip's divorced wife. She had asked Salome to dance for Herod Antipas. Then as a favor she was to ask for the head of John the Baptist.

As the time for praying was appropriate, the disciples asked Jesus to teach them the prayer of John the Baptist. It was customary on the anniversary of a Jewish death, to publicly pray the Kiddush. The Lord's Prayer is similar to the blessing of wine.

DEATH (Luke 9:1-9, 23-26, Luke 12:16-21, What shall I do? John, authority, good news, who?, Genesis 12:1-3, Isaiah 26:19 Aland notes that Luke 9:7-8=3:19,9:19 and Luke 9:9=23:8. Herod Antipas thought that John the Baptist had risen from the dead. The people knew that Jesus had something to do with Lazarus being risen from the dead. Herod wanted to see Jesus. Jesus had taught that those who sought to save their lives would lose them, but those who lost their lives for his sake would save them.

Pilate was seeking a way to better himself. Jesus asked him about wealth after one dies.

AFTER THE DEATH (Luke 16:14-17, 24:13-22,, John, authority, good news, mighty, what, Genesis 25:23, cf Isaiah 42:11, cf Acts of Pilate 5:32) The Law and the Prophets were honored and taught by both John and Jesus. John's preaching and baptism had brought many into a relationship with God. Some like Peter questioned the wisdom of so many followers. Jesus explained that being a follower was more like being a servant than a member of an elite group. More followers would be better. He increased the number of disciples by seventy.

PART TWO: THE LORD'S PRAYER

If Pontius Pilate prayed, this is what he might say. Pontius Pilate was believed to be the illegitimate son of Tyrus of Mayence who became a hostage in Rome. When Tyrus was defeated by the Romans, Pilate was taken to Rome. He attended school with Tiberius, Aretas IV and Herod Philip. After the unsolved murder of one of the Caesars, Pilate was sent to serve in the Roman army in the Black Sea region 'amongst cannibals'. Returning to Rome in honor, he married Claudia, an illegitimate 'granddaughter of Caesar's'. In 26 c.e. he was sent to Judea as Governor. He considered himself a Caesar. About 34 c.e. he was recalled to Rome to answer to Caesar for John's death. It broke pax romana. Now Tiberius in 37 c.e. sent for Pilate to answer for Jesus's death. At the same time he sent for Herod Antipas and Aretas IV because they were both rulers of Roman possessions but carrying on a border war against each other.

Pilate was warned he must crucify Jesus if he wanted to be a friend of Caesar. (cf John 19:12) The word play is philos (friend) which is a near homonym to the name Pilate. The reader should note the frequent use of Philos (friend) in Part III.

OUR (Luke 3:1-12, John, Tiberius Caesar, Pilate, Genesis 6:6, Isaiah 40;3-5) Aland notes that Luke 3:2=1:80, Luke 3:3=20:4, Luke 3:7,12=7:30 and Luke 3:7=7:29) Tiberius Caesar had retired from Rome, but he had discussed Jesus with Mary Magdalene. The darkness on the day of Jesus's death intrigued him. Nevertheless he was considering adding Jesus to the Roman pantheon. He was hoping to find a non-military peace in Jerusalem and Judea. (Martin, PHJ). The Roman Senate declined, Tiberius died and Nero destroyed all records bearing the name of Tiberius. (James, ANT, 156)

FATHER (Luke 2:1-7, Caesar Augustus,, good tidings, cf Acts of Pilate 2:2,7:8,8:5) Aland notes that Luke 2:6=1:27. In 42 b.c. Cassius (Longinus) left his nephew in Syria. He went his way, but he was defeated by Marc Antony. Then he commited suicide. (Schurer, HJP, I. 1. 338-339) The Longinus who commented about Jesus could have been a relative.The Caesars had many illegitimate children. Perhaps Mennius of Tyre or Tyrus of Mayence was one. Pilate was illegitimate, but he was taken to Rome as a hostage. After an unexplained murder,

Pilate was sent as a soldier to Sinope on the Black Sea. Seneca's third son was Governor (later Bishop) there. Pilate defeated the cannibals there and returned to Rome.

NAME (Luke 13:1-9, 'wicked Caesar to perish', Pilate, Numbers 23:10, Isaiah 38:18, cf Acts of Pilate 2:15) The name Caesar means 'severed', and the name Pilate means 'close pressed' as a piece of felt. (Jackson, DSPN, 20, 75) As a youth Pilate had been given the name Pontius Pilate. He married Claudia, the protégée of Seneca the Elder's second wife, Pomponia. She was the widow of Aulus Plautus, a Roman general who served in what is now Great Britain. Claudia was the daughter of British King Cogidunus. She and Pomponia were Christians. Confusion exists between two Claudia's, the wife of Rufus Pudens and the wife of Pontius Pilate. She was the protégée of Second the Elder's second wife Pomponia, a Christian. (Griffin, PIP, in passim.)

Mandaeans called their scripture the Treasury of Life. (Mead, GJB, 86-89) Pilate, believing that the Mandeans were carrying the lost treasures of Moses up Mounts Ebal and Gerizim, had his soldiers attack and kill Samaritans. Their asses were only carrying bales of hay. (Ferguson, EEC, 561, Josephus, 380)

KINGDOM (Luke 23:1-5,, Caesar, Exodus 30:12, Isaiah 7:14, Acts of Pilate 2:8-13) Aland notes that Luke 23:2=20:25.. In the Acts of Pilate, fifteen witnesses testified as to the legitimacy of the infant Jesus. Because some of them had gathered for the census, many knew he was of the lineage of David. However when King David had allowed a census of the people, he had been reproved for it. (II Samuel 24, I Chronicles 21) Mary and Joseph, being of the lineage of David, go to Bethlehem for the census. Jesus's claim to authority is supported by the fact he was a descendant of David. John the Baptist was not.

Pilate brought the adult Jesus before him for trial. Some accused him of forbidding them to give tribute to Caesar. Then Pilate asked him, "Are you King of the Jews?" He replies, "Whatever you say…" Pilate then announced that he found no fault in the man.

EARTH (Luke 23:50-52, Pilate, Exodus 19:6, Isaiah 53:9) Pilate respected the Jewish Sabbath to the extent that he allowed Joseph of

Arimathea to take the body of Jesus down from the cross. Otherwise it would have been hanging there on the Sabbath.

Pilate may have made errors in judgment about Galileans, but Jesus teaches that the people should be more concerned about God's judgment than about earthly treasures.

BREAD (Luke 23:6-12, Herod, Pilate, friends,, John, Deuteronomy 22:29, Isaiah 29:14) Aland notes that Luke 23:7=3:1 and Luke 23:8=9:9. Herod supposedly wrote to Pilate as follows, "Therefore gird up your loins, and receive righteousness, thou with thy wife remembering Jesus night and day; and the kingdom shall belong to you Gentiles, for we the (chosen) people have mocked the Righteous One." (Hone, LBB, 270) He placed a gorgeous robe and crown on Jesus to mock him. It may have been the same one that Herod wore at the Olympic games. Herod died a few days later, but the robe caused many to think he was a god. (Josephus, 412)

EVIL (Luke 9:7-9, Herod, who?) Reincarnation was a more common belief amongst the Jews than resurrection. Herod kept hearing about Jesus. He wondered if he were John whom he had beheaded or Elijah, an earlier incarnation of John.

FORGIVE US (Luke 23:13-26,, Pilate, Exodus 26:31-33, Isaiah 60:2, cf Acts of Pilate 3:9,14, 8:12-15) Aland notes that Luke 23:2=20:25. Pilate asked Jesus 'What is truth?' (John 18:38) Jesus said that his kingdom is not of this world. Jesus said to Pilate, 'Believe that truth is on earth among those, who when they have the power of judgment, are governed by truth, and form right judgment. (Hone, LBB, 67) Pilate served as procurator from 26 to 36 c.e. (Schurer, HJP, I. 2, 82-87)

Thinking like a Roman, Pilate knew that the water system of Jerusalem needed repairs so he took the necessary funds from the Temple. The priests and the people became very angry because it was from dedicated funds. At one place water flowed from time to time. The water came from the Virgin's Spring. Sick people would lie on the banks of the place where the water would gush in. When it did, they would enter the water for a blessing. When Pilate repaired the water system, the water conduits broke and killed many who were waiting.

Moreover, when Pilate heard of the protest, he sent his own soldiers dressed in regular clothing to beat the Jews. More died. (Josephus, 479)

The Jews could not under Roman Law carry out a sentence of death. Pilate's wife Claudia had told Pilate to have nothing to do with Jesus. However, Tiberius had warned him against any outbreak in civil order. He gave the people a choice of releasing Jesus or Barabbas, and they chose Barabbas. He could have been more protective of a man who

had done no wrong. The irony is that in the clamour of shouting, he could not have distinguished Bar Abba (Son of God) from Barabbas (son of Gamaliel).

AS WE FORGIVE (Luke 20:19-26, Caesar, Exodus 20:4, Proverbs 18:10)

Pilate offended the chief priests and scribes. They deliberately made trouble for him. He would have been somewhat sympathetic when the chief priests and scribes tried to make trouble for Jesus. Jesus showed no personal animosity toward Caesar. He said, 'Render unto Caesar what is Caesar's and unto God what is God's.' John 19:12 states that the people reminded Pilate that if he released Jesus, he was not Caesar's friend. Pilate forgave the people for their obstinence. Legend and the Acts of Pilate say that Nicodemus became a Christian. When accused he said, 'Let my lot be with him.' The Abyssinian Church has made a saint of Pilate, perhaps for his post-ascension life. Most Christians cite a creed that includes 'crucified under Pontius Pilate'. (Comay and Brownrigg, WWB, II, 358)

AMEN (Luke 23:50-56, Pilate) Pilate allowed the body of Jesus to be taken down because the Sabbath was approaching. Nicodemus gave ointments and herbs to be used in the preparation of the body. The body was covered in linen which was recycled from its use as scrolls or scroll covers. (Eisenman, JBJ, 307-308, 228) The infant Jesus had been wrapped in swaddling clothes, probably linen from the same source.

PART THREE: THE TEN COMMANDMENTS

Isaiah 53:11 in the ELS has a phrase that includes the word 'power'. It becomes the key word for Part Three as it refers to Jesus. The same commentary that James ben Zebedee had for the Ten Commandments was used by Pilate. Only those about Jesus are given below, but John's commentary is given in scattered placees above. The word 'philos' means 'friend' and it is similar in sound to the name Pilate. ONE GOD

(Luke 10:19-20, power, Luke 11:5-10, friend, idea of what, Exodus 20:3, Psalm 91:13, Isaiah 27:1, Acts of Pilate 4:7) Aland notes that Luke 11:7,8=18:5. Although it is no longer obvious, the plural of tanna (biblical scholars) and serpents (tannaim) are a word play. One of the priestly families was that of Phineas (serpent's mouth). Perhaps Pilate had a spy in the seventy that Jesus sent out.

IDOLS

(Luke 9:37-45, powerless , Luke 15:8-10, friend, what, Exodus 20;4, cf Isaiah 1:26, 40:29, cf Acts of Pilate 5:34-37) The Caesars had health problems which were called incurable, so this would have intrigued Tiberius Caesar. Incest had caused certain physical problems to exist. The question as to why the disciples could not help the son could be that they could deal with disease and breaks, but not congenital defects. Jesus could.

HOLY NAME

(Luke 5:17, power, 21:10-19, friend, what, perish, Exodus 20:7, Isaiah 64:7, I Samuel 14:45) Aland notes that Luke 21:12=12:11, Luke 21:14-15=13:29 and Luke 21:18=12:7.The people came from many places to see Jesus and be healed. He had the power to heal them.

SABBATH

(Luke 6:1-5, Lord implies power, Luke 7:1-10, friend, idea of what?, Exodus 8, I Samuel 21:6) The stringent laws of Jewish Sabbath would have irritated Roman soldiers. Certain Jewish soldiers refused to fight on the Sabbath. Maybe Pilate thought if they could 'harvest', maybe they could fight, too.

PARENTS

(Luke 1:5-25, 35, power, Luke 14:12-15, friend, Exodus 20:12, Isaiah 7:14, cf Acts of Pilate 2:12-13) Aland notes that Luke 1:15=1:41, 45, Luke 1:20=1:45 and Luke 14:15=13:29. The issue in the Acts of Pilate appears to focus on the legitimacy of the lineage of Jesus, not the miraculous aspect of his birth.

KILL

(Luke 12:1-12, power, friend, what, Exodus 20:13, Isaiah 28:15, Acts of Pilate chapter 15-18) Aland notes that Luke 12:7=21:18 and Luke 12:11-12=21:14-15. In the Acts of Pilate, Jesus goes into hell and rescues those imprisoned there.

ADULTERY

(Luke 16:18, idea of power, Luke 15:3-7, friend, what, Exodus 20:14, Isaiah 55:7, Acts of Pilate chapter 2) Jesus is charged with being born as a result of fornication, but the Acts of Pilate refutes the charge. Cyborea, once a prostitute for Herod the Great, became the mother of Judas Iscariot with the name Lost Sheep of the House of Israel.

STEAL

(Luke 22:52-53, power, Luke 16:9-12, friend, who, Exodus 20:15, Isaiah 21:11, 1:23, Acts of Pilate 20:7) The guards that arrested Jesus did not arrest him openly, but in the dark of night. Thieves are arrested in the night. Judas Iscariot, the instigator, was a thief, but not Jesus. Although the significance is no longer clear, the Mandaeans preferred darkness. (Mead, GJB, in passim)

LIE

(Luke 4:5-8, power, Luke 7:29-35, friend, what, Exodus 20:16, Isaiah 44:3) Aland notes that Luke 7:29=3:12 and Luke 7:30=3:7,12. The devil promises to give Jesus what is not his to give—all the kingdoms of the world.

COVET

(Luke 22:67-71, power, Luke 14:7-10, friend, who, Exodus 20:17, Isaiah 40:29, Proverbs 25:6-7) The members of the Sanhedrin were envious of the following of Jesus. They break their own obedience to the Commandments by charging Jesus with blasphemy. They ask, 'Are you the Christ?' He answers, 'Ye say that I am.' Then they say he has admitted to blasphemy.

PART FOUR BIBLIOGRAPHY

Aland, Kurt, et al.,eds. The Greek New Testament. United Bible Societies. (New York:1975)

Comay, Joan and Ronald Brownrigg.Who's Who in the Bible. 2 parts. Wings Books (New York: 1980)

Eisenman, Robert, James the Brother of Jesus. Viking Press (New York:1996)

Ferguson, Everett,ed. Cyclopedia of Early Christianity. Garland Reference Library.(New York:1990)

Griffin, Miriam T. Seneca, a Philosopher in Politics. Clarendon Press (Oxford:1976)

Hall, Manly P. The Secret Teachings of All Ages. Pb. Penquin (New York:2003)

Hone, William. Lost Books of the Bible. Crown Publishers (Cleveland, Ohio:1979)

Jackson, J. B. A Dictionary of Proper Names…being a literal translation. Pb. Loizeaux Brothers (Neptune, New Jersey;1979)

James, Montague Rhodes, tr. The Apocryphal New Testament. Clarendon Press (Oxford:1973)

Josephus. Complete Works. Translated by William Whiston. Kregel (Grand Rapids, Michigan:1985)

Marshall, I. Howard. The Gospel of Luke. William B. Eerdmans Publishing Company

(Grand Rapids, Michigan:1978)

Martin, Harry V. Proving the Historical Jesus. Free America Press (n.a.:1995)

Mead, G.R.S. The Gnostic John the Baptizer. John M. Watkins (London:1924)

Rambsel, Yacov. His Name Is Jesus. Pb. Word Publishing (Nashville:1999)

Schurer, Emil. A History of the Jewish People in the time of Christ. 5 vols. Hendrickson (Peabody, Massachusetts:1994)

XII. JOSEPH JUSTUS BARSABAS- JESUS- JOB (TROUBLE)

Isaiah 53:2 is the verse that begins the Equidistant Letter Sequencing for the name Joseph. Also beginning at that point is ELS for the name Job, trouble, ram of sacrifice, mountain of grace, prophets of God, and Levites. (Rambsel, HNJ, 25,7, 36, 39, 40, 46) Joseph was an older brother of James the Less. James the Less was probably so-called because his mother's name was Escha (last, least). He was three years old when she died after being married to Joseph of Nazareth fifty years. (Hall, STAA, 585-586) Escha was a member of the Haggai-Phabes family that also included Zechariah and Zebedee. She was descended from Aaron, therefore she was a Levite, so James could call himself a Levite.

Joseph (Joseph Justus Barsabas of Tiberius) was a former employee of Herod Agrippa, historian. However, Joseph himself wrote a Chronicle of Israelite Kings. (Eisenman, JBJ, in passim.) James Justus (the Less) became Head of the Circumcision Party of the Jews which may have affected his interpretation of Law. (Eisenman, JBJ, 197) The things he did were Rechabite customs similar to Arabian customs. Rechabites were called the Blessed or Beloved Ones. ("History of the Rechabites" in Charlesworth, OTP, II, 443-462) Joseph was descended from a priestly family, that of Aaron . His stepbrother Jesus was descended from a royal family, that of David of the Tribe of Benjamin (or Judah). In their time the people expected the Messiah to come, and this testimony in part discusses which lineage he would have.

The family of Joseph of Nazareth is sometimes called Barsabas. Sabazian

Mysteries in Rome seem unrelated to Christianity. Their sign was a golden serpent and initiation included dragging a live snake over the chest. (Hall, STAA, 89) Since Son of the Father is Bar Abba, Barsabas may allude to God.

PART ONE: STATIONS OF THE CROSS

Notes for a dual biography written by Joseph Justus compare his brothers James Justus (James the Less) and Jesus. One unifying phrase for Part One is 'brothers' and the other is 'which of you'.

SUBJECTS (Luke 3:21-23, beloved, Isaiah 42:1; 22:32, brothers, 17:7-11, which of you, Jerusalem, James 2:14) Aland notes that Luke 3:22=9:35 and Luke 3:23=4:22. James was head of the Circumcision Party in Jerusalem. Jesus had been born to the Virgin Mary when James was only four years old.

Aaron was brother to Moses and his spokesman. However, at one time he and Miriam, their sister, opposed Moses. Moses still declared that all priests be descended from him. Then there was Melchisedek and Phineas. David in his time further narrowed the choice of priests to descendants of Zadok.

The budding of the rod of Aaron portends a story about Joseph of Nazareth. After it had been decided that Mary should marry, the High Priest took the rods of all eligible men present. Nothing happens so he returns the rods. Immediately after Joseph of Nazareth takes back his rod, a dove flies to the rod and sits on it. He is told that God has chosen him. (Hastings, DOB, II, 776)

FAMILY (Luke 11:5-10, which of you, 11:27-28, brothers, James 1:5) Aland notes that Luke 11:7-8=18:5. Upon the death of his father, Jesus promises to bless all who give bread to the poor on the anniversary of his death, all who write out the story of Joseph's body being incorrupt for a thousand years, but all who are too poor to do anything else should name a son Joseph. (Hastings, DOB, II, 776-777)

Once Mary's proclamation was associated with the mother of Eleazar ben Hyrcanus. Christians associate it with James 1:22. Keepers of the Covenant is a term used more by Arabians and Muslims than by Christians who use it to mean only Nazoreans or Nazarites. (Eisenman, JBJ, 952)

One Jacim (Alcimus) was High Priest about 162-169 b.c., and he was a descendant of Aaron. (Jeremias, JTJ, 187, fn 127) He was called illegitimate by some other priests. Alcimus died tearing down a wall in the temple that separated the women from the men during worship. (Schurer, HJP, I. 1. 236) At Qumran every priest's tomb except that of Alcimus faced North-South. (De Vaux, ADSS, 46) James was called Oblias, Wall or Protection. (Eisenman, JBJ, 353)

GENEALOGY (Luke 9:46-56, Which of you, Luke 20:27-38, brothers, Jerusalem, James 4:10) Aland notes that Luke 9:46=22:24, Luke 9:48=10:16 and Luke 9:47=5:22. As Aaron was brother to Moses, James Justus was stepbrother to Jesus. His mother Escha (last, least) and Elizabeth the mother of John the Baptist were descended from Aaron. Moses ordered that only Levite descendants of Aaron could serve as priests. In David's time eligibility was further decreased to descendants of Zadok. Physically defective men were not allowed into the Temple to worship, much less serve as priests. Herod the Great further reduced their numbers by massacre. Prophecy said the Messiah would be a son of Joseph. James was a son of Joseph eligible for the priesthood. His religious fervor was so great that he was even allowed to enter the Holy of Holies. (Eisenman, JBJ, 240) The name Aaron means 'enlightened or illumined'. The word for Ark (aron) is similar.

SERMON (Luke 4:16-22, Joseph's sons, Luke 12:16-34, which of you, least=Escha, mother of James, James 4:15) Aland notes that Luke 12:24=12;7 and Luke 12:32= 22:29.

At Nazareth Jesus preached from Isaiah 61:1-2, but he left out the part about vengeance. Even his brothers did not believe. (John 7:3-5) At Capernaum some said that he was beside himself. (Mark 3:21) Then at another time he preaches about the dangers of treasures and riches. His brother James was allowed to go into the Holy of Holies on the Day of Atonement. As usual he wore white linen, only adding a diadem (sacrificial plate) on his head. (Eisenman, JBJ, 311-312)

MARVEL (Luke 9:27-36, which of you, face, Jerusalem, stand, Jeremiah 19:35) Aaron's Rod was part of Moses being able to create the Plagues of Egypt. (Exodus 7-8)

Jesus performed miracles without a rod.

As Aaron appeared with his brother Moses and his son Eleazar on Mount Hor shortly before his death, Jesus appears on the Mount of Transfiguration shortly before his death with Moses and Elijah. (Hastings, DOB, I, 3)

Rechabites were not to live in houses under roofs, because possessions caused cities that were evil. Peter was present when Jesus was on the Mount. He thought of making three tents, but he remembered his vow. He was not to live under a roof until the Messiah came. Jesus was the Messiah. Moreover, honoring his prophets as his equal would be idolatry.

FAME (Luke 5:12-26, which, Jerusalem, face, Isaiah 43:25, Luke 8:19-21, James 1:17) Aland notes that Luke 5:22=9:47. Joseph of Nazareth had four sons by Escha (Simon, Joseph, Jude and James). The content of this periscope is like that of Luke 11:27-28. James cared very much about appearances. To be turned away would have been embarrassing to him.

News about the healing Jesus did spread quickly. Jesus healed and then withdrew into the wilderness to pray, but James stood before a throne to pray. (Eisenman, JBJ, 310) Jeremiah had promised the Rechabites they would never lack a man to stand before His throne. (Jeremiah 35:19)

PROPHECY (Luke 14:28-35, which of you, 17:1-6 brothers, James 2:10) Aaronite priests had authority over other Levite priests. (Numbers 3:10, 16:40, 18:1-7) Aaron was with his brother Moses when he led the people out of Egypt. Their negotiations with the Pharoah could be called prophecies.

John Hyrcanus retired from war to build his dream home at Bathyra (Araq el-Emir). He ran out of funds and commited suicide. There is a tower there. Herod the Great offered it to Babylonians to protect his border. Hillel and Gamaliel built a dual academy there, to teach scripture and warfare. (Lapp in Perdue, ABI, 165-184)

Gideon had dared to fight impossible battles. (Judges 7:2-7) In gospel times the sons of Gamaliel favored different policies toward the Romans. Judas of Galilee formed the zealot Fourth Philosophy. His twin Joshua organized the Peace (or appeasement) Party.

LAST WEEK (Luke 22:21-27, which of you, 14:25-27, brothers, James 4:7) Aland notes that Luke 22:24=9:46, Luke 14:26=9:23, and Luke 14:27=9:23. As Moses pronounces the plagues that caused the Egyptians to release the Israelites, it is Aaron who speaks. Aaron helps Moses to hold up his rod at the defeat of Amalek. (Exodus 17:10, 12)

Jesus told his disciples that the hand of his betrayer was eating with them. Each asked which one would do such a thing. He reminded them that he had said his disciples must not show greater loyalty to family than to him. Also descendants of the brothers Jacob and Esau must worship him, not worship their ancestors.

DEATH (Luke 7:36-49, which, Luke 16:19-31, brothers, James 5:6). James prayed so much on his knees that they were calloused like those of a camel. (Eisenman, JBJ, 310) James had a throne, but it was for standing before, not for sitting on. (Jeremiah 19:35) The Patriarch Aaron was to bring the names before the Lord. (Exodus 28:12-13) Among those who saw the crucifixion of Jesus was Simon bar Cleophas who was one of the priests of Rechab, a son of the Rechabites. Simon says on the occasion of the stoning of James, "Stop, he is uttering the most marvelous prayers for you." Eusebius describes the same event calling him the Just One. (Eisenman, JBJ, 313) Simon was cousin to James. (Eisenman, JBJ, 467) Their mothers may have been sisters.

AFTER THE DEATH (Luke 21:14-24, brothers, Jerusalem, Luke 24:30-31, knew which one, James 2:23-24) Aaron became the spokesman for his brother Moses. He interpreted the law for the occasion. James was noteworthy in interpreting the law for evangelists going into foreign lands. Mohammad used James' directives in his works. (Eisenman, JBJ, 135-136)

James recognized Jesus after the Resurrection when he was breaking bread. (Kraeling, TD, 108) His conversion is connected with seeing Jesus after the Resurrection. (I Corinthians 15:7-9)

PART II: THE LORD'S PRAYER

If Joseph Justus were to pray, this might be what he said. Variations on 'just' like the family name Justus (Barsabas) and 'righteous' relate to Aaron, brother of Moses. .

OUR (Luke 7:24-34, justify, great, James 1:22) Jesus spoke of John with high praise, but he then uses the word 'least' to suggest a greater one. Joseph of Nazareth was married to Esca (last, least) for fifty years. He may have been saying that the Christian movement would be in the hands of James after his death. Jacob (James) had had his name changed from Jacob to Israel. (Genesis 32:28) In their day, Aaron made it possible for Moses, his brother, to lead the people. (Exodus 28)

Usually people rejoiced at a wedding, but the forthcoming wedding of Herodias and Herod Antipas caused the people to feel shame. Usually people mourned at a death, but Lazarus had died. The people rejoiced when Jesus restored him to life. John the Baptist and James used no wine just as the Rechabites used no wine. Jesus, however, used wine in religious celebrations.

FATHER (Luke 2:25-38, Joseph not Simon, Jerusalem, face, James 5:8) Aland notes Luke 2:38=24:21. Luke 2:35, 38=23:51) Joseph of Nazareth was present when Jesus was presented at the temple. Simeon announced that Jesus was a light to lighten the Gentiles. The name Aaron means 'he enlightened'. Although Honi is associated with rain, James received the name of the Just One after he brought rain. He prayed, then lifted up his hands and it rained. (Eisenman, JBJ, 368)

Joseph of Nazareth married Escha when he was forty years old. They were married 49 years which made him 89 or 90 when he married the Virgin Mary. By Escha he had four sons and two daughters. Mary, the daughter of Hannah like Samuel, had lived in the temple since she was three, perhaps 9 to 11 years. To find out which single man he should give Mary to, the priest took the rods of all. Nothing happened. Then he returned Joseph's rod to him. A dove came to sit on his rod which was taken as a sign. (Hastings, DOB, II, 776)

NAME (Luke 23:50-51, Joseph Justus not Joseph of Arimathea, James 1:8) Aland notes that Luke 23:51=2:35, 38. Luke does not specify Joseph of Arimathea. This verse could have been so similar when it referred to Joseph Justus that one of the two verses was dropped. One legend is that he drank a deadly poison, but suffered no harm. (Hastings, DOB, II, 778)

Justus of Tiberias (fl 66-67 c,e,) and Joseph Justus (fl when Jesus was born) might be the same person and might not. He was imprisoned twice by Agrippa. Vespasion condemned him to death, but Bernice who touched the hem of Jesus's garment intervened. She had her brother Agrippa spare his life. Justus had worked with him on a history while he was writing his own history. Justus wrote, A Chronicle of the Jewish Kings from Moses to Agrippa II. (Schurer, HJP, I. 1. 65-69) Josephus and others used his information in their works.

Joseph Justus was considered as a replacement for Judas Iscariot in the twelve, but Matthias (Zacchaeus) was chosen instead. (Acts 1:23) Josephus has much to say about Joseph Justus, especially in relation to Bernice and Agrippa. (Josephus, 17, 18)

KINGDOM (Luke 20:20-26, Caesar, just, James 1:12) Aland notes that Luke 20:20=11:54. The Kenites were ironworkers who lived in tent cities. Those who more or less settled at Petra called themselves the 'monks of Aaron in the valley of Moses." (Bromiley, ISBE, III, 820) Similar if not the same as Rechabites they made a singing sound that used echoes. (Hastings, DOB, IV, 204)

Pretending to be following the commandment against idolatry, the priests of Annas forbid the use of faced coins in worship inside the temple. Since James almost lived inside the temple, he had to know. The priests took faced coins and exchanged them for rare faceless coins for personal profit. Worshipers put them in the collection only to have to buy them back before the next worship service. (Edersheim, LTJM, I, 371-372)

EARTH (Luke 10:25-37, justify, Jerusalem, James 2:8) Samaritans pretended to be the posterity of the Patriarch Joseph. (Josephus 244) At one time many Jews were exiled into Babylon. When they returned, they considered Samaritans unworthy to be Jews "for they had not suffered."

A lawyer, perhaps James, asked Jesus what he should do to have eternal life.

Jesus said to obey the Ten Commandments and love his neighbor as himself. Then Jesus tells the Parable of the Good Samaritan. A priest passes by without helping the victim of

a robbery. Then a Levite passes by. Last of all, a Samaritan stops to help. James was a Levite who was prejudiced against Samaritans. The lesson was not an easy one.

BREAD (Luke 14:12-15, just, brothers, James 4:6) Aland notes the Luke 14:15=13:29. Judgment Day was visualized as a great banquet. Jesus invited those who gave hospitality to those in need to come to his great banquet.

EVIL (Luke 16:1-13, unjust, James 5:12) Aland notes that Luke 16:10-12=19:17-26. Agrippa accused Joseph Justus of wasting time when Joseph was his secretary. Bernice interceded and Agrippa allowed him to continue as a secretary.

FORGIVE (Luke 18:9-14, justified, James 2:15) Aland notes Luke 18:13=23:48 and Luke 18:9-14=16:15. Before he became a Christian, James was extreme in his religious fervor. He was honored to the extent he was allowed to go into the Holy of Holies, an experience allowed only to priests. Indeed 'keepers of the Covenant' meant 'Sons of Zadok'. (Eisenman, JBJ, 940)

AS WE (Luke 15:3-7, just, Isaiah 53:6, James 4:4) Cyborea, mother of Judas Iscariot, was known as the Lost Sheep of the House of Israel. James would have been astonished that the forgiven woman should worship with Christians. Jews often put sinners out of their congregations. God rejoices when the unjust come back into fellowship. Concern for animals on the Ark can be part of a pun for 'aron'.

AMEN (Luke 16:14-17, justify, hearts, James 1:12) Aland notes that Luke 16:15=21:37, 18:9-14. God looks upon the heart, and he knows what is in the heart. James had done all he knew how to earn God's favor. However, if Jesus were the Messiah, James felt unappreciated. Joseph was a widower when he married the Virgin Mary. Levite wives had to be pure, and James from time to time may have had doubts. (Jeremias, JTJ, 215) A few sources say that James married the wealthy widow of Judas of Galilee. Judas of Galilee was the zealot son of Gamaliel, and he started the Fourth Philosophy. Others say James nevertheless died a virgin.

Rechabites were ascetic Jews. James was comfortable as a leader in Jerusalem of religious Jews. Later as Bishop of the Church at Jerusalem, he also led Gentiles. Recalling that Moses brought the Law down from Mount Sinai, Luke uses the unifying word 'mountain' to discuss the Law.

ONE GOD

(Luke 22:39-43, mountain, James 2:23-24) Aland notes that Luke 22:39-21:37. Jesus goes to the Mount of Olives to pray. An angel comes from heaven to strengthen him. Jesus asks that God's Will be done. In one sense, father and son were one. Jesus willed the same as his father.

IDOLS

(Luke 4:1-13, mountain, James 1:13) Jesus is tempted by the devil. The second test is that he is taken up a high mountain to see all the kingdoms of the world. Rechabites saw cities as evil because they were based on wealth and power. He only asked that Jesus worship him. Jesus would not, for he knew a greater power.

Last of all, the third temptation sounds like a story told about James. James was enticed to go up the side of the Temple to proclaim his faith. Then he was cast down into the Kedron Valley below. (Eisenman, JBJ, 946) Jesus did not go up. James fell on the fifth step of the temple, breaking his legs. (The Patriarch Jacob limped.) Not a bone in the body of Jesus was ever broken. The History of the Rechabites tells how Zosimos, the Blessed One of Christ is tempted of the devil. (Charlesworth, OTP, II, 461, fn c)

HOLY NAME

(Luke 8:26-37, mountain, James 1:24) Aland notes that Luke 8:28=4:34. Since the prophecy of Zechariah 8:23, Jerusalem had been the religious center for the Jews. Even in exile, the people would say 'next year in Jerusalem'. Fortunatus (Legion, Troop) although mad called Jesus Son of God most high. Jesus sent the demons from him into swine feeding on a mountain. Hezir (swine) was the family name of priests in the time of David. (Peloubet, PBD, 255)

SABBATH

(Luke 6:6-12, mountain, pray, James 2:7,14) Aland notes that Luke 6:7=14:1 and Luke 6:8=5:22, 9:47. Jesus healed a man with a withered (shortened) hand. The rumor was that the man refused to serve as priest. To avoid it, he had cut the nerve in his hand. James was admired so much that sick people wanted to touch the hem of his garment. (Eisenman, JBJ, 239) The same is told about Jesus (Luke 8:44)

PARENTS

(Luke 23:27-31, mountain, Jerusalem, James 5:1) Aland notes that Luke 23:29=21:23. Jesus had not completed the last part of Isaiah 61:1-2 when he preached at Nazareth. Now he describes the Day of Vengeance. He warns parents that they shall be concerned about their children.

KILL

(Luke 19:11-30, Mount of Olives, Jerusalem, keep, stand, James 2:19) Aland notes that Luke 19:26=8:18 and Luke 19:17-26=16:10-12. A triple word play is used in this periscope. Minas (money), minyahs (cities) and minyehs (quorum for worship) are supplemented by minim (curses).

ADULTERY

(Luke 21:34-38, Mount of Olives, temple at Jerusalem, stand, James 4:4) Aland notes that Luke 21:37=22:39. Herod the Tetrarch was commiting adultery with Herodias (his brother's ex-wife) in Jerusalem. Aaronites considered mating with Gentiles adultery. Aaron's grandson Phineas killed backsliders and thus saved the camp. (Numbers 25:7, 11) The backsliders were Jews who had married Gentiles. (Eisenman, JBJ, 373)

STEAL

(Luke 19:41-48, Dominus flevit=cliff on side of mountain, temple at Jerusalem, James 5:4) Aland notes that Luke 42=8:10 and Luke 19:44= 21:6, 1:68) Dominus flevit is the name given the area above the Garden of Gethsemane. A church stands there. (Duffield, HBL, 110) The sons of Annas were making a profit from not allowing coins with images in the temple offering. When Jesus was asked about using such a coin in worship, he said, "Render unto Caesar what is Caesar's and unto God what is God's.

LIE

(Luke 24:13-27, Emmaus may have been a mountain instead of a village, Jerusalem, James 3:8) Rechabites avoided cities, and the village with the name of Emmaus has not been found. The resurrected Jesus pretends he does not know what has happened in Jerusalem. He meets two cousins of James, but he wants to hear what they think happened.

COVET

(Luke 21:20-24, Jerusalem, Gentiles, Isaiah 12:12-15, James 5:9) James held the Jerusalem assembly until the 40's, perhaps until the 60's. As the new Christians and Jews interacted, it was difficult not to covet. Paul needed the support of the Jerusalem Christians, but they feared his reaching out to include Gentiles. (Matthew 10:5 contra John 7:35)

BIBLIOGRAPHY

Aland, Kurt, et al., eds. The Greek New Testament. 3rd ed. United Bible Societies (New York:1975

Barnstone, Willis, ed., "Protoevangelium Jacobi" in The Other Bible. Pb. HarperSanFrancisco (New York:1984)

Bromiley, Geoffrey W., gen. ed. The International Bible Encyclopedia. 4 vols. William B. Eerdmans Publishing Company (Grand Rapids, Michigan: 1982)

Charlesworth, James H. The Old Testament Pseudepigrapha. 2 vols. Doubleday & Company (Garden City, New York:1983)

De Vaux, Ronald. Archaeology and the Dead Sea Scrolls. Oxford University Press (London:1973)

Duffield, Guy P. Handbook of Bible Lands. Pb. Regal Books (Glendale:1969)

Edersheim, Alfred. The Life and Times of Jesus the Messiah. Wm. B. Eerdmans Publishing Company (Grand Rapids, Michigan:1976)

Eisenman, Robert. James the Brother of Jesus. Viking (USA:1996)

Hastings, James. Dictionary of the Bible. 5 vols. Charles Scribner's Sons (New York:1909)

Hall, Manly P. The Secret Teachings of All Ages. Pb. Penquin (New York:2003)

Jeremias, Joachim. Jerusalem in the Time of Jesus. Pb. Fortress Press (Philadelphia:1969)

Josephus. Complete Works. Kregel Publications (Grand Rapids, M ichigan: 1985)

Kraeling, Emil G. The   Disciples. Rand McNally & Company (USA:1966)

Lapp, Nancy L. "Araq el-Emir" in Perdue, Leo G. et al., eds. Archaeology and Biblical Interpretation. John Knox (Atlanta, Georgia: 1987)

McClintock, John and James Strong. Cyclopedia of Biblical, Theological and Ecclesiastical Literature. 12 vols. Baker Book House (USA:1981)

Peloubet, F. N. Peloubet's Bible Dictionary. Universal Book and Bible House. (Philadelphia:1947)

Rambsel, Yacov. His Name Is Jesus. Pb. Word Publishing (Nashville:1999)

Schurer, Emil. A History of the Jewish People. 5 vols. Hendrickson (Peabody, Massachusetts:1994)

XIII. MATTHEW BEN THEOPHILUS BEN ANNAS (LEVI)-ABRAHAM-JESUS

Isaiah 53:8 has the beginning of ELS for Matthew and 'let him be crucified'. (Rambsel, HNJ, 45) ELS for Satan, bind up, weighed, 'from prison', 'burnt offerrng' and 'from the great whip', Messiah, Jesus and Joseph, the husband of Mary, begins with the same verse. (Rambsel, HNJ, 17, 22, 30, 35, 36) The unifying word for the whole testimony is children, sometimes substituted for by son. The phrase, "Blessed is he that cometh in the name of the Lord" comes from Psalm 118:26. Included in it is the beginning of ELS for Messiah and Yeshua. (Rambsel, HNJ, 193)

Matthew (Levi) was one of the twelve disciples. When the Apostles Creed was composed, Matthew's name was attached to, "From thence he shall come to judge the quick and the dead". (Hone, LBB. 91) Matthew (Levi) was called by the words 'follow me." (Luke 5:27) As a publican, Matthew was required only to follow the laws of Noah. The part of the Apostles Creed associated with Matthew is "to judge the quick and the dead." (Hone, LBB, 91) Matthew the grandson of High Priest Annas was a Levite.

Two magi were terrorizing Ethiopia. Matthew undid their mischief so Candacis hails him as divinely appointed. Matthew had brought fire-breathing dragons to sit at his feet. Then a man wants the head of a convent to leave it to marry him. Matthew refused to order her to leave her work, so Hyrtacus stabbed Matthew. (Kraeling, TD, 163-164)

The Gospel of Matthew is arranged to be a commentary on the Pentateuch, the first five books of the Old Testament. Perhaps he followed the example of Ezra or Isaiah. The synoptic gospels result because someone rearranged Luke for sake of comparison. Modern minds do not appreciate the duplication, but law is based on the agreement of three or more witnesses.

PART ONE: STATIONS OF THE CROSS

Notes for a dual biography are related to the Patriarch Abraham and the Gospel writer Matthew. The unifying phrase in Part One is Abraham. Matthew emphasizes that Jesus is the Son of God. Levites like the famous Chanina (Annas) family of priests claimed to relate to God through Abraham.

SUBJECTS (Luke 1:70-80, Abraham, child, Genesis 22:16) Aland notes that Luke 1:80=1:27 and Luke 1:80=2:52. Joseph as a name means to add or increase. Abraham was willing to sacrifice his beloved son, so God did not require that of him. He promised to multiply Abraham's seed as the stars in the heavens.

Matthew went to Ethiopia, probably not present day Ethiopia, perhaps a place on the way to Egypt. Scriptures say, "Out of Egypt have I called my son, for he shall be called a Nazarene." (McBirnie, STA, 175) Matthew's Gospel is written as a commentary on the Ezra Lectionary. It relates the teaching of Jesus to the reading for the day at the Temple in Jerusalem for three years. (Goulder, EC, in passim.)

FAMILY (Luke 1:39-56, Abraham, babe, Genesis 17:19) Jesus treated women differently from the Jewish customs of his day or of their history. Abraham listened to Sarah and sent Ishmael into the desert to die. Sarah had born a child named Isaac. God promised that he would make a covenant with Isaac and his seed. The Patriarch Joseph was not blessed with his encounter with Potiphar's wife, for she had him thrown into prison. The Virgin Mary was called blessed. She replied that all who hear and keep the Word are blessed.

GENEALOGY (Luke 20:34-38, Abraham, child, Exodus 3:6,14) Moses was afraid to look upon the face of One who claimed to be the god of Abraham, Isaac and Jacob. Two of Aaron's sons were put to death for burning a strange fire on the altar. Jacob's twelve 'sons' became the progenitors of the twelve tribes of Israel (Jacob). When John the Baptist baptized Jesus, a voice from heaven said, "Thou art my beloved son, in thee I am well-pleased." When the Apostles Creed was formed, Matthew's name was associated with "From thence he shall come to judge the living and the dead." (Hone, LBB, 91)

SERMON (Luke 10: 25-37, like Abraham, more=increase=Joseph, Genesis 18) Aland notes that Luke 10:25=18:18. Hospitality was typical of Abraham. Once he entertained angels unawares. When the angels left, they promised that Sarah would bear a son.

Jesus gives the parable of the Good Samaritan. Matthew would have been attentive to the mention of a Levite and the Priest. The Chanina family of priests was headed by his grandfather Annas and five of his uncles served as High Priest. His Uncle Zacchaeus (Matthias) was overlooked because his size was considered a deformity until 65 c. e.

Women could not pass a partition within the temple. Only able-bodied men could. Any man considered deformed could not worship in the temple. He certainly could not become a priest.

MARVEL (Luke 13:10-17, Abraham, daughter, Genesis 17:5) Aland notes that Luke 13:16=19:9. When Abraham was 90 years old, Jesus asked him to walk before him and to be perfect. Being stooped over was associated with the curse of having to work. Jesus saw a woman stooped over. Even though it was the Sabbath and she was working, he healed her. In Jerusalem the issue was the proper posture for each prayer, such as morning and evening. She had been unable to pray in the correct posture for some prayers.

FAME (Luke 13:23-30, Abraham, last=least, Genesis 6:8) Noah was a perfect and just man in a corrupt society. God would use him and his faith to save a few people, his family. Jesus is asked if many (Qumran) or few (Sadducees) would be saved. Jesus answers that the covenant God made with Abraham, Isaac and Jacob still stands. As in the days of Noah, many are hypocrites. They may have lineage from Abraham, but they lack faith. Abraham's faith was counted as righteousness (perfection).

PROPHECY (Luke 17:22-32, Lot, Son of Man, Genesis 18:25-33) Aland notes that Luke 17:23=21:8 and Luke 17:25=9:22, 18:32-33. Lot was Abraham's nephew which he brought with him from Ur (Basra). They separated and Lot went to Sodom where there was an evil lifestyle. Lot called for Abraham to come save him. Abraham knew that if the town were destroyed, the righteous would die with the wicked. He tried to bargain with God. If he could find fifty righteous men, then would God save Sodom. He could not, so Sodom would be destroyed because of its own wickedness. Jesus says that a nation can still be destroyed by its own wickedness. The Second Coming will be a blessing and a curse.

LAST WEEK (Luke 19:1-11, Abraham, Son of Man, Genesis 15:6) Aland notes that Luke 19:9=13:16. Theophilus ben Annas was brother to Zacchaeus (Matthias) so Matthew was a nephew to Zacchaeus. Matthew had been High Priest 5-4 b.c. and Zacchaeus (Matthias) would be offered the High Priesthood in 65 c.e. (cf Jeremias, JTJ, 377-378) Since one assumes the nephew is younger, this is evidence of discrimination.

Zacchaeus repents of any overcharging he has done as a tax collector for the Romans. He offers to do more than Jewish law reguires. Jesus mentions his ancestor Abraham, which may be an allusion to faith counting as righteousness. Above and beyond sacrifice, faith is an essential to salvation. Judas Iscariot was nephew to Zacchaeus's wife. When Judas commited suicide, two men were proposed as his replacement, Joseph Justus and Zacchaeus. By lot Zacchaeus was chosen.

DEATH (Luke 16:19-31, Abraham, brothers, Genesis 22) Abraham was willing to sacrifice his beloved son Isaac. God provided a substitute, so that Isaac lived. In gospel times Jesus was willing to be a sacrifice for the sins of the world. Although he died, God had mercy and he was resurrected in three days.

Jesus talks about hell. One of Matthew's uncles, perhaps one who was High Priest and has died, asked Abraham if they could return to warn the family about hell. He replies that they have Moses and the prophets. Jesus ponders whether his return from the dead will cause people to believe.

A. D. (Luke 3:7-9, Abraham, child, Genesis 15:6) Certain Jews thought they had no responsibility. God had promised good to them. He had but he asked them to walk in his ways. They needed God more than he needed them, for the Creator could turn rocks into sons of Abraham (faith) should he choose.

PART TWO: THE LORD'S PRAYER

When Matthew prayed, these may have been his thoughts. When Matthew (Levi) was tried, the question was raised, "Is Matthew (mathai=when) to be put to death? It is written, 'When shall I come and appear before the Lord?' " (Psalms 42:3) The sentence was "... Mathai is to be executed, for it is said, 'When shall he die and his name perish?' " (Psalm 41:6) Matthew was at a writing table when Jesus called him to follow. The unifying word in Part Two is 'follow'. The word paraclete (Holy Spirit) means 'to follow alongside.'

OUR (Luke 9:46-50, follow, child, Matthew 18:1-5) John asks about healers who are not part of their following. Essenes, for example, recommended an ascetic life without faith. Ironically several years later Christians were called Essenes. (Szekely, GE, in passim.) Since the days of Moses eighteen blessings were read for the Jews and eighteen curses for Gentiles. According to Josephus, Matthew, son of Theophilus, was in Jerusalem when the Jewish War with the Romans began. (Josephus, 425) Matthew's father-in-law, Simon ben Boethus, was father to Joazar who was High Priest in 4 b.c. Matthew and Joshua ben Gamla married daughters of Simon ben Boethus. (Jeremias, JBJ, 154-155) The term Alphaeus may refer to the first of a 'pair' which would bring questions before the Sanhedrin . The phrase 'ox and ass' refers to priestly lineages. The word for ox (bous) is similar to Boethus, and the word for ass (onos) is similar to Annas. They were two of four priestly lineages in gospel times.

FATHER (Luke 1:1-7, course=following, cf Matthew 2:1) Theophilus ben Annas was High Priest 37 c.e. when Pilate, Caiaphas and Annas were taken to Rome to be tried for breaking the peace. (Jeremias, JBJ, 194) Rome recognized Judaism as a legal religion, but allowed punishment for illegal religions which they called pagan. It would be to Pilate's benefit to prove followers of Jesus were not good Jews. For this former Jewish High Priests were the ideal witnesses.

NAME (Luke 5:27-35, follow, child, Matthew 9:9-17) Levi (Matthew) was also called Nittai of Arbela when he served the Sanhedrin as one of the 'pairs'. For example, he spoke for the laying on of hands at festival sacrifices. (Schurer, HJP, II, 1, 180,357)

Matthew was appointed High Priest after Herod Antipas accused his wife (Matthew's sister-in-law) of trying to poison him. (Josephus, 360)

Matthew ate nuts and vegetables, but no meats. He stayed in Jerusalem 15 years preaching to Jews, maybe longer because he was in Jerusalem 65-67 c.e. Then he went to Syria, Persia and Ethiopia. In Ethiopia, Matthew healed a girl named Iphigenia of leprosy. Her father a king may have beheaded him out of anger. On the other hand, there are reports he (or his uncle Matthias Zacchaeus) died a peaceful death. (McBirnie, STA, 180)

KINGDOM (Luke 18:31-43, pass by= follow, Son of Man, Matthew 19:16-30) Jesus was to sit on the throne of David. According to the apocryphal Acts of Matthew and Andrew, Matthew was captured by cannibals who attempted to put his eyes out and put him in prison 30 days before eating him. Andrew came miraculously by a storm at sea and saved him. After escaping Matthew returned to 'save' the cannibals. He worked many miracles, so many the king became jealous. He ordered that dolphin oil, brimstone, asphalt and pitch cover Matthew. Then he surrounded him with 12 gods of the people. The king set a fire which melted the idols before turning into a dragon that captured the king. Matthew rebuked the fire and converted the king who became a priest. (McBirnie, STA, 177)

Jericho was a site for tax collection. A blind man calls out to Jesus calling him the son of David. Hananiah (Chananiah) returned from

Babylon with Ezra to perform the functions of a priest in Jerusalem. (I Esdras 8:48) Ananias (version of same name) was a musician and head of one of the courses of temple service under David. (I Chronicles 25:4,25) Not only that, but Herod the Great had killed as many descendants of Levi and Aaron that there were not enough left to carry out temple services.

EARTH (Luke 9:22-26, follow, Son of Man, Matthew 16:21-26) Aland notes that Luke 9:24=17:33. Tax collectors bid on a geographical area with the high bid winning. Since there was no given tax rate, they used their own judgment about the amount to charge. The temptation to overcharge the taxpayer was great, but Jesus reminds us of the other side. Since God created the heavens and the earth, he asks what a man profits if he gains the whole word, but loses his own soul. Moses advocated one measure, the same measure, to be used for buying and selling, the golden rule of economics.

BREAD (Luke 22:7-18, follow, Passover Lamb, Matthew 26:17-20) In Egypt, Moses asked the Pharoah to set his people free from slavery. He did not so several curses came upon his people. The last was the death of the oldest sons. Jews smeared blood on their doorposts so the Angel of Death would pass them by. Each year at Passover this is remembered. At the Last Supper in Jerusalem, Jesus drank from a cup. He said a Nazarite vow that he would not drink wine again until the Kingdom of God came.

Levites turned to tax collecting when the Temple cheated them of a living. Their ability to read, write and translate made them invaluable to Rome as tax collectors..

EVIL (Luke 12:49-59, send henceforth=follow, children, prison, Matthew 20:18) Matthew was thought to be a collaborator with Rome because he was a tax collector. Because the people are already deciding for themselves what is right, Jesus asks why they do not get things like weather right. He warns that people will pay for their sins.

FORGIVE (Luke 22:33, go with=follow, prison, baptized, not in Matthew) Aland notes that 22:33=22:54. At several places Luke uses words from one witness inside the witness of another. Matthew did not go to prison with Jesus, for he and the other disciples hid Newly baptized Christians were called Mikros (children).

AS WE (Luke 3:18-20, expectation=follow, prison, Matthew 3:1-12) Matthew heard John the Baptist rebuke Herod Antipas's affair with Herodias. Matthew's wife's sister was mother to Judas Iscariot. His faith was tried as he tried to be faithful to Jesus and to his own family. Matthew forgave his family 'for they knew not what they did.'

AMEN (Luke 23:27-30, follow, children, Matthew 27:33-38) Jesus is speaking of his death which will follow shortly. He warns women that they will weep for their children, implying that God weeps for his lost children. After the death and resurrection, the fall of the temple was devastating.

PART THREE: THE TEN COMMANDMENTS

The two unifying words in Part Three are 'Son of God' and the name Jesus.

ONE GOD

(Luke 3:21-23, Son of God, Jesus, Matthew 3:13-17) A voice from above says, 'This is my beloved son.' Matthias became High Priest in 65 c.e. just a few years before the Romans attacked Jerusalem. Matthew was still in the area preaching Christ. (Harrison, NUBD, 563) Matthew was highly skilled in oration and writing, so he could have been of use in negotiating with the Romans. The warning Jesus gives is fulfilled. As an evangelist in Ethiopia, he demonstrated his belief that thegospel was for both Jews and Gentiles.

IDOLS

(Luke 4:38-41, Son of God, Jesus implied, Matthew 8:14-17) Aland notes that Luke 4:41=4:34, 8:28 and Luke 4:43=8:1. Matthew married one daughter of Simon ben Boethus and Zacchaeus married another. Their brother-in-law was Eleazar (Lazarus) who was High Priest in 4 b.c. replacing his brother Joseph (Joezer). (Jeremias, JBJ, 377)

Lazarus died and was entombed. Although foul play was suspected, it was not investigated. Jesus caused him to rise from the tomb. (John 11, 12:1)

The family of Jesus had the potential for strife because of the marriage of Joseph who was old. His new teen-aged wife is found to be pregnant. The whole family has to go to Egypt to escape the jealousy of Herod, who is a kinsman .

HOLY NAME

(Luke 8:28-39, Son of God, Matthew 28-34) Aland notes that Luke 8:28=4:34, 4:41. Gadara was once a beautiful university town where the Book of Nehemiah was kept. In gospel times, Greek columns lay on their sides beside crumbling buildings. Remains of a former garden bloomed. The area was unsafe because of earthquakes and landslides, so only outcasts lived there. Fortunatus was there but not in his right mind. Still he called Jesus the Son of God. Jesus healed him. He went back to India with Thomas.

SABBATH

(Luke 9:27-36, Son of God, Jesus, Matthew 17:1-8) Aland notes that Luke 9:35=3:22. On the eighth day, Jesus went up on the Mount of Transfiguration. The disciples followed him partway. He spoke with Moses and Elijah about his coming crucifixion. The disciples went to sleep. Perhaps Matthew was not with them. A voice from heaven said, "This is My beloved Son, in whom I am well pleased." When Jehovah was asked to give His Name, he said it was I Am. (Exodus 3:14) If a single I has been omitted, this would be easily translated, I who am I Am.

Matthew was separated from his kin. He grew up at Arbela near Tiberias where the ruins of an ancient synagogue stands. (Schurer, HJP, II, 180, 357) To the Jews the Law forbid certain activities from the instant that the sun sat on Friday evening. To be sure that the Law was followed, a watchman on a mountain at the border built a fire. When the dusk became dense enough, he had a fire burning. When the watchman at the synagogue could see the fire, he somehow notified the Temple in Jerusalem. Probably it was a chain of runners.

Peter returned a longlost son to Theophilus and was given a tall chair. (Kraeling, TD, 106) One may suppose that at the time of the slaughter of the Innocents, Matthew was hidden at the ancient synagogue in Arbela. Even his father did not know where he was. Maybe even Matthew did not know who he was.

PARENTS

(Luke 1:26-38, Son of God, Jesus, Matthew 1:18) The virgin Mary was willing to do God's will. Although it seems strange, many Jewish girls prayed to become the mother of the Messiah. (Also Luke 2:40-52, increase, fulfil=follow, days) A father is responsible for the religious education of his sons. Joseph once asked Matthias Zacchaeus to teach Jesus, and Matthias was an uncle as well as brother-in-law to Matthew. Then when Jesus was twelve, his parents took him to Jerusalem. He was found in the Temple asking and answering questions. Annas, the grandfather of Matthew, may have been there.

KILL

(Luke 4:31-37, Son of God, Jesus) The Hebrew word for exorcism is Saba, but it can also mean 'oath'. The family of Joseph of Nazareth sometimes were called Barsabas. Perhaps the name relates to their orientation to God rather than to a place. (cf Bromiley, ISBE, 242)

Caiaphas was uncle to Judas Iscariot, so it is likely that he was involved in the plot to kill Jesus. The third day after the Crucifixion, Jesus was seen alive by Levi Matthew. After praising Mary and Joseph, Levi is told to bring three witnesses of the resurrected Jesus to Jerusalem. They were Adas (Thaddeus), Phineas, and Angaeus, all Rabbis. (Acts of Pilate in Schneemelcher, NTA, I, 519)

ADULTERY

(Luke 20:27-33, Jesus inverse 34, children, Matthew 22:23-33) Susanna was a Jewish woman who had married many brothers. Each died before she bore him a child. The name Susanna is listed among those women that Jesus forgave and healed. (Luke 8:1-3) She was not the historical Susanna, however.

Herod Antipas was married to the daughter of Aretas IV, Governor of Edom, and they had two sons. Herod went to Rome where he met his brother Philip's divorced wife. He brought her back to Jerusalem where he lived with Herodias openly. John the Baptist spoke out about the sin of adultery. Herodias more or less tricked Antipas into beheading John the Baptist.

STEAL

(Luke 23: 32-49, God, chosen=beloved son, cf Matthew 27: 44) Aland notes that Luke 23:49=8:2-3. As the Holy Family escaped to Egypt, two robbers wanted to take the gifts that the wise men had given to them. Mary and Joseph told their story and the men returned their gifts. About thirty years later, one of them was crucified alongside Jesus. (Schneemelcher, NTA, I, 512) Jesus forgave and promised him the equivalent of eternal life.

The part of the Apostles Creed associated with Matthew was "From thence He shall come to judge the quick and the dead'. (Hone, LBB, 91)

LIE

(Luke 22:66-71, Son of God, Christ, Matthew 26:59-68) Aland notes that Luke 22:70=4:3,9. Jesus was questioned before the Sanhedrin. When he was asked whether or not he was the Son of God, he answered, "Ye say that I am." One recalls that God calls himself I Am. (Exodus 3:14) The Sanhedrin called Jesus a blasphemer or liar rather than evasive.

COVET

(Luke 4:1-9, Son of God, Jesus, Matthew 4:1-11) Aland notes that Luke 4:3,9=22:70.

Jesus goes into the wilderness and he is hungry. The devil tempts him to change stones into bread. Then he tempts him to accept power gained by evil. Last of all, the devil tempts Jesus to test (tempt) God. Each time Jesus responds with scripture. Matthew was very much a scholar of scripture. He wrote a gospel that clearly relates the story of Jesus and the Old Testament.

BIBLIOGRAPHY FOR MATTHEW

Aland. Kurt, et al., eds. The Greek NewTestament. United Bible Societies (New York:1975)

Bromiley, Geoffrey W., ed. The International Bible Encyclopedia. 5 vols. William B. Eerdmans Publishing Company (Grand Rapids, Michigan:1979)

Edersheim, Alfred. The Life and Times of Jesus the Messiah. Eerdmans (Grand Rapids, Michigan:1976)

Harrison, R. K, ed. The New Unger's Bible Dictionary. Moody Press (Chicago:1988)

Hone, William. Lost Books of the Bible. Bell Publishing (New York:1979)

Jeremias, Joachim. Jerusalem in theTime of Jesus. Pb. Fortress Press (Philadelphia:1969)

Josephus. Complete Works. William Whiston, Tr. Kregel (Grand Rapids, Michigan:1985)

Kraeling, Emil G. The Disciples. Rand McNally & Co. (n,a,:1966)

McBirnie, William Steuart. The Search for the Twelve Apostles. Pb. Tyndale (Wheaton, Illinois:1977)

Rambsel, Yacov. His Name Is Jesus. Pb. Word Publishing (Nashville:1999)

Schneemelcher, Wilhelm. New Testament Apocrypha. 2 vols. James Clarke (Westminster:1992)

Schurer, Emil. A History of the Jewish People. 5 vols. Hendrickson (Peabody, Massachusetts:1994)

Szekely, Edmond B. The Gospel of the Essenes. Pb. C. W. Daniel Company (Essex, England:1982)

XIV. SIMON BAR JONAH (PETER)-JONAH-JESUS

Moses ordered that an annual recitation of blessings and curses be given between the Mounts of Ebal and Gerizim. (Deuteronomy 27:9- 28:62) Blessed Peter may have once belonged to a Jewish sect called the Blessed Ones (Rechabites). They claimed the sons of Jonadab ben Rechab as their founders. Their history can be found as the History of the

Rechabites. (Charlesworth, OTP, II, 443-461.. Equidistant Letter Sequencing finds that Jonah is spelled out from verse Isaiah 52:7 and Peter is spelled out beginning at Isaiah 53:10, a verse in harmony with the Beatitudes. From Isaiah 52:7, the additional words are signature (name) and Jonah. Among other expressions, "wicked" (woe) and "weighed in the balance"are spelled out from Isaiah 53:10. (Rambsel, HNJ, 7, 21, 28, 42) For this analysis, 'praise the Lord' becomes blessed.

Ebionites (the poor) did not accept the divinity of Jesus and questioned the miracles, a sign of the divine. (McClintock, CBTEL, III, 21) Perhaps Peter addressed them in his preaching, for the first section has to do with signs. Rechabites are mentioned in Jeremiah 35. Jeremiah gave shelter to a number of Jews who had sworn not to build houses nor drink wine until the Messiah came. Jeremiah promised them that they would never lack a man to stand before the throne of God forever. (Jeremiah 35:19) Unitarians and Ebionites may be compared with Rechabites. (McClintock, CBTEL, III, 21)

The letters 'on' are part of the name Jonah (H and J are silent). Woe may refer to On (awen=wickedness) (cf Ezekiel 30:17, Bromiley, ISBE, III, 604). To further the code, the name Jonah means dove . (Rambsel, HNJ, 255) J is silent in Hebrew so the names On, Onias, Honi and Jonah may be a word play. Simon means sign, so the sign of Jonah is Simon bar Jonah. Moreover the word for 'name' is onoma, and 'nomos' is similar (law). The overall clue to Peter's testimony herein is the word 'name'. The Maccabees were religious rebels. At some point their leaders betrayed each other. Onias III fled to Egypt after Andronicus, the King's deputy tricked him out of his temple. (Bromiley, ISBE, III, 605) Ptolemy gave him land at On on which to build a temple called Leontopolis. (Josephus, 269,280,425)

In this testimony 'weighed in the balance' reflects God's blessing and curse. Unlike Matthew regarding the Sermon on the Mount, Luke cites both in one sermon. Relevant works cited: The Gospel of the Ebionites seems to have been known (Schneemelcher, NTA, I, 166-170) as well as the Apocalypse of Peter (Schneemelcher, II, 620) and Kerygma Petrou (Schnemelcher, NTA, II, 531-541) I and II Peter naturally contain some references to the same material.

PART ONE: STATIONS OF THE CROSS

SUBJECTS (Luke 11:29-30, Jonah, Exodus 3:14, Mark 8:11, Jonah 3:8,10, I Peter 2:9, KP 539-540) Simon Peter and his brother Andrew were fishermen. Fish were salted and taken to Cyprus where miners ate them. Peter's father-in-law Aristobulus sometime of Cyprus was brother to Barnabus (Menachem) who was uncle to John Mark. (Harrison, NUBD, 146) Peter had a daughter with withered limbs which could be compared to the withered plant that Jonah grieved. (Lost Gospel According to Peter, in Hone, LBB., **282-286**)

FAMILY (Luke 2:21-25, dove=Jonah, I am, name, Leviticus 12:3, Jonah 3:11, II Peter 21:15,16) Aland notes that Luke 2:21=1:59. Jesus was circumcized as an infant. Debate between Christians and Jews was over whether the doves were a sin offering or a ritual of naming. When the Apostles Creed was written, the words, "I believe in the Father Almighty" were associated with Peter. (Hone, LBB, 91)

The people of Nineveh were warned by Jonah to repent which they did. Thus by believing, they saved their nation for a time. (Jonah 3:11) Some early Christians thought of the whale as God the Father who was sheltering Jonah. Others thought the whale represents ignorance. Remembering God can overcome ignorance. (Hall, STAA, 264)

GENEALOGY (Luke 3:21-23, dove= Jonah, 'name', I am, It came to pass, Exodus 3:14, Mark 9:7, Jonah 1:10, II Peter 1:17) Aland notes that Luke 3:22=9:35. God spoke to Jonah, saying "Arise, go to Nineveh." When John baptized Jesus, a dove (the voice of Jonah?) spoke for God, "Thou art my beloved (blessed) Son."

SERMON (Luke 6:20-38, name, blessings, woes, weep, Deuteronomy 27,28, Mark 4:36-41, Jonah 3:8, I Peter 3:9,4:14) Aland notes that Luke 6:23=11:47. The Beatitudes are quite a contrast to the responsive reading Moses required annually between Mount Ebal and Mount Gerizim which was designed to be unchanging . The organizer of the Rechabites was Jonadab. Their end would be the arrival of the Messiah. They split up into four self-governed Essene groups. Peter according to the Talmud belonged to a rival sect to that of John the Baptist. Mandaeans thought in terms of Good and Evil. Later Mandaeans became Nazarenes.. (Blavatsky, IU, 127) Jesus thought of evil as the thing to overcome.

Jonah took a ship to Joppa in the midst of a storm at sea. The shipmaster blamed someone on board for having displeased his God. Jonah admits he has sinned against his God, and he is thrown overboard. Despite the storm, Jonah had been asleep. (Jonah 1:5)

MARVEL (Luke 8:19-25, Peter, asleep, stand, name, 'sign', Exodus 15:19, Mark 4:36-41, Jonah 1:17, cf I Peter 3:20) Jesus was sleeping during a storm. He was awakened and calmed the sea. Jesus called Peter to him walking on water, but Peter lost his focus and began to sink. The point was that Jesus could command natural forces if he would. As the sea swallowed Peter, a great fish swallowed Jonah. Then when Jonah remembered God, the fish put him ashore.

FAME (Luke 8:40-56, Peter, James and John Aland notes that Luke 8:42=7:12, Luke 8:48=7:50, 17:19, 18:42 , Luke 8:52=7:13, Luke 8:52=7:14 and Luke 8:56=5:14.

PROPHECY (Luke 5:1-11, Peter, James and John, Mandaeans used the term fishers of men. The sign was the miraculous catch after catching nothing all night. Jonah complained when God allowed the gourdvine to wither. God reminded him that a much greater good had just happened in Nineveh to others.

Jonah wanted to preach but he wanted to choose where he preached. Peter told Jesus he was willing to go to prison with him. Jesus warned him that he would deny him three times before the cock crew. This could mean before he was beaten. It could mean before dawn. Near Nazareth was the spot where priests watched for the dawn and signaled the rest of the land. As a boy Jesus must have seen Jonah's grave on that mountain. (Dalman, SSW, 110-111) To him, that grave was ironically a sign of a new day.

Jesus warns his followers that there will be trouble for Christians.

LAST WEEK (Luke 22:7-15, Peter and John, Mark 14:12-16) Aland notes that Luke 22:13=19:32. Rechabites did not build houses, but waited until the Messiah came. Peter recognized Jesus as the Messiah and thought of building three tents. Then he realized the Messiah had come so houses could be built instead of tents.

The man that Peter was to ask for the upper room was Simon Cantheras. In Egypt the family made a jug with little handles on large rounded cheeks, and it was called a cantheras. Kanatha was also the name of a town in Israel.

DEATH (Luke 9:27-36, Peter, James and John ,) Luke 22:29=12:32, Luke 22:33=22:54 and Luke 22:34=22:61. Rechabites thought that angels came to take away the bodies of the dead. Perhaps like the Maccabaeans, they placed the bodies on high towers so the birds would carry them away. Jonah was in the belly of the whale three days. When Jonah warned Nineveh. It took him three days because of its size. When Jesus died, he was in the tomb three days before he was resurrected. Jonah caused the city to repent within forty days. Moses (whose name means 'saved from the water') took forty days to present the Law. (Exodus 24:18)

Rechabites were promised that they would never lack a man to stand before the throne of God. (Jeremiah 35:19) Jesus refers to those standing by.

AFTER THE DEATH (Luke 24:9-12, Peter, name, Jonah 3:9) Aland notes that Luke 24:10=8:3. Mary Magdalene lived at the Valley of the Doves. (Picknett, TR, 280) Priests living there had not been allowed to own land, but that area was taxfree to them. They lived there, trapped doves and later sold them to worshipers. For whatever reasons, Peter could not accept her faith as genuine. (Picknett, TR. 65, 82, 95, and 353)

PART II: THE LORD'S PRAYER

The unifying words are the name Peter and 'remember'. If Peter prayed, these are possible thoughts he might have prayed .. God gave an oath to Abraham, and all Israel should remember it. God will remember it. (Genesis 9:15) "Remember" may also refer to a Levitical musician named Zacchur. (I Chron icles 2:52, Nehemiah 12:35, Unger, NUBD, 1376)

OUR (Luke17:32, remember, Lot, Genesis 19:26) Lot's wife looked back and was turned into a pillar of salt. Petrer's wife was being led to persecution and death. Peter said to her, "O Thou, remember the Lord." When Jonah remembered the Lord, he was saved. (McBirnie, STA, 75)

FATHER (Luke 1:69-75, remember, Abraham, David, Genesis 22:16, Jonah 3:8,10) The names of Honi, Jonathan ben Uzziel and Jonadab ben Rechab are somehow related toPeter. Honi, the rainmaker, drew a circle and said that he would not leave it until it rained. He was also known as The Righteous. The difficulty of associating him with Jonah father of Peter is that he lived 200 B.C. (Eisenman, JBJ, 379-384) Honi's heir was thought to be John the Baptist, and Jonah was a sometime form of the name John. Peter's father or Grandfather may have been John Hyrcanus who committed suicide after building up an expensive estate at Bathyra (Araq el-Emir). In gospel times, Babylonian immigrants like Gamaliel and Hillel lived there. (Lapp in Perdue, ABI, 165-184)

The Oniads were a priestly family (cf. Daniel 9:26) but they were not allowed to serve as priests in Jerusalem. (Modrzejewski, JOE, 128) When the Maccabees had been strong, the members of the Onias family opposed each other to get into office. One Onias had been tricked out of his temple at Daphne before he was murdered. Another Onias went to Alexandria about 162 b.c. Another Onias fled to Alexandria where he gained the support of King Ptolemy to build a temple which was not closed until 73/74 c.e. (cf Isaiah 19:19, Modrzejewski, JOE, 129) Alexandria had been the site of the translation called the Septuagint Bible in the 3rd Century b.c. (Bromiley, ISBE, IV, 400)

NAME   (Luke 22:50-56, remember the holiday, Joseph, Mark 15:42-47) Jesus was buried in the tomb of Joseph of Arimathea. Rechabites did not place their dead in tombs. They believed that angels took the body away. In one sense the Maccabees also said the angels took the body away. They put the corpse on a top ledge of a tower at Modein so the birds would carry the body away.

Places called the Rock including Petra in the South and Tyre in the North. The miraculous catch of fish confirmed to Peter that Jesus was the Messiah because he was a follower of John the Baptist. Mandaeans used that metaphor to mean believers caught by fishers of souls. However, the Song of the Poor seems to be supporting the Ebionites. (Mead, GJB, 71-93) Peter is so overcome that he confesses himself to be a sinner and forsakes all.

John Mark was a member of Peter's wife's family from Cyprus. Mark was Peter's amanuensis and later interpreter in Rome where they were in prison together. (Colossians 4:10) Earlier Paul and Barnabas disagreed about Mark's going with them on the second journey. (Acts 15:36-39)

KINGDOM   (Luke 1:41-62, remember, name, sign, three, I Samuel 2:1-10, cf Mark 11:1-10) Dominus flevit was a cliff above the city and Jesus would weep there. It was also called Elijah's Roost. Zealots watched the road into Jerusalem from there. To signal his approach, a friendly person made the sound of a dove.

Hannah's song became a battlesong for the Maccabees. (Bromiley, ISBE, III, 220) The Virgin Mary sings it anticipating a king who will sit on the throne of David. (Luke 1:32) Elizabeth has miraculously conceived despite her age. The child in her womb (John) reacts to the child in Mary's womb (Jesus). The Septuagint Translation of the Bible states that the Messiah will be born of a virgin. The Hebrew translation is that he will be born of a young woman which is the belief of the Ebionites.

EARTH (Luke 24:6-12, Peter, remember Mary Magdalene) An early manuscript mentions Mary in a passage which has been translated as "kiss". It can also mean "touch". A hole in the manuscript does not say what Jesus touched or kissed. To stop an other from talking, sometimes a finger is placed on the speaker's lips.

Those who come to the tomb of Jesus are told that he is not there. This is what the Rechabite expected. Peter is told to remember what Jesus had told them. He would rise on the third day.,

EVIL (Luke 4:31-44, Peter, knew=remembered Aland notes that Luke 4:41=4:34 and Luke 4:43=8:1. Peter had two people heconsidered enemies, Mary Magdalene and Simon Magus. (Schneemelcher, NTA, II, 512-514)

BREAD (Luke 22:14-20, Peter present, remembrance, idea of I Am, Mark 3:6, 14:22-25. At the Lord's Supper, Jesus asked the followers to repeat it in remembrance of him.

FORGIVE (Luke 22:54-62, remember, Peter, wept, Mark 14:53-54, 66-72) Aland notes that Luke 22:61=22:34. Jesus had told Peter that he would deny him three times before the cock crew. In this verse it was poultry, but Peter may have understood the warning differently. A Roman beating was said to make the cock crow because it caused painful cries. Jews believed God would forgive lying about a matter only two times, not three times.

Jonah started to go the wrong way to Nineveh, but he did go. Peter tried to hide, but later he became a great leader in the early churches at Antioch of Syria and in Rome.

AS WE (Luke 23:39-49, remember, father, Mark 15:37, I Peter 2:23) Two thieves had tried to rob the Holy Family when Jesus was an infant. They were on their way to Egypt carrying the gifts of the

Wise Men. They were being crucified on either side of Jesus. One believed and asked Jesus to remember. Jesus said he would meet him in Paradise.

AMEN (Luke 14:34-35, Mark 9:50) Cyprus, the island home of Peter's in-laws, imported salted fish from Israel and Edom. This saying makes several plays on words. Salt (praise) is good, but if the salt has lost its savour (ability to make a difference), wherewith shall it be salted. It is neither fit for the land (enemies salted land to kill crops), nor yet for the dunghill (cast out=shouted), but men cast it out (shout).

PART THREE THE TEN COMMANDMENTS

The unifying word is "awen=wickedness", a homonym for On, the site of the Temple in Alexandria. One can recall that Jonah went to "wicked" Nineveh.

ONE LORD

(Luke 8:1-3, Peter present, wicked, name=Mary Magdalene of the Valley of Doves, Exodus 15:26, Mark 1:38) Aland notes that Luke 8:1=4:43 and Luke 4:41=4:34. The passage comments on Jesus's universality, including women. Peter's animosity to Mary Magdalene continued even until they were both in Rome. Once she had spoken to Tiberias hoping the Roman Senate would declare Jesus a God. He was intrigued because he had seen a dark cloud when Jesus was crucified. At the time he thought it smoke from a fire, but his soldiers found nothing. Perhaps Peter objected to her because she was female or because of her past or because of her influence. (Picknett, TR, 65, 82, 95, 353)

Rechabite men often wore a loincloth or apron of the Masonic type. Mary Magdalene on occasion hid her body with her hair. (Charlesworth, OTP, II, 454)

IDOLS

(Luke 10:13-16, woe, Peter was born at Bethsaida) Jesus condemns the cities for their lost opportunities. Rechabites were forbidden to use wine and alchohol. They can become idols. Rechabites considered all possessions evil, so cities which depended on possessions were considered evil. How ironic that Peter served in the great city of Rome.

HOLY NAME

(Luke 7:1-18, not worthy=wicked, woe, remember to repay him, Jesus) Usually Jesus healed with a touch, but this time he healed a man with a word. He healed by the power of his name. When James died, two Rechabites protested, perhaps Peter and John (Unger, NUBD, 914)

Jesus restored to life the son of a widow . N was a sign for spirit, and "ain" meant a well. In time in Rome, Peter became the mentor for Maternus. (McBirnie, STA, 60-61).,l

SABBATH

(Luke 5:8-11, sinful=wicked, Simon Peter) Peter was fishing on the Sabbath when Jesus called Peter, James and John to be disciples. (Edersheim, LTJM, I, 344ff. Although Rechabites called every seventh day the Sabbath, they did not count years. To celebrate Passover and the Jubilee Year, years must be counted. (Charlesworth, OTP, II, 456)

PARENTS

(Luke 21:12-24, woe, name, Peter present, Pharisees, Exodus 20:7, Mark 13:14) Jesus warns of evil days which are to follow. He tells them to go to the mountains, so many Christians went to Pella after the fall of Jerusalem. Rechabites limited sex to the goal of producing children and limited the number of children to one or two. (Charlesworth, OTP, II, 456)

KILL

(Luke 11:45-48, woe, II Kings 10:15ff) At one time the Rechabites killed the followers of Baal. (II Kings 10:15 ff.) They had either been Kenites or had close association with them.Kenites had the ability to make metal tools and swords. Ironically the Rechabites did not plow nor raise vineyards which would have been benefited by such knowledge. (Charlesworth, OTP, II, 459)

ADULTERY

(Luke 10:13-16, woe, name=Chorazin, Exodus 20:14, Mark 8:23, I Peter 5:6, AP 24, 629) Peter followed John the Baptist before he followed Jesus. John was beheaded because he preached against adultery. Herod Antipas was sleeping openly with Herodias. Jonah protested the sinfulness of Nineveh. Nineveh listened, but Antipas did not.

STEAL

(Luke 11:39-44, woe, clues to names, Mark 12:38, Apocalypse of Peter 31,631. The phrase "clean platter" refers to Isaac Pinas (Phineas). He was an opponent to Gamaliel in the Sanhedrin advocating interpretation of law as strict as the Rechabites. He preached "messianic woes". (Hengel, TZ, 175, 245f.) God gives but he requires a tithe and some other fees. Not to pay is tor rob God. Mint (Meahem), rue (Rufus), cumin (Cumanus), judgment (James Justus) and love of God (Theophilus) had not been treated correctly according to the law(nomos) which is similar to onomas (name).

LIE

(Luke 11:51-54, woe, Zacharias,) The staff which was used to hold up a scroll during a worship service was called the key of David. Peter was the obvious choice to hold the key because of his heighth. Jesus was saying he would build his kingdom based on the scriptures that Peter held up. A Christian should act harmoniously with the scriptures.

Once when Jeremiah became disgusted because of the sins of God's people, he threw away the keys to the temple. (Hastings, DOB, III, 759) He contrasted the behavior of the Rechabites and those living in Jerusalem. (Jeremiah 35:19.

COVET

(Luke 22:21-23, woe, Judas Iscariot not named, Peter present) At the Lord's Supper, Jesus says that the hand of one who will betray him is at the table. The custom was that eating with another was a sign of peace and friendship..

PART FOUR BIBLIOGRAPHY

Aland, Kurt et al. trs. The Greek New Testament. American Bible Society (New York:1975)

Apocalypse of Peter. See Schneemelcheer.

Blavatsky, Helen. Isis Unveiled. Pb. 2 vols. Theosophical Publishing House (Wheaton, Illinois:1972)

Bromiley, Geoffrey W. The International Bible Encyclopedia. 5 vols. William B. Eerdmans (Grand Rapids, Michigan:1979)

Charlesworth, James H. "History of the Rechabites' in The Old Testament Pseudepigrapha. 2 vols. Doubleday & Company (Garden City, New York:1985)

Dalman, Gustaf. Sacred Sites and Ways. Society for Promoting Christian Knowledge. Macmillan Co. (New York:1935)

Eisenman, Robert. James the Brother of Jesus, Viking Press (New York:1996)

Gospel of the Ebionites. See Schneemelcher.

Hall, Manly P. The Secret Teachings of All Ages. Pb. Penguin (New York:2003)

Harrison, R. K., ed. The New Unger's Bible Dictionary. Moody Press (Chicago:1988)

Hastings, James, ed. Dictionary of the Bible. 5 vols. Charles Scribner's Sons (New York:1900)

Hengel, Martin. The Zealots. Tr. David Smith. T & T Clark (Edinburgh:1989)

Hone, William, ed. The Lost Books of the Bible. Bell (New York:1979)

Lapp, Nancy L. "Araq el Emir" in Perdue, Leo G. et. al, eds. Archaeology and Biblical Interpretation. John Knox (Atlanta, Georgia:1987)

Josephus. Collected Works. Tr by William WHiston. Kregel (Grand Rapids, Michigan:1985)

McBirnie, William Steuart. The Search for the Twelve Apostles. Pb. Tyndale House Publishers (Wheaton, Illinois:1977)

McClintock, John and James Strong. Cyclopedia of Biblical, Theological and Ecclesiastical Literature. 12 vols. Baker Book House (Grand Rapids, Michigan:1981)

Mead, G. R. S. The Gnostic John the Baptizer. John M . Watkins (London:1924)

Modrzejewski, Joseph Meleze. The Jews of Egypt. Tr. By Robert Cornman. Jewish Publication Society. (Philadelphia:1995)

Packer, James I. et al. eds. All the People and Places of the Bible.Pb. Thomas Nelson Publishers (New York:1982)

Perdue. See Lapp above.

Picknett, Lynn and Clive Prince. The Templar Revelation. Pb. Simon and Schuster (New York:1998)

Rambsel, Yacov. His Name is Jesus. Pb. Word Publishing (Nashville:1999)

Schneemelcher, Wilhelm, ed. New Testament Apocrypha. John KnoxPress (Louisville, Kentucky:1991)

Unger, Merrill. Unger's Bible Dictionary. Moody Press (Chicago:1978)

XV. JOSEPH OF ARIMATHEA (OBODAS II)-JESUS-DAVID

Obed (=servant) was an ancestor of David and Samuel an ancestor of Joseph of Arimathea (Obodas II, Lawlor, NHP, 91-101, 103-105, 141-143). The Equidistant Letter Sequencing for Obed begins at Isaiah 53:7 as well as for David, Galilee, life (living), 'was afflicted' and 'for my brothers'. (Rambsel, HNJ, 11, 25, 36, 46) The theme of Jesus as suffering servant is developed. (cf I Corinthians 9:19) Ebed or Obad means 'servant', perhaps inspiring the name of a sect called Ebionites (the poor). They believed Jesus was a mere man yet the son of David and the true Messiah. (McClintock, CBTEL, III, 21) Concerns about lineage suggest a tie with Branch Davidians. Joseph encased the Holy Grail with a design of branches and preached in Ireland from an altar of branches. (McBirnie, STA, 207-234) As husband of the Queen of Edom, Joseph of Arimathea was Treasurer of the Temple at Jerusalem and in charge of the balsam groves. The Queen of Sheba had brought the original cuttings to King Solomon, son of David.

Imma Shalom was married four times or her husbands used aliases: Eleazar Hyrcanus, father of Jairus, Simon of Cyrene, father of Rufus and Alexander, stepfather of Jairus, Simon of Arimathea (Asira), father of Sylleus, Saul and Joseph of Arimathea. The confusion of names allowed Herod the Great's sister Alexandra Salome to become Queen of Edom instead of the rightful heiress. Her brother Herod the Great then had her married to their uncle Joseph. (Obodas I) She had that Joseph killed, and Herod married her to their nephew Joseph of Arimathea. Thus Joseph became Obodas II, Governor of Nabatea, for the throne descended mathriarchically. As Governor of Edom, he was Treasurer of the Temple at Jerusalem.(Lawlor, HNP, in passim.) To be fair to Herod, his relative Cypros had been Queen of Edom. (Hastings, DOB, I, 355)

Herod had first asked his brother Sylleus to marry his sister. Sylleus refused, but Joseph married her and had the required children, including the disciple Simon Zelotes. To improve the economy of Edom (Nabatea), he traveled over seven years. He neglected the Temple and left the work in Edom to Sylleus. Then Sylleus wanted to marry Alexandra Salome even if it meant circumcision which he refused earlier. Saul who would become Paul was their brother, and Domitilla, mistress of Titus, was their sister.

At his trial, the question was, "Is Netzer to be put to death? His defense was Isaiah 11:1, "A branch (netzer) shall spring up out of his roots." The sentence was death for Isaiah 14:19 reads, "Thou shalt be cast forth from they sepulcre, like an abominable Netzer." (Dalman, JCT, 72) It was known that Jesus had been buried in the sepulcre that had been prepared for Joseph of Arimathea by his brother who wished him dead. Then he had Joseph deified to enchance his own reputation. Sylleus declared the death iof Joseph of Arimathea in 9 b.c. (Lawlor, HNP, 101) In fact Joseph of Arimathea died in Ireland after 60 c.e. (McBirnie, STA, 213)

Carrington triads include thorn, neck, merry and David.

PART ONE. STATIONS OF THE CROSS

These are notes to be used to write a dual biography about Jesus and David.The Book of Obadiah condemns Edom (Nabateans or Arabians) for the mistreatment of Jacob by Esau. From Obadiah 1:4 comes the key word 'where'. From Isaiah 61:3 comes the key word 'glorified'. Throughout this testimony place names are given with Galilee emphasized in Part One. ELS for Obed and Galilee begin in verse Isaiah 53:7.

SUBJECTS (Luke 1:26-39, Galilee, David, where=hill country) Qoz was the traditional Edomite god of healing. Cos was an island in the Aegean Sea that had a school for physicians and a museum of anatomy. A work entitled 'History of the Rechabites' written in the 1st to 4th Century would be consistent with Edomite worship of a god of healing. Cos fits the description of their ancestral home. (Charlesworth, OTP, II, 443-462) Herod the Great went to Cos and knew of the Temple there. (McClintock, CBTEL, II, 499) Although Ebionites denied Jesus divinity, his healing was impressive enough to call him the Messiah. Cos also meant 'thorn'. Either Joseph of Arimathea or his grandfather was called Costobarus, named for the healing god. (Josephus, 319)

were part-time residents of Petra, the capital 'city' of the Nabataeans. They got around the Rechabite prohibition of roofs by making caves do. Since the site of the city of Arimathea can not be identified, it could have been the name of a traveling encampment for miners. Moses had a traveling encampment, for the Tabernacle of Worship was a tent.. Obed (servant) was an ancestor of David. The Virgin Mary calls herself a handmaiden (servant). King David was Israel's second king, and he was chosen by Samuel. David married Saul's daughter Michal and Saul's son Jonathan was his lifelong friend. (Harrison, NUBD, 280-281) The angel Gabriel announced that a virgin espoused to Joseph of the lineage of David would bear a child to be named Jesus (Joshua). He would fulfill the Davidic Covenant. (II Samuel 7:16)

Although some sources say that Joseph of Arimathea was Mary's uncle, too little is known about Joachim and Anna to affirm that. It is believed that Joseph accompanied the Holy Family on the trip to Egypt. Unlike the Hebrew scriptures, the Egyptian Septuagint translated Isaiah 7:14 to mean virgin. The gossip that Mary had been impregnated by Pantheras was false in that she was still a virgin. Moreover, the name may have been Cantheras (thorn) that was intended. (Eisenman, DSSFC, fn 53)

When the priests sought a husband for the Virgin Mary, Joseph of Nazareth was chosen when a dove sat on his rod. Some even said that the rod blossomed. When Joseph of Arimathea stuck his rod into the ground at Glastonbury, it grew. Legend says that the thorn tree of Glastonbury blossoms every Christmas. (Bromiley, ISBE, II, 1132)

FAMILY (Luke 2:4-20, Galilee, David, alive, where=Bethlehem, Exodus 3:6, Ruth 4:22, Isaiah 8:19, Psalm 110:1) David was from the Tribe of Benjamin (or Judah). When women in their tribe became scarce because of war and famine, Benjaminites were allowed to date-rape-marry women from other tribes or pagans attending religious festivals at Shiloh. (Judges 21) Joseph of Arimathea was of the lineage of Samuel, a Levite. The lineage of Jesus was traced down through Nathan rather than Solomon for this reason.

The first husband of Alexandra Salome was her uncle Joseph Costobaris, and her second her nephew Joseph of Arimathea who was of the lineage of David. Ever since Eve and certainly since Delilah, women had been blamed for any wrong. A wrong commited by David was having a census. (II Samuel 24) The census Luke recalls worked to God's advantage, for it confirms that Jesus was of the lineage of David.

SERMON (Luke 8:1-15, 'where seeds are sown', thorns) Aland notes that Luke 8:8=14:35. Two words for thorn are 'syr' and 'akantha' which suggests the Word of God was given to the Syrians and Cantheras. Other seed fell on the rock which suggests Petra and Tyrus of Tobias (Bathyra, Araq el-Emir). Without water (baptism), the seed could not develop. The saying, "He that has ears to hear, let him hear", could refer to Joseph's relative in Alexandria who sold jugs. One was called a 'cantheras' for its shape was that of a fat-cheeked person with tiny ear-shaped handles. The 'good' ground could be an allusion to the name Lebonah because 'bonus' means good in Latin. During the Maccabaean wars, their enemies cut off their ears to make them unfit to serve as priests. No one with a deformity was allowed in the Temple as priest or worshiper..

As husband of the Queen of Edom, Joseph of Arimathea was Treasurer of the Temple of Jerusalem. One such Treasurer was Costobaris. Herod the Great gave the profit from the balsam groves to Mark Antony who gave them to Cleopatra. Herod was to collect from Edom and pass the profits on. At first Costobaris paid, then he. told

Edom ites to underreport profits. He hoped Cleopatra would blame Herod for skimming. (Josephus, 319)

MARVEL (Luke 17:7-19, Galilee, where=Samaria and Galilee, glory) Aland notes that Luke 17:19=8:48, 18:42, 7:50. Joseph of Arimathea was married to the Queen of Edom, so in that sense he was as outcast from the Temple at Jerusalem as a Samaritan. The priests at Jerusalem accused all Samaritans of impure lineage. When the Jews went into exile in Babylon, those left in the country intermarried with other tribes, with Edomites who were descended from Ishmael and Esau, and with pagans. Since information was lacking, the priests banned all Samaritans, but accepted their gifts.

Ten men who were lepers asked Jesus for mercy. He healed them all and sent them to the priests. The priests would declare the lepers healed and reinstate them into Jewish society. However, one was a Samaritan who hesitated to go to the Temple. He thanked Jesus by falling down on his face.

Jesus had healed Simon Zelotes, the son of Joseph of Arimathea, of snakebite in Egypt while they were boys, and then he healed his brother James of snakebite. Although Saint Patrick is usually given credit for driving all the snakes out of Ireland, Joseph of Arimathea was credited with that earlier than when Saint Patrick went to Ireland. (Bromiley, ISBE, II, 1132)

The healing of the blind man is important because he recognized Jesus as the son of David even before he was healed. Perhaps he was Bava ben Buta, the physician that Herod the Great had blinded. (Josephus, 327) One recalls the slogan, 'Physician, heal thyself.' Bava could not heal himself.

Samuel anointed David to become the second king of Israel. Nob Hill (Bethany) was given to Samuel's heirs forever. In gospel times that included Simon ben Boethus and his children. Herod the Great had married Simon's daughter, and Joseph of Arimathea's wife Alexandra Salome was Herod's sister. The apostle Simon Zelotes (may refer to Shiloh or Sela, an ancient name for Petra) was Joseph of Arimathea's son. The reason that Samuel went to live at the temple at Shiloh was that High Priest Eli's eyesight was failing.

FAME (Luke 5:15-26, Galilee, where=Galilee, Judah and Jerusalem, glorified God) The man who was healed of palsy is believed to have been either Ptolemy or his brother Nicodemus. (Bromiley, ISBE, I, 183)

On at least one occasion David feigned madness.

PROPHECY (Luke 13:1-9, Galilee,) Joseph of Arimathea, by virtue of being married to the Queen of Edom (Nabatea) was Treasurer of the Temple at Jerusalem. (Josephus, 323) The drowning of the sick who waited at the Pool of Siloam was blamed on Pilate. He had taken money from the treasury of the Temple to repair the water system of Jerusalem. (Josephus, 379) Additional water pressure caused the overhead conduit to break. Some died. Jesus prophesied that unless the people repented, they would all perish. Joseph was traveling.

LAST WEEK (Luke 22:39-46. where=Mount of Olives, area going to Galilee) The Garden of Philogenes was the place where Jesus went to pray. It either belonged to Joseph of Arimathea or one of his ancestors called Philogenes. During that last week, Jesus went to the Garden of Gethsemane which belonged to Joseph of Arimathea. (Schneemelcher, NTA, I, 555) David once expressed the desire for a cup of water from home. His men risked their lives to get it, but he poured out the water as being too precious to drink. During the last week, Jesus drank from a cup that came to be known as the Holy Grail. It was said that Joseph of Arimathea designed a covering for it embellished by a twig design and the names of the original twelve disciples. His son Simon Zelotes was one of the twelve. He and his son Simon took the cup to Ireland where it became an inspiration for Arthur and the Knights of the Round Table. (Cahill, HISC, in passim.) Joseph's oratory at Glastonbury was made of entwined branches or twigs. (McClintock, CBTEL, IV, 1020)

DEATH (Luke 23:45-49, Galilee, where=the temple) On the day that Jesus was crucified, the sun darkened. A centurion called Longinus declared that Jesus was a righteous (innocent) man. Sylleus desired to marry his brother Joseph of Arimathea's wife. Joseph was absent from the Kingdom of Nabatea many years, and Sylleus had to do whatever work there was. Cleverly, Sylleus had his brother declared divine and then he had him declared dead. The tomb was elaborate saying "Divine Inside'. Then Joseph surprised his wife by reappearing. Alexandra Salome was angry and divorced Joseph, but Rome would not allow her to marry Sylleus. She married her daughter's father-in-law and died within the year, about 9 b.c.. (Lawlor, HNP, 99, 101) Thus Obodas II resumed his former name of Joseph.

AFTER THE DEATH (Luke 24:1-6, Galilee, where=tomb of Joseph of Arimathea) Jesus was buried in the tomb prepared for Joseph of Arimathea, the nephew of Herod the Great, who had not died nor used the tomb. (Lawlor, NHP, NHP, 101) Earlier Hyrcanus had taken gold from David's sepulcre. Then Herod the Great had robbed the tomb of King David of golden furniture. (Josephus, 279, 345) Just as the Book of Obadiah, Jesus had predicted a Day of Judgment. The effect of Jesus's death on the cross was that sinners can ask for and receive mercy while still in this life.

PART TWO THE LORD'S PRAYER

The ELS for Obed (servant) begins at Isaiah 53:7 as does the phrase 'for my brothers'. (Rambsel, HNJ, 36)

OUR (Luke 6:41-45, brother, thorn, where=in eye, II Samuel 3:18, Psalm 27:13) Bethany was the estate of the Bethany Band which included Joseph of Arimathea, Saul (Paul), his brother, Domitlla, his sister, and Simon Zelotes, his son. Jesus visited High Priest Simon ben Boethus there as well as his son Lazarus and daughters Mary and Martha. Thr estate was given to the descendants of Samuel when it was called Nob Hill. (McBirnie, STA, 289) Samuel had anointed David and these were descendants of Samuel.

FATHER (Luke 22:7-16, brothers in Christ, where=city, Ezra 2:61, Isaiah 55:13) Aland notes that Luke 22:13=19:32. John Hyrcanus, the last of the Maccabees died in 30 b.c. His ears had cut so that he could never again serve as high priest. (Harrison, NUBD, 796) Simon Cantheras (akantha=thorn) also had had his ears cut by the enemy so that he would never again serve as a priest. His relative was Simon ben Boethus of Bethany who blessed the infant Jesus.

Peter and John are sent into Jerusalem to prepare for a last supper. They meet a man carrying a jug. That was a saying about a man whose ears were ridiuculously high and tiny. Simon Cantheras had such ears. In Alexandria the Boethus family had manufactures jugs called Canteras that had highrounded cheeks and tiny earlike handles.

Imma Shalom, the mother of Joseph, either was married five times or married a man who took many aliases over time. After Eleazar ben Hyrcanus died, all her other husbands had the first name of Simon. Their names were Simon of Cyrene, Simon of Arimathea, Simon Cantheras and Simon Boethus (of which there were two)...

NAME (Luke 23:50-56 Galilee, where=Arimathea, cf. Eccles 6:3, Isaiah 14:19) Aland notes that Luke 23:51=2:25,38. Joseph of Arimathea, nephew to Herod the Great, married Alexandra Salome, sister to Herod the Great. When she was made Queen of Edom, Joseph became Obodus II, Governor of Edom. Obed (servant) was an ancestor of Joseph of Arimathea. Earlier Herod the Great had had his sister Alexandra Salome married to their uncle Joseph Costobaris (note cos=thorn) making him Obodas I. Then Joseph of Arimathea married her and he became Obodas II. (Lawlor, HNP, 143) As Governor of Nabatea (Edom), the Governor of Edom was Treasurer of the Temple at Jerusalem and overseer of the balsam groves. (Josephus, 327)

The men of the Sanhedrin interpreted the Law and the Prophets. When a faction wished to try Jesus, Gamaliel, Nicodemus and Joseph of Arimathea were not notified. Furthermore, a death sentence had to follow a night of sleeping on the evidence. This custom was not observed. After the Romans were involved, Jesus was crucified. Joseph of Arimathea offered his tomb which had never been used. He wrapped the body in linen removed from the scriptures when it became worn. (Lightfoot, CNT, III, 214-215) This was despite the prohibition about touching a dead body. According to The Gospel of Nicodemus, some Jews stalked him in the days that followed. (Barnstone, OB, 359-380) Simon Zelotes (Simon of Sela=Petra=the Rock) would go with Joseph to Ireland as an evangelist. (McBirnie, STA, 213) The similarity between the names of Simon Peter the Rock and Simon Zelotes is too much to be a coincidence. Perhaps Jesus called one rock for Petra, the Nabataean or Edomite capital. It might have been useful at one time. After the Resurrection Jesus appears to one of the Simon's who recognizes him when he is breaking bread.

KINGDOM (Luke 13:18-19, where=garden, mustard seed) Several plays on words are in this passage. Mustard seed (sinapis) and Sinope, great tree and Black Sea, and fowls (Assyrians=Syrians or Arabians=orebim).

EARTH (Luke 12:13-21, I Timothy 6:9-10, Obadiah 1:6, brother, where=land) Aland does not n ote that Luke 12:19=15:24,32. The Day of Judgment or Armageddon is to be feared by all nations. Obadiah correctly predicts the end of the kingdom of the Nabataeans. As with the fall of the temple at Shiloh, the cause is sin. (Judges 21:25) Every man did what seemed right in his own eyes.

The Nabataean kingdom had descent by matriarchal inheritance. Herod the Great became its Governor by marrying Mariamne the Hasmonaean. Then he killed her out of jealousy and lost his claim. Not to be outdone he used the name of his sister Alexandra Salome to lead Rome to declare her Queen of Edom. To preserve his power, he had her married to their Uncle Joseph. She killed him and Herod had her married to their nephew Joseph of Arimathea. By the time of the crucifixion, Aretas IV was Governor of Edom on behalf of his daughter Shaqailath, the wife of Herod Antipas. When she became queen, Herod Antipas thought he would rule his kingdom and hers. Before that could happen, Herod Antipas met his brother's divorced wife Herodias in Rome. They lived together openly after they returned to Jerusalem. Border warfare erupted between Aretas and Antipas.

Joseph of Arimathea traveled extensively while Governor of Edom. Since he left Sylleus his brother behind, Sylleus made any required decisions. Eventually Sylleus wanted to actually be the Governor married to Alexandra Salome. He would become Treasurer of the Temple at Jerusalem. He wanted Jesus to decide.

Because Herod the Great married the daughter of High Priest Boethus, Mariamne the Hasmonean became an aunt to his nephew Joseph of Arimathea. In time Herod ordered the death of her sons, but Joseph of Arimathea and his wife Alexandra Salome protected them for years. Then Alexandra became angry and betrayed them. Herod Antipas ordered them killed. (Edersheim, LTJM, I, 120, 126)

BREAD (Luke 22:25-30, brother Leviticus 19:10, I Samuel 15:24, Psalm 16:9) Aland notes that Luke 22:29=12:32. Jesus upholds the idea that service is a superior calling over consuming. The person who wanted to retire in Luke 12:16 may have been John Hyrcanus, but it did not work out that he could eat, drink and be merry. Jews were forbidden to store a harvest more than they needed for two and a half years. Even so, it was generally known that Joseph the Patriarch had stored grain for seven years in Egypt The rest was to be given to the poor or left in the field for gleaning. Levites were forbidden to own farmland.

EVIL (Luke 6:12-19, brother, where=Tyre and Sidon) Simon Zelotes, the son of Joseph of Arimathea, was one of the original twelve. In time Philip would send both to what is now England as evangelists. They carried the Holy Grail with them. One Asira had written a book of maxims which may have suggested the saying to forgive seventy times seven. (Schurer, HJP, II, 3. 23-27) The words 'increase our faith' could be an allusion to Joseph Pistus. Josephus has much to say about Pistus. (Josephus, 9) When a soldier refused to cut off Clitus's hand, Josephus told Clitus to cut off his own hand or die.

FORGIVE US (Luke 15:11-24, brother, neck, eat, drink and be merry, where=far country, servant, Deuteronomy 32:36, II Samuel 19:15, Psalm 90:13) Aland does not note that Luke 15:24=15:32, 12:19. Nabatea (Edom) prospered when Joseph was Governor. (Lawlor, HNP, in passim.) Joseph was said to have traveled to Africa and the British Isles. Joseph had taken his share of his inheritance which he 'wasted'. He asked if he could return home to his father—as a servant, not as a son.

AS WE FORGIVE (Luke 15:25-32, brother, eat, drink and be merry, where=field) Aland does not note that Luke 15:32=15:24, 12:19. Sylleus had taken care of Joseph's responsibilities. He wanted Joseph's wife and his position. He planned to have Joseph declared a deity before he had him pronounced dead. He did this to enhance his own position. He built a tomb for Joseph and put a sign on it, 'The Divine Inside'. Sylleus (Silas?) had prepared to announce the death of his brother Joseph and to announce his wedding to the widow. Instead Joseph returned and their father embraced Joseph, Sylleus sulked. (Lawlor, NHP, 347, 352)

AMEN (Luke 17:1-6, brother, mustard seed) The word "neck" suggests Trachyonitis. The words "mustard seed" suggest Sinope, a city on the Black Sea in what is now Russia. Joseph of Arimathea became a follower of Jesus. An early saying was that a wife could be a millstone about one's neck..

PART THREE: THE TEN COMMANDMENTS

The theme of the Messiah as a Suffering Servant begins with the name Benjamin (son of my sorrow, Gen. 35:16), the youngest son of Jacob. He was born at Bethlehem. Isaiah 53:3 further prophesies that the Messiah will be a man of sorrow. ELS for Obed (servant) begins at the same verse as the unifying words above.

ONE GOD

(Luke 16:13, servant, Exodus 20:3, Isaiah 52:10, Psalm 98:2). No man can serve two masters. Simon ben Boethus recognized the infant Jesus as the messiah. How Simon ben Boethus was related to Joseph of Arimathea is possibly confused because he had a son Joezer who preceded him as priest. Another son Simon Cantheras was priest in 41 c.e. (Jeremias, JTJ, 377-378) However, they were descended from an earlier Cantheras. Both Joseph of Arimathea or his grandfather were called Costobarus. (Josephus, 319) The name was dropped when the Edomites stopped worshiping Cos and worshiped Jehovah.

IDOLS

(Luke 19:12-27, servant, Exodus 20:4,) Aland notes that Luke 19:17=16:10, and Luke 19:26=8:18.. Any object or practice can become an idol in the biblical sense. No thief can touch the treasure which one stores up in heaven. The treasury at Petra is in a cave. Its façade is carved from red sandstone to look like a Greek-columned building. When the owner sends for what is his, the servants may kill the messengers. If he sends the son, they may consider killing him, too. (cf. Josephus, 3-4)

HOLY NAME

(Luke 7:1-18, servant, Exodus 20:7, Isaiah 53:12, Psalm 33:9) Aland notes that Luke 7:12=8:42, 7:13=8:52 and 7:14=8:54. Intercession occurs when a third party requests God to do something for the second party. In most pagan religions, this involves cursing rather than blessing. Now healing miracles were accompanied usually by a touch. Jesus first heals the servant without a touch; that, in His Name.

The second healing is Maternus, the son of Leah. Maternus goes to Rome where he becomes a disciple of Peter. Then he builds a church dedicated to the Virgin Mary beyond the Alps. (McBirnie, STA, 60-61)

SABBATH

(Luke 6:1-5, David, Exodus 20:8, Isaiah 1:23, Psalm 50:18, I Samuel 21:1-6) Jesus took grain and rubbed it in his hands on the Sabbath. By definition, that is harvesting on the Sabbath.

PARENTS

(Luke 2:25-35, servant, Isaiah 40:1,5, Psalm 98:2) Many thought the Messiah would be the son of Joseph. Of course, Simon Zelotes was the son of Joseph of Arimathea and James was the son of Joseph of Nazareth.

KILL

(Luke 22:50-53, servant,) Aland notes that Luke 22:52=22:37 and Luke 22:53=19:47, 21:37. Malchus (chus=cos) was the servant of the high priest. His family had suffered because Cantheras's ears had been cut off. They could no longer enter the sanctuary to worship. Jesus restored his ear.

ADULTERY

(Luke 7:36-50, acted as a servant, Simon, forgive, Psalm 119:64, Psalm 23:5) Aland notes that Luke 7:48-49=5:20-21 and Luke 7:50= 8:48, 17:19, 18:42. Jesus could have been in the home of Simon Zelotes. The identity of the woman is vague, but she anointed Jesus with her tears. She may have been the daughter of Simon Boethus who married Herod the Great. Joseph of Arimathea had a sister named Domitilla who was mistress to Titus. She thought Titus would take her to Rome after the fall of Jerusalem. He did not.

When Joseph of Arimathea was in charge of the balsam groves, Judas Iscariot and his wife assumed power. They cared for Joseph's two-year-old infant son who spoke out against Judas's mother. (Schneemelcher, NTA, I. 555)

STEAL

(Luke 19:45-48, 'servants of the temple', Exodus 20:15, Isaiah 56:7, Psalm 16:2,3) Aland notes that Luke 19:47= 21:37, 22:53 and Luke 19:47-48=20:19, 22:2. The 'sons of Annas' were money-changers who took advantage of their near-monopoly of ancient faceless coins. They required faceless coins for worship and recycled the coins. They charged a higher exchange rate than the public did. Joseph of Arimathea had once been Treasurer of the Temple, but his brother Sylleus was more involved than he was. Moreover, they found blemish in sheep the worshipers brought from home for sacrifice. They sold them one of theirs instead, even though they were not supposed to own pastures. (Edersheim, LTJ, I, 368-369) Although out of the country, Joseph of Arimathea was Treasurer of the Temple part of the time that Annas was High Priest.

LIE

(Luke 20:9-16, servant, Isaiah 5:1, Psalm 118:22,, Exodus 20:16, Deuteronomy 32:4, Isaiah 59:14, Psalm 51:6) Aland notes that Luke 19:30=23:53 and Luke 19:32=22:13. Cos was a forbidden name after Herod Antipater conquered the Nabataeans for a time. Cos was the

Nabataean god of healing. The identity of Costobaris is either Obodas I (Joseph, uncle of Herod the Great) or Obodas II (Joseph, nephew of Herod the Great.) Each became Governor of Nabatea by marrying Alexandra Salome, Herod the Great's sister.

Although the gardens were in Nabatea, they belonged to the Temple. Herod the Great illegally gave them to Cleopatra and Antony. Costobaris was to collect her share of the proceeds from the gardens and send them to Herod the Great who would send them to her. Costobaris short-reported so that she would accuse Herod of skimming. (Josephus, 319)

COVET

(Luke 12:37-53, servants, blessed, II Samuel 11:13, Psalm 69:12) Aland notes that Luke 12:37=17:7,8 and Luke 12:51=2:14. The relationship between the Creator and the Created is like the one between a master and his servant. The master is not pleased with servants who eat, drink and get drunk at his expense. He expects them to do as he says even when he is not present physically.

The inclusion of Gentiles and Edomites into the Covenant was hard to accept. Jews had kept to themselves to protect purity and reduce temptations. Jesus was asking them to reach out to the Gentiles and the Gentiles to reach out to them. Their whole concept of identity was threatened. Later Philip in France would send Joseph of Arimathea and his son Simon Zelotes to Gentile Great Britain. (McBirnie, STA, 211)

Obadiah the prophet had predicted the fall of the Arabians (Nabataeans) because of their sins against the sons of Jacob. As God had allowed Shiloh to fall because of Israel's sin, he would judge the nations. Israel needed to forgive the Samaritans and forget their genealogical purity or lack of it.

BIBLIOGRAPHY

Aland, Kurt, ed. et al. The Greek New Testament. United Bible Societies (New York:1975)

Barnstone, Willis, ed. The Other Bible. Pb. Harper & Row (San Francisco:1984)

Bromiley, Geoffrey W., ed. The International Standard Bible Encyclopedia. 4 vols. Eerdmans (GrandRapids:1986)

Cahill, Thomas. How the Irish Saved Civilization. Nan A. Talese Doubleday (New York:1955)

Charlesworth, James. Old Testament Pseudepigrapha. 2 vols. Doubleday & Company (Garden City, New York:1985)

Dalman, Gustaf. Jesus Christ in the Talmud, Midrash, Zohar and the Liturgy of the Synagogue. Arno Press (New York:1973)

Edersheim, Alfred. The Life and Times of Jesus the Messiah. Wm. B. Eerdmans (Grand Rapids, Michigan:1976)

Eisenman, Robert. The Dead Sea Scroll and the First Christians. Castle Books (New Jersey:2004)

Harrison, R. K. The New Unger's Bible Dictionary. Moody Press (Chicago:1988)

Hastings,James, ed. A Dictionary of the Bible. 5 vols. Chas. Scribner's Sons (New York:1909)

Jeremias, Joachim. Jerusalem in the Time of Jesus. Pb. Fortress Press (Philadelphia:1969)

Josephus. Complete Works. Tr. William Whiston. Kregel (Grand Rapids, Michigan:1985)

Lawlor, John Irving. The Nabateans in Historical Perspective. Pb. Baker Books (Grand Rapids, Michigan:1974)

Lightfoot, John. A Commentary on the New Testamen t from the Talmud and Hebraica. 4 vols. Hendrickson (USA:1995)

McBirnie, William Steuart. The Search for the Twelve Apostles. Tyndale (wheaton, Illinois:1977)

McClintock, John and James Strong. Cyclopedia of Biblical, Theological and Ecclesiastical Literature. 12 vols. Baker Book House (Grand Rapids, Michigan:1981)

Rambsel, Yacov. His Name Is Jesus. Pb. Word Publishing (Nashville:1999)

Schneemelcher, Wilhelm. New Testament Apocrypha. 2 vols. James Clarke (Westminster:1992)

Schurer, Emil. A History of the Jewish People in the Time of Christ. 5 vols. Hendrickson (Peabody, Massachusetts:1994)

XVI. JONATHAN ANNAS (ELIJAH BEN ASIRA)-ELIJAH-JESUS

The names Joel and John (gift of God) in the Equidistant Letter Sequencing begin at Isaiah 54:1 as does the ELS for the name Elijah. (Ramsel, HNJ, 40) Jonathan Annas followed Joseph Caiaphas as High Priest for only fifty days. (Jeremias , JTJ, 195, also Acts 4) He used the name Elijah ben Asira. Possibly he was also known as Jochanan ben Zakki. When he was asked to be High Priest, he again recommended that Matthias (Zacchaeus) replace him as High Priest in 65 and it was done. (Jeremias, JTJ, 194-195)

Jochanan ben Zakki led a Christian school at Jabneh after the fall of the temple in Jerusalem. When he (Jonathan Annas) went to Rome, he opened a Levitical school and used the name Elijah ben Asira. (Hastings, DOB, II, 682) Perhaps the Carmelite nuns who thought themselves spiritual descendants of the Prophet Elijah owe more to Elijah ben Asira (Jonathan Annas). (McBrien, HCEC, 228-230) His relatives had religious training at On (Alexandria) which contained courses on healing. The Therapeutae were an Egyptian religious order that taught preventive medicine, practiced chastity and sang psalms. (Ferguson, EEC, 896) He founded an order of nuns.

In the middle of the first Century, I and II Kings were written about by one Jonathan ben Uzziel (Asira, Azariah) which might have been Jonathan. (Schurer, HJP, 1. 2. 178)

Using a fig tree (or just a sacred tree) to center worship was practiced in I and II Kings. (I Kings 15:13, I Kings 18:19 and II Kings 21:7) Such a tree was called 'asherah' which sounds like Asira. Jesus spoke to Nathaniel under a fig tree. (John 1:48) (Jeremias, JTJ, 197) Using the name Eleasar Ben Asariah (cf Elijah ben Asira), he went to Rome in 37 c.e. with Gamaliel, Joshua ben Gamla and Rabbi Akiba. (Schurer, HJP, 2.1.370)

The overall unifying expression is "it came to pass".

PART ONE; STATIONS OF THE CROSS

In Part One the key or clue word is the name Elijah.(my God is Jehovah). In some ways the hope for the return of Elijah is similar to the Christian's hope for the Second Coming. Elijah (El and yah) and Joel ('O' and el) are the same as a double vocative for God like 'Lord, Lord'. Elijah left Elisha with a double portion of spirit. (II Kings 2:13)

SUBJECTS (Luke 1:13-25, Elijah, it came to pass, behold, Numbers 6:3, I Kings 21:20, II Kings 1:8, Malachi 3:1, 4:5-6, Psalm 103:20) Aland notes that Luke 1:15=1:41 and Luke 1:20=1:45. Elijah ben Azariah was a name taken by a Christian who went to Rome, most likely Jochanan ben Zakki. (McClintock, CBTEL, IV, 938) There is a problem because his birthdate is given in 50 b.c. His death date is confused with that of John ben Zebedee. Perhaps High Priest Annas had both a son and a grandson named Jochanan ben Zakki. (cf Josephus, 411) This Jonathan established a Christian academy at Jabneh where he was when the temple at Jerusalem fell about 68 c.e. (McClintock, CBTEL, IV, 938) He was in Ephesus at the same time as John ben Zebedee and Philip. Philip had four daughters who may have been proto-nuns. After Ephesus, he went to Rome where the daughter of Rufus became a nun. There he established a Levitical-Christian academy which seemed to be influenced by both Essene or Therapeutae beliefs. Possibly the teaching lessons followed the Ezra cycle of readings for special days in the calendar. The Gospel of John, according to Aileen Guilding, is a sequential Christian commentary for Jews. It is arranged as a calendar of special holy days for three years. (Guilding, FGJW, in passim) Accordingly, the Gospel of John could have been taken from Ephesus to Rome. Then a curriculum could be based on it for a Levitical academy similar to what he had in Jabneh, but adding Christian service.

Hope for the return of a reincarnated Elijah is expressed in Malachi 4:5.   Jonathan ben Uzziel, translator from the Chaldee, revealed the meaning of certain scriptures, especially Haggai, Zechariah and Malachi. He flourished about 30 b.c. and would have been more than 67 years old in 37 c.e. (McClintock, CBTEL, 997) The name John the Presbytyr would fit him.

FAMILY (Luke 9:18-26, Elijah, himself, idea of reincarnation, it came to pass, Exodus 3:14, John 6:68-69, cf 11:23-24, II Kings 9:36, 10:10, Psalm 8:3) Aland notes that Luke 9:19=9:7-8. Again there is the theme of reincarnation. In some cultures knowing the name gives one power over another. Elijah the Tishbite was called the Thunderer or troubler of Israel, for thunder precedes lightning. Jesus called James and John ben Zebedee the sons of thunder. (Hastings, DOB, Ext, 544) Whenever Israel was in trouble, it expected Elijah to return to save them. (Malachi 4:5-6)

GENEALOGY (Luke 3:21-23, Heli=Elijah or Elxai, cf. John 1:1, 6:42, 8:29) Aland notes that Luke 3:23=4:22.   Less obvious is the Mandaean association of the name of Jonah (dove) and the name John. Among the Mandaeans there was a class or level called perfect and/or Doves.(Mead,GJB,18) At Qumran, ten judges-four from the tribes of Levi and Aaron and six from Israel, evaluated persons as either 'Master' or 'perfect'. (Burrows, DSS, 232) The voice of the dove informs the listeners that Jesus is the Son of God. Many supposed that Joseph of Nazareth was his father.

Evangelists who talked with those who had never heard of Elijah had a problem. They solved it by abbreviating the name Helios (the sun god) to Eli. (Schurer, HJP, II, 1, 23)

SERMON (Luke 4:24-30, Elijah, pass, I Kings 17:7-9,18:1, Deut 6:4-9, II Kings 7:3, 5:1-14, John 6:42,44, 2:12, 7:46, Psalm 45:2) Certain Prophecies said that the messiah would be the son of Joseph. Jesus reads from Isaiah 61:1-2 which has a 'healing' theme. Jesus omits the last part of the quotation from Isaiah 61:1-2 which refers to violence. Even so, his message like that of Elijah is rejected.

The therapeutae of Egypt used artificial respiration like Elijah and Elisha, but also prayer, contemplation, herbs, minerals, diet and exercise to prevent illness. A document entitled '4Q Therapeia' was found at Qumran which indicates the scope of medical treatment done there. (Allegro, DSSCM, App. 1,235-240)

Elijah's life was in danger. He was miraculously fed at Cherith. Then he went to the home of a widow where meal and oil were miraculously supplied. Elijah's follower Elisha caused Naaman to be healed. The passage quoted is about healing.

MARVEL (Luke 9:51-56, Elijah, it came to pass, Genesis 19:21, II Kings 1:10,12, Isaiah 50:7, cf John 4:9, cf. 7:2-10, 12:47, Psalm 74:7) Jesus was asked by James and John, the sons of Zebedee, to burn up an unfriendly Samaritan village. Elijah had brought down fire from heaven in his time. Jesus replied that he would save, not destroy. Perhaps the legendary Levitical academy of the South was further to the south than is generally supposed. Egypt and its Temple On were far to the south.

FAME (Luke 9:7-9, Elijah, II Kings 1:3,16) Aland notes that Luke 9:7-8=9:19 and Luke 9:9=23:8. Herod kept hearing about Jesus, so he wanted to see for himself. Some even said Jesus was Elijah reincarnated. Others said he was John the Baptist who had been beheaded.

Once Elijah was told by God to go to the messengers of the king. He was to ask them if there were no God in Israel that they could ask about the future. King Ahaziah eventually died because he sought out information from the wrong source.

PROPHECY (Luke 7:11-23, cf Elijah, visit, I Kings 17:17, 21) Aland notes that Luke 7:12=8:42, Luke 7:13= 8:52, Luke 7:14=8:54 and Luke 7:16=19:44, 1:68. Jesus resotores the life of Maternus, the son of Leah. Later Maternus becomes a follower and builds a church beyond the Alps. (McBirnie, STA, 60-61) He studies in Rome.

Elijah restored the life of the son of another widow, possibly using prayer and artificial respiration. Those were skills used by the

Therapeutae. Mandaeans associated healing with the constellation called the Great Bear N'ash. A bier is being carried between the mourners. At the same time, the mourners are seeking a murderer. (Hastings, DOB, I, 192)

LAST WEEK (Luke 9:28-36, Elijah, it came to pass, cf Exodus 4:"0-13. John 1:14, Psalm 2:7) Aland notes that Luke 9:31=9:22, 13:33. Moses symbolizes the Law, Elijah the Prophets and Jesus the Savior. The shining is the shekinah glory which appeared on Moses face after he had seen God. (Fabatus, Phabes, Phiabi=shining).

Mount Hermon was called Sirion by the Sidonians because of the frequency of thunder and lightning which prevented building there. Syrians used the top of the mountain as an altar and fire-signal. (Harrison, NUBD, 554-555) One notes the similarity between Sirach and Asira with Sirion. Mount Carmel was the site of Elijah's sacrifice. It was intended to show the superiority of his God. There was a great shining as his sacrificial fire burned.

DEATH (Luke 23:6-12, Elijah, themselves, II Kings 2:13) Aland notes that Luke 23:8=9:9. Herod wonders if Jesus is the reincarnation of Elijah or John the Baptist. Too late Herod Agrippa sought to learn more about Jesus. Although Herod Antipas was the one who beheaded John, Agrippa takes credit. Herod Agrippa appeared in a robe so shining that the onlookers thought he was a god. The event was the beginning of the 'Olympic Games'. Within days he was dead, eaten up inside with worms. (Josephus, 412)

Elijah's prophecy about the chariot of Ahab was fulfilled when the dogs lapped up the water used to wash the chariot. Absalom, son of David, rode in beautiful chariots with fifty men running alongside. (II Samuel 3:3) He set up a pillar in the King's Dale to honor himself. Because he had sinned against David, Jews threw stones at the pillar which had the form of a hand at the top. (Bromiley, ISBE, I. 19) The names of Zechariah ben Phabes and Zebedee ben Phabes have been carved upon that pillar. Both names are associated with thunder (Barak).

AFTER THE DEATH (Luke 24:50-53, like Elijah, it came to pass, II Kings 2:11, Psalm 20:7, Exodus 14:6, John 14:28,16:22, Rev

3:21) Because Elisha watched Elijah rise up into the sky, he was given a double portion of his spirit. After Jesus rose up into the sky, he asked them to tarry in Jerusalem until they too were filled with spirit. Jesus went to Bethany near Bethphage to ascend into the sky. Levites stayed at Bethphage, the city of figs.

PART TWO; THE LORD'S PRAYER

As stated above the author noted that Nathaniel was under a fig tree when Jesus spoke to him. (John 1:48) In Elijah's time, a tree connected with worship was called an 'asherah'. Jonathan ben Annas took the pseudonym of Elijah ben Asira. A Carrington triad for the word 'physician' occurs in Part Two of this testimony.

OUR   (Luke 4:23, physician, thyself, Leviticus 14:2-32). At Alexandria, there was a drama called Exogogue based on the story of Moses. The Therapeutae had a similar celebration every 50 days (7 x 7 + 1). They called themselves 'healers of their own souls.' They ate no meat, drank no in toxicating beverages and were celibate. They composed psalms and studied the Torah. (Ausubel, BJK, 295) At intervals the whole Community would dance a reel. A 'Miriam' would lead the women, and a 'Moses' would lead the men in a reel. The feet would slipslide as if walking on deep sand. When tired, they would read their original psalms, then dance again the rest of the night. They claimed that the drama Exogogue was written by Ezekiel. (cf Philo, 704 and Encyclopedia Judaica, XI, 314) Politically, the Therapeutae were opposed to slavery.

FATHER (Luke 19:1-10, tree, I Kings 21) Aland notes that Luke 19:7=5:30, 15:1-2 and Luke 19:9=13:16. When Elijah called Elisha to follow him, Elisha asked to go tell his father farewell. Nathaniel's and John's names can be translated as "gift from God'.

The Asira family of scholars lived at Tiberias where there was some association with the masoretic Bible, the sole known surviving source of Isaiah's equidistant lettering system.

Christ's birth occurred in the sign of Pisces (Fish), an era of 2150 years. (Seymour,BC,96) Christians referred to this sign to identify themselves.When meeting a stranger, the Christian drew the letter

Alpha which is shaped like a fish in the sand. The stranger if a Christian drew Omega shaped like waves beneath the alpha. Then the sand was shifted so no one else could see. Zacchaeus ben Annas was asked to teach Jesus the alphabet, so his son Jonathan may have been present. (Schneemelcher, NTA, I, 445)

NAME (Luke 11:13, fig tree in John 1:48) Jesus spoke to Nathaniel under a fig tree. As Jonathan Annas became High Priest in Jerusalem in 37 c.e. and served fifty days, the number of days between Therapeutae celebrations. (Jeremias, JTJ, 197) In 52 c.e., Jonathan Annas sponsored Felix for office. (Jeremias, JTJ, 157) As Jochanan ben Zakki, he opened a school-shelter for Christians escaping Jerusalem in 68 c. e. As Elijah ben Asira he opened a school-hospital for suffering Christians in Rome. This probably became the order of Carmelite sisters. (Hastings, DOB, II, 682) Acts 4:5-6 suggests that Jonathan was in Jerusalem at that time. Later he chastised Felix for laziness. Felix conspired with his own enemies to have Jonathan Annas assassinated. (Schurer, HJP, II. 1. 199)

Elijah the Tishbite valued contemplation of scripture, healing the sick and comforting the poor. Carmelite nuns have assumed their inspiration came from him. It did indirectly.

KINGDOM (Luke 19:28-30) Bethphage was an area given to the priests such as Annas. Boethus was nearby in Bethany. Bethphage means 'city of green or unripe figs.' (Unger, AOT, 114) Jonathan Annas was one of three summoned to Rome in 37 c.e. about Pontius Pilate, for he was High Priest at the time. He accompanied his father (not brother) Zacchaeus (Matthias) and friend Joshua ben Gamla of the Peace Party to Rome. (Roth, Encyclopedia Judaica, X, 280)

One recalls that Elijah accused Jezebel of wrong after she took the vineyard of Naboth by false accusation. A favorite description of Israel is that each man will sit under his own vine and fig tree. (cf II Kings 18:30-31)

EARTH (Luke 5:30-35, physician, II Kings 5:20) Aland notes that Luke 5:30=15:1-2, 19:7. Elijah healed and did not take money nor gifts, but his servant Gehazi tried to collect anyway for a healing. Gehazi was stricken with leprosy.

The Carmelite sisters took contributions of money to support their order, but they did not charge sinners or the sick for their services.

BREAD (Luke 8;40-56, physician, II Kings 5) The Therapeutae would have said, 'Give her bread', but Jesus said, 'Give her meat.' At Gilgal, the prophet Elisha fed a hungry crowd. After they had eaten, there was still some left over. Jesus did the miracle of the loaves and fishes. There was still some left over. On another occasion, Jesus had said 'I am the bread of life.'

Herod's sister Bernice (Veronika) was healed by touching the hem of Jesus's garment.

In Elisha's time, Naaman had to humble himself to go into a river not of his choosing. He was healed. Elisha charged nothing.

EVIL (Luke 13:6-9, fig tree, I Kings 17:17-24) Aland notes that Luke 13:16=19:9. The widow whose son Elijah restored believed then that he was a man of God. Jesus says a fig tree will be cut down; that is, its potential blessing stopped. When the people were eating, a woman who was bent over served them. Jesus healed her so she could stand up straight. The priests were arguing about the proper position for several kinds of prayers. Without being able to stand up straight, she could not follow their instruction.

Elijah was protected from Jezebel. John was not protected from Herodias. Jesus promised the seventy protection from evil, and to some, that meant protection from the evil influence of women, the daughters of Eve. Monastaries came into being.

FORGIVE US (Luke 21:29-33, fig tree, pass, ownself) Aland notes that Luke 21:33=16:17. Figs have two seasons, early and late. Jesus curses a fig tree which appears healthy but does not produce fruit. (Mark 11:21) Jesus was saying that time lost can never be regained in this life. They needed to evangelize and serve God's people in the present age. Since they were unable to stop the worship of the Syrian sun God named Helios, some evangelists preached that the Jewish Elijah was reincarnation of Helios. (Schurer, HJP ,2. 1. 23.)

AS WE FORGIVE (Luke 6:39-46, fig tree, thyself, Lord Lord, II Kings 13:21) Elisha's bones were used to heal, and Jesus's spirit would heal even after he ascended into heaven. Charity, a strong motive for Carmelite orders, is praised by Jesus. Jonathan ben Uzziel was a student to Hillel I about 30 b.c. Hillel was active in promoting translation and interpretation of scripture to improve the status of women. (Charlesworth, H&J, in passim and McClintock, CBTEL, IV, 997) Jonathan Annas needed to forgive those who did not accept women as equals. They were to be judged by the work for the Lord if at all.

The name Isaac Pinas (clean platter) refers to a translator possibly opposed to the translations of Jonathan ben Uzziel. His overly literal interpretation included preventing women from their rights as widows unless two living witnesses attested to seeing the corpse. In battle this was often impossible. Faenius Rufus was appointed procurator before Pilate held the position. (Griffin, SPP, 95) Could he and Pinas be the same man and/or somehow related?

AMEN (Luke 23:28-31, fig tree, yourselves) Elijah was associated with hope like the hope one feels in the spring. Trees that look dead and barren spring to life. If all else failed, the Jews believed that Elijah would return. (Malachi 4:5) When Jesus leaves this earth, he promises to return. Perhaps he meant his followers to recall that one season follows another.

PART THREE; THE TEN COMMANDMENTS

The key or clue word is 'Lord God', often the translation for a double vocative. One problem that Jerusalem had with Jonathan Annas was his appointment of women into office. In Rome Pudentia, the daughter of Rufus Pudens, was a nun. (Griffin, SPP, 294) John and Philip were evangelists in the vicinity of Ephesus and Hierapolis. Philip had no daughters so the virgin daughters may have been nuns. His daughter Hermione was a physician. (McBirnie, STA, 123-124) Jonathan Annas was at Ephesus where John and Philip were evangelists. A triad like those of Philip Carrington exists for the word 'visit'.(Carrington,PCC, in passim)

ONE GOD

(Luke 4:1-8, Lord God, living) Jesus goes into the desert. Therapeutae went into the desert. The devil tempted him to take shortcuts in winning over the world. Jesus resists the devil. Some made much of the fact that John the Baptist was born at the summer solstice and Jesus at the winter solstice. Mandaeans accepted a treatise on 'astrology' which they might have assimilated from the worship of Mithras. (discussion in Gilbert, M, 229-230) God is maker of heaven and earth, so the worship of the sun God Helios is to be considered a temptation from the devil.

IDOLATRY

(Luke 4:9-13, Lord God) After hunger and ambition did not work, the devil tries what appears to be a magic trick. Jesus is dared to jump from the pinnacle of a temple. At Alexandria this trick was accomplished with a pulley and invisible ropes. Jesus will not do that either. In Rome Simon Magus, father of Judas Iscariot, tried to use this trick he had learned at Alexandria. Peter had the rope cut and Simon fell. (Schneemelcher, NTA, II, 512)

HOLY NAME

(Luke 1:59-68, Lord God, it came to pass, visit) Aland notes that Luke 1:68=7:16, 19:44. Zacharias believed that the child to be born was indeed a gift from God. He wrote, "His name is John (gift from God)." He added, "Blessed be the name of the Lord God, for he has visited and redeemed his people."

SABBATH

(Luke 13:10-17, Lord and God in different verses) Aland notes that Luke 13:16=19:9. Hillel recognized the general teaching that medication that could wait should not be given on the Sabbath. Bond servants were released after seven years, but she had been bent over eighteen years. It mattered to disciples of Hillel because morning and evening prayers required positions she could not perform.

KILL

(Luke 19:31-44, King Lord, visit) Aland notes that Luke 19:44=1:68, 7:16. Herod Antitipas did not wish to kill John the Baptist, but Herodias tricked him into saying he would, so he did. Jezebel tricked King Ahab into taking Naboth's vineyard. Elijah prophesied the manner of their deaths. (II Kings 9:30) Herodias was exiled to France with Herod Antipas about 37 c.e.

ADULTERY

(Luke 20:27-38, Lord God, living, Judges 21:19) The Tribe of Benjamin when Shiloh was the central sanctuary was depleted of people. They asked permission to intermarry with other tribes. Permission was not granted. However, all tribes met at Shiloh several times a year. The men of Benjamin were given permission to date-rape-marry single women of other tribes. Sometimes pagan girls were taken back to Benjamin. Since David was of the tribe of Benjamin, the Sadducees did not forget. Qualifications for priesthood specified that a priest could not marry the widow of an illegitimate man. (Jeremias, JTJ, 317-319) Jesus said there is no marriage in heaven.

STEAL

(Luke 19:45-48, Mark 11:15-21 associates the temple and fig tree) The priests of the family of Annas benefited themselves by selling figs and lambs to those who came to worship. Jesus said they had made the temple a den of thieves. Priests lived at Bethphage where they were not supposed to catch doves or raise animals.

LIE

(Luke 24:1-12, Lord Jesus, themselves, living) After the Resurrection, several people went to the tomb. The women were accused of telling idle tales.

COVET

(Luke 16:13-17, two masters=two gods, yourselves) Aland notes that Luke 16:17=21:33. The people liked the teaching about mercy, but they had not understood in their hearts. Jesus reminds Jews and Christians alike that the letter of the Law stands. The Pharisees were happy with 'Once a sinner, watch out.' John the Baptist preached against Herodias who was living openly with Herod Antipas, husband of the Queen of Edom. The Queen escaped to Nabatea to rule, and Herod Antipas and Herodias were sent into Gaul as exiles. Jonathan Annas was a witness along with Zacchaeus and Joshua ben Gamla. (Roth, Encyclopedia Judaica, X, 280)

Note: Jonathan ben Zakki was involved in the 37 c.e. trial of Pontius Pilate. Perhaps Jonathan was the mentor or grandfather of John. Harnack seems to think that John the Presbyter and not John of Zebedee was the stronger witness for Christ. (Delff in Hastings, DOB, II, 699) Jonathan ben Uzziel using another name lived in a cave because he was a leper. The Pillar of Absalom was near the cave. The names of Zebedee ben Phabes and Zechariah ben Phabes have been discovered by archaeologists on a piece of that pillar. Originally the Pillar of Absalom had a top shaped like a hand. Once Uzzah put out his hand to steady the Ark. For that he was sentenced to death. (Unger, AOT, 212) The names Azariah and Uzziah were synonymous on some occasions. (Finkelstein, BU, 233) Lacking other evidence, Uzziel influenced Jonathan Annas to emulate Elijah by his study and his commentaries on I and II Kings.

PART FOUR BIBLIOGRAPHY

Aland, Kurt, et. al. eds, The Greek New Testament. American Bible Society (New York:1975)

Allegro, John. The Mystery of the Dead Sea Scrolls Revealed. Gramercy (New York:1981)

Ausubel, Nathan. The Book of Jewish Knowledge. Crown Publishers (New York:1964)

Barnstone, Willis, ed. The Other Bible. Pb. HarperSanFrancisco (SanFrancisco:1977)

Bromiley, Geoffrey W. ed. The International Standard Bible Encyclopedia. 5 vols. William B. Eerdmans Publishing Company (Grand Raids, Michigan: 1988)

Burrows, Nukkar, The Dead Sea Scrolls. Viking (New York:1960)

Carrington, Philip. The Primitive Christian Calendar. University Press (Cambridge:1952)

Charlesworth, James H. and Loren L. Johns. Hillel and Jesus. Fortress Press (Minneapolis:1997)

Delff. See Hastings

Edersheim, Alfred. The Life and Times of Jesus the Messiah. Wm. B. Eerdmans Publishing Company (Grand Rapids, Michigan:1976)

Ferguson, Everett, et al. eds. Encyclopedia of Early Christianity.Garland (New York:1990)

Finkelstein, Israel and Neil Silberman. The Bible Unearthed. Free Press (New York:2001)

Gilbert, Adrian G. Magi, the Quest for a Secret Tradition. Bloomsbury (London:1996)

Griffin, Miriam T. Seneca, a Philosopher in Politics. Clarendon Press (Oxford:1976)

Guilding, Aileen. The Fourth Gospel in Jewish Worship. Clarendon Press (Oxford:1960)

Harrison, R. K., ed. The New Unger's Bible Dictionary. Moody Press (Chicago;1988)

Hastings, James, ed. Dictionary of the Bible. Charles Scribner's Sons (Edinburgh:1908)

Jeremias, Joachim. Jerusalem in the Time of Jesus. Pb.Fortress Press (Philadelphia:1969)

Josephus. Complete Works tr. By William Whiston. Kregel (Grand Rapids, Michigan: 1985)

McBirnie, William Steuart. The Search for the Twelve Apostles. Pb. Tyndale House Publishers (Wheaton,Illinois:1977)

McBrien, Richard P., gen.ed., The HarperCollins Encyclopedia of Catholicism. HarperSan Francisco (San Francisco:1995)

McClintock, John and James Strong. Cyclopedia of Biblical, Theological and Ecclesiastical Literature. 12 vols. Baker Book House (Grand Rapids, Michigan:1981)

Mead, G. R, S. The Gnostic John the Baptizer. John M. Watkins (London:1924)

Peloubet, F,N, Peloubet's Bible Dictionary. Universal Book and Bible House (Philadelphia:1947)

Philo. The Works of Philo. Tr. By C. D. Yonge. Hendrickson (Peabody, Massachusetts: 1993)

Rambsel, Yacov. His Name is Jesus. Pb. Word Publishing (Nashville:1999)

Roth, Cecil,ed. Encyclopedia Judaica. 17 vols. (Israel:1973)

Schneemelcher, Wilhelm, ed. New Testament Apocrypha. 2 vols. James Clarke & Company (Westminster:1992)

Schurer, Emil. A History of the Jewish People in the Time of Christ. 5 vols. Hendrickson (Peabody, Massachusetts: 1994)

Seymour, P,A, H. The Birth of Christ. Virgin Publishing Limited (London:1998)

Szekely, Edmond Bordeaux The Gospel of the Essenes. Hillman (Essex:1976).

Unger, Merrill F. Archeology of the Old Testament. Zondervan Publishing House (Grand Rapids, Michigan:1954)

XVII. HEROD AGRIPPA I-JESUS- SAMSON

Beginning at Isaiah 53:6, 'the man Herod' , Nazarene, tola (worm,red), Pharisee, and 'his cross' can be found in Equidistant Letter sequencing. (Rambsel,HNJ,17,25,45) The case can be made that Samson was a Nazarite and Jesus a Nazarene, but the similarity without vowels to Nazareth is clear. The word Nazirite (separate) could be confused with the name Pharisees (separate). There have been multiple translations of the Aramaic over time. Herod Agrippa I, can be considered 'the man Herod' and Luke 9:23-26 uses the term 'his cross'. Tyre was the center for purple color, but the Elkesaites who wore red robes had to have a source of red color, perhaps 'tola'. The name Zharephath (Sarepta near Tyre) is derived from the phrase 'to dye red'. (Blaiklock, DBA,483) "And he said unto them" is a unifying phrase in a gospel associated with the testimony of Agrippa I. It was only called the Gospel of Philip because Philip is the only disciple mentioned in it. (Isenberg in Robinson, NHL, 139-140) Part One is an encomnia comparing Samson and Jesus. Hercules was the Greek and Roman strong-man-god seen as the equivalent to the Jewish Samson. Part Two is more information about the eyewitness Herod Agrippa, and it is arranged in the sequence of words taken from the Lord's Prayer and the word 'blood'. Part Three compares the Ten Commandments and Herod Agrippa's understanding of the teachings of Jesus. Most of the chreia in this report are associated with the words 'and he said unto them' with the relevant verse is noted in parentheses. The relevant work called the Gospel of Philip is extant. (Schneemelcher, NTA, 179-208)

The Sampsitae were similar to Ossians and Essenes. They turned to the sun at dawn to pray although most Jews turned toward Jerusalem to pray. (Schurer, HJP, II. 2. 213, 221) The name Samson is similar to Samsitae. Agrippa was striving to please the Jews. Although Herodians and Pharisees were different, Agrippa would have had access to the Pharisees and their ideas.

Herod Agrippa died from intestinal worms, which had led to the shedding of blood. This was only five days after a royal appearance. His shining robes were so beautiful that the crowd acclaimed him as a god. (Harrison, NUBD, 563) Below the number of the verse that contains, 'and he said unto..' is enclosed in brackets [].

Although it is no longer clear, Samson was once called a solar deity. He fought with the Nubian Lion, the Philistines (Power of Darkness) and carried off the gates of Gaza. When fall came, Samson entered into Virgo (Delilah). (Hall, STAA, 137, 139)

One Aristobulus was son of Herod the Great and Cleopatra of Jerusalem. His son Agrippa I was considered to be Idumaean. The word for behold was "idou" which sounds much like Idumaean. The overall unifying word is "behold" as in John 1:29, "Behold the Lamb of God." It also occurs in Jeremiah 23:5.

PART ONE ENCOMNIA COMPARING SAMSON THE NAZARITE AND JESUS

Samson was captured by the Philistines in connection with his marriage. Within a few years, the church was called the bride of Christ. Samson, Jesus and Agrippa I had this in common. They were mocked. Nazareth is a village, and its inhabitants were called Nazarenes. A Nazarite has taken a vow for a given time as Samson's parents did for him. At the end of a vow, the hair is cut and burned under an altar as a sacrifice.

SUBJECTS (Luke 1:26-38 [30], Nazareth, behold, impossible=suggestion of mockery, Judges 13:7) Aland notes that Luke

1:27=2:5 and Luke 1:30-31=3:6. Manoah and his wife agreed with an angel that Samson would be a Nazirite all his life. The Virgin Mary spoke with the angel Gabriel knowing that she had not had a sexual experience to produce a child. (Isaiah 7:14) Jesus also would live a life of dedication much like that of a Nazirite..

FAMILY (Luke 2:1-14, {10}. Nazareth, behold, Judges 13:25) Aland notes that Luke 2:5=1:27 and Luke 2:14=19:38. Psalm 118:26 is cited at Luke 2:14, 13:35 and 19:38. The Spirit of the Lord was moving in Samson as he grew up. Jesus was revealed as a descendant of the House of David. Manoah and his wife knew the angel was from God because it went up above the altar. Mary and Joseph heard the angels singing.

GENEALOGY (Luke 2:33-42 [42], Nazareth, behold, Deuteronomy 18:18) Aland notes that Luke 2:40=2:52. Anna, who may have been married to the first King Aretas of Edom, would have been kept in the Temple in Jerusalem by the Herods. She prophesies that the infant Jesus is fulfillment of God's promise in Deuteronomy.

Agrippa had to wait a long time to get his inheritance. Although Agrippa I claimed descent from Abraham, he was mocked and not considered a Jew. He grew up in Rome after his father Aristobulus was killed. Once when he was returning from Rome to Israel, he stopped at Alexandria. The people mocked him as a Jewish king by crowning a halfwit and parading him with pomp. (cf. Unger, NUBD, 562)

SERMON (Luke 4:1-16 {8}, Nazareth, showed him=he beheld, cf. Isaiah 7:12, Deuteronomy 34:1-4, Judges 16:1-3) Aland notes that Luke 4:3, 9=22:70. Instead of testing his spiritual strength, Samson exercised his physical strength. He tore down the gate and carried it, posts and all. Jesus was tempted by the devil to make a mockery of his position as a son of God. Samson lost a puzzle contest at his wedding. Samson killed thirty men to get their robes to pay off the debt. It took so long that his would-be wife was given to another.

MARVEL (Luke 2:41-51, [49], Nazareth, behold, Judges 16:13) Aland notes that Luke 2:51=2:19. Manoah and his wife are given instructions by an angel so that Samson will be a lifelong Nazarite. They marveled but did not fear.

At the age of twelve, Jesus amazed the doctors at the Temple with his questions an d and answers. Then he goes back to Nazareth with Mary and Joseph.

FAME (Luke 4:31-37, Nazareth, hold, Judges 15:4-13) Aland notes that Luke 4:33-34=8:28 and Luke 4:3=44:41. Jesus healed a man from demons. His fame spread.

Samson took 300 foxes. He tied. Their tails together and lit them. As they ran through the fields of the Philistines, their grain caught fire. Soon three thousand men of Judah came to Samson to question him and warn him.

PROPHECY (Luke 17:20-24 [22], behold, Pharisees, Judges 16:6-14) Aland notes that Luke 17:23=21:8. This is the theme of betrayal. A Nazarite did not cut his or her hair until the vow was completed or broken. Delilah found out that Samson's hair was the secret of his power. The Philistines cut his hair. Jesus warned the Pharisees that the kingdom of God was within them.

Agrippa I told his friend that he wished the emperor of Rome dead. He thought his friend would be emperor. The real emperor heard of this and put Agrippa in iron chains. Then one day the emperor did die and the friend became emperor. He gave Agrippa I golden chains and removed the iron ones..

Agrippa I had returned to Israel from Rome, so broke that he contemplated suicide. At that time his title was Prefect. Jesus answers a certain ruler who asks about eternal life. He is said to be very rich, for that is the image that the spendthrift Agrippa I always gave.

LAST WEEK (Luke 18:31-43 [42], Nazareth, behold,, Deuteronomy 32:29) 22:63-71 [67]. Judges 16:25) Aland notes that Luke 18:38=17:13 and Luke 18:42=7:50, 17:19. Jesus heals a blind man who may have been physician to Herod the Great. He ordered him blinded immediately after he saw his sons being killed. One of Baba's sons was Aristobulus, father of Agrippa I. (cf. Edersheim, LTJM. 126)

The Philistines mock Samson whom they blinded. They have him pulling around a millstone as if he were an ox. Jesus was blindfolded and asked to identify who it was that was hitting him. He also prophesies that he will be mocked. After his death, others will come claiming to be either Jesus, the Son of God or the Messiah. The Star Prophecy was to be one of those.

DEATH (Luke 23:35-38 [34]. mocking sign, behold, Judges 16:30) During a festival, the Philistines tie Samson to the pillar of their temple. His hair has grown back. His strength has returned. He kills more Philistines at his death than in his lifetime. Jesus is crucified beneath a sign that says He is King of the Jews in three languages. Ironically this was done to mock him, not to praise him. Jesus saves more people at the time of his death than he did during his lifetime. Samson killed more people at the time of his death than he killed during his lifetime.

A.D. (Luke 24:13-24 [19], Nazareth, behold, Judges 17:31) Samson judged Israel for twenty years, but Jesus judges all men for eternity.

PART TWO THE LORD'S PRAYER

If Agrippa I were to pray the Lord's Prayer, these are some ideas he might have. Rambsel found the name Herod in ELS beginning at Isaiah 53:6. ELS for 'tola' begins at the same verse. Tola was associated with 'worm' and the red of blood. For some reason Luke uses the word "mock" as well as using Herod as the unifying word in Part Two.

OUR (Luke 3:1-6, Herod, see=behold, the Herodian bloodline) Aland notes that Luke 3:1=23:7. Agrippa I was grandson to Herod the Great and son of Cypros (Bernice) and Aristobulus. They were first cousins, and he also married his own first cousin. The Book of Acts does not call him Agrippa, but just Herod. (Acts 12:1, 6, 11, 19-21) Herodians were Sadducees when it served their purpose. It served Agrippa I to call himself a Pharisee.

FATHER (Luke 8:41-48 [48], behold, bleeding) Aland notes that Luke 8:48=18:42, 7:50, 17:19. Aristobulus was a son of Herod theGreat who became the high priest at the age of seventeen. He married Bernice I daughter of Alexandra Salome I and Salome's uncle Joseph. Salome's second husband was Joseph of Arimathea. When Herod the Great ordered the death of Aristobulus in 6 b.c., Salome and Joseph hid him in Edom long enough for him to grow up and marry. Then

Antipas heard of his being alive and killed him. . (Edersheim, LTJM, I, 120, 126, 370, 372)

Bernice, either Aristobulus's wife or daughter, was healed when she touched the hem of Jesus's garment. Knots in its hem were tied as the person recited promises from the Old Testament scripture. The children of Aristobulus included Agrippa I, Herodias, Herod of Chalcis and Bernice. Both Agrippa I's mother and sister were each called Bernice at times. As Jesus was on his way to the home of Jairus, Bernice touched the hem of his garment. Its fringe had had each knot tied separately while the tier recited a promise from the scriptures. Bullfighters call their capes Veronikas for her. The sister Bernice was engaged to Marcus, the son of Alexander. He died and she was married to her uncle the King of Chalcis. She was accused of an incestuous relationship with her brother Agrippa II. The she married Poemon for a short time before becoming mistress to Vespasion and his son Titus. (Harrison, NUBD, 564)

NAME (Luke 9:7-9, Herod, see=behold, bleeding of John the Baptist) Aland notes that Luke 9:9=23:8. The first Herod is Herod Agrippa I and the second Herod is Herod Antipas who takes credit for beheading John the Baptist. Herod Antipas had more reason. Others described Agrippa as vain, but a kindly spirit with gracious manners and great eloquence. (Harrison, NUBD, 561) Because he had spent most of his life in Rome, he was not well known in Israel. Before he returned to become an official, he had returned earlier to borrow money. He was so desparate that he planned to commit suicide. (Schurer, HJP, 1.2.151) Agrippa I (Herod) did not die until 44 c.e. He is named in Acts 12:1, 6, 7, 11 and 23.

KINGDOM (Luke 20:17-26 [25]., beheld, Mark mentions that this refers to Herodians. (Mark 12:13-17) Agrippa ruled at the pleasure of friends in Rome three years over Palestine. Then he received the additional territory of Herod Philip. When he left Rome to go to the area, he went by way of Alexandria, Egypt. His bodyguard and clothing decorated with gold and silver amused the Egyptians. To mock him, they took Carabas, a boy of the streets. They stripped him and put a paper crown on his head and a stick in his hand. They had fun calling him the new king. However, when Agrippa I reached his kingdom, he was welcomed with respect. (Harrison , NUBD, 562)

EARTH (Luke 11:39-41 [39]. Behold, Josephus compared Agrippa I to this chreia and said that it fit. (Josephus, AJ, XIX, 6) He vainly tried to appear perfect in religious matters. Luke uses this passage to say that he mistreated Menahem (mint), Rufus,(rue), Cumanus (cumin), Joseph Justus (judgment) and Theophilus (love of God). Joseph Justus, son of Joseph of Nazareth was secretary to Agrippa I. They were both writing books.

BREAD (Luke 22:19-20 [19], behold, blood) Jesus offered the cup to his disciples, saying 'This is my blood." ELS for "tola" could mean "red" or "blood".

EVIL (Luke 22:63-71 [70], blindfolded him=he could not behold, Blasphemy is evil. The enemies of Jesus said many blasphemous things. Then the Sanhedrin accused him of blasphemy when he only said, "Ye say that I am." Note that Exodus 3:14 states that the name of God is I Am.)

In Rome Agrippa I had wished that the Emperor might die so that his friend would become emperor. He was imprisoned for that. (Schurer, HJP, 1, 2, 155) When his friend did become Emperor, he exchanged the iron chains with those of gold. Agrippa I in time gave them to the Temple of Jerusalem.

FORGIVE (Luke 23:6-14, behold,), Herod and Pilate wished to question Jesus. They had been students of Seneca together in Rome. They wanted to see him perform a miracle as magic. He would not answer. The Romans had taken all robes of authority into custody. As a ruler he used a royal robe to mock Jesus. Ironically Herod would be seen wearing a beautiful shining robe at the games just prior to his death by worms (tola?) (Josephus, 412) By then he had heard that Jesus wore a shining robe on the Mount of Transfiguration.

AS WE FORGIVE (Luke 13:31-33 [32].behold) Agrippa I may have sent a Pharisee to warn Jesus that his brother Herod Antipas intended to kill him. An other possibility is that theoriginal Luke divided the above passage so that Luke 23:12-14 belongs in AS WE FORGIVE.

AMEN (Luke 23:27-31 [28], behold) Agrippa I would in time kill James ben Zebedee who was related to him through his mother. Marriages in his family were quite confusing. Herod Philip married Salome, the daughter of Herodias. She left him to marry another son of Herod the Great. Herodias married another Herod Philip whom she left for his brother Herod Antipas.

PART THREE; THE TEN COMMANDMENTS

As stated above, the word for Nazarite is 'separate' and the word for Pharisee is 'separate'. The word "Nazarene" is found in ELS beginning at Isaiah 53:6. Pharisees lived according to Jewish custom and valued worship and sacrifice. During a religious celebration within his territory, the prohibition of the presence of a Gentile was read. Although Agrippa I was present and heard this, the Pharisees said to him, "Fear not. Thou art our brother." (Harrison, NUBD, 562 and Eisenman, DSS, 209) Pharisees is the unifying word in Part III.

ONE GOD

(Luke 12:1-12, Pharisees,) Nazarites cut their hair at the start of the vow and again when the vow is completed. Then the hair is burned under an altar. Samson's hair was cut by Delilah. It grew back and he regained his strength. Jesus promised his followers that the hairs of their heads were numbered and safe.Agrippa I enjoyed money and s Agrippa I spent more than he had. He borrowed money frequently. When he first became a Jew, he paid the cost for many who wanted to carry out Nazarite vows, he gave his golden chain to the Temple, and he punished those who erected a statue. (Hastings, DOB, II, 359)

IDOLS

(Luke 15:1-10 [3]. Pharisee) Agrippa I had coins made that said "Agrippa the Great, Lover of Caesar" on its face with an image. (Harrison, NUBD, 562) This was against the second commandment. Agrippa I persuaded Petronius to remove a statue of the Emperor from the Temple at Dora. The Pharisees praised him for that. (Hastings, DOB, II, 359)

HOLY NAME

(Luke 5:29-35 [31], Pharisee) Aland notes that Luke 5:29-30= 15:1-2. Agrippa I's title was Prefect, not Perfect. Jesus calls himself the Bridegroom. Agrippa had married Cypros, daughter of Phasael, brother of Herod. The name Herodian was important to Agrippa I, it was through the Herods that he received his inheritance.

SABBATH

(Luke 14:1-6 [3], Pharisee, behold) Aland notes that Luke 14:1=11:37, 7:36. Pharisees would not light a lamp before dark on Friday evening lest they defile the Sabbath with work. Jesus healed on the Sabbath. Some said dropsy was divine retribution. Defecation was forbidden on the Sabbath, and occasionally there were several consecutive Sabbaths.

PARENTS

(Luke 7:11-18, Nain=well of Nazareth, behold). Agrippa I had five children, but Drusus died. That left Bernice, Drusilla , Mariamne and Agrippa II. Drusilla's son Agrippa died when Mt. Vesuvius erupted. (Hastings, DOB, II, 361)

Jesus took pity on the mot her of a child that died and restored Maternus to life.

KILL

(Luke 13:31-35 [32]. Pharisee, behold) Aland notes that Luke 13:35=19:38. Agrippa I had James ben Zebedee killed, imprisoned Peter and perhaps would have seen to it that Jesus was killed at Passover. At the time he was in Rome. In 36 c.e. he unwisely told his friend that he wished the Emperor would die so that his friend could become Emperor. For this he was chained and placed in prison in Rome 6 months. (Hastings, DOB, II, 359) When Jesus was about to be killed,

Jesus calmly said that he would fulfil his mission. Years later, Paul says to Bernice and Agrippa I, "I know that you do not believe." Agrippa replies, "A little more and you would have made me a Christian." (Eisenman, DSS, 235)

About Paul, Agrippa would say, "This man has done nothing to deserve death nor imprisonment." (Eisenman, DSS, 235) That echoes what Pilate said about Jesus.

ADULTERY

(Luke 3:18-20, Herod) In 37 c.e.. Agrippa I was in part responsible for the exile of his brother Herod Antipas and Herodias. He exaggerated if he did not lie about them at the trial in Rome.. Antipas and the daughter of Aretas IV had been married and a treaty between Edom and Israel confirmed by the Roman Senate. In 37 c.e. Antipas and Herodias were living together openly in Jerusalem. Pharisees objected because Herodias was his brother Philip's ex-wife and because Herod Antipas had had two sons by his own wife, the daughter of Aretas IV.

STEAL

(Luke 18:9-14 [9], Pharisee, look up=behold) Aland notes that Luke 18:9-14=16:15, Luke 18:13=23:48 and Luke 18:14=14:11. Costobar, Governor of Edom, had falsely reported the balsam crop of Edom to Herod the Great. Agrippa I boasts that he is not guilty of extortion.

LIE

(Luke 23:1-14, behold) Aland notes that Luke 23:2=20:25. The first lie was that many supposed that Jesus was the son of Joseph. The second was that Jesus was an enemy of the state. Note some overlap with Luke 23:6-12.

COVET

(Luke 19:37-44 [40], Pharisee, beheld, impossible) Aland notes that Luke 19:38=2:14. This is the third use in Agrippa's testimony of

Psalm 118:26. Luke 3:8 says that Abraham can raise up children from stones. In this passage, the people are told that the stones under the donkey on which Jesus rode represent those who would rise up after Palm Sunday. Brothers should not covet each other. Perhaps Agrippa I coveted the territory assigned to Herod Philip. Then it was given to Agrippa I, almost restoring his kingdom to the size of the kingdom of his grandfather Herod the Great.

BIBLIOGRAPHY

Aland, Kurt. The Greek New Testament. United Bible Societies (New York:1975)

Blaiklock, E. M. an d R. K.Harrison, eds. The New International Dictionary of Biblical Archaeology. Zondervan (Grand Rapids, Michigan:1983)

Edersheim, Alfred. The Life and Times of Jesus the Messiah. William B.Eerdmans Publishing Co. (Grand Rapids, Michigan:1971)

Eisenman, Robert. The Dead Sea Scrolls and the First Christians. Castle Books (Edison, New Jersey:2004)

Eisenman , Robert. James the Brother of Jesus. Viking (New York:1996)

Hall, Manly P. The Secret Teachings of All Ages. Pb. Penguin (New York:2003)

Harrison, R. K., ed. The New Unger's Bible Dictionary. Moody Press (Chicago:1988)

Hastings, James. Dictionary of the Bible. 5 vols. Charles Scribner's Sons (NewYork:1909)

Isenberg. See Robinson.

Josephus. Complete Works. Tr William Whiston. Kregel (Grand Rapids, Michigan1985)

Rambsel, Yacov. His Name Is Jesus. Pb. Word Publishing (Nashville:1999)

Robinson, James M. The Nag Hammadi Library. Harper and Row (San Francisco:1988)

Schneemelcher, Wilhelm, ed. New Testament Apocrypha. 2 vols. John Knox Press (Westminster:1992)

Schurer, Emil. A History of the Jewish People. 3 vols. in 5 books. Hendrickson (Peabody, Massachusetts:1994)

Unger. See Harrison.

XIX. HEROD PHILIP - ADAM-JESUS

This testimony is not like the others in this study. Rambsel gives Isaiah 53:5 for the Apostle Philip, but there is no additional equidistant letter sequencing that fits this testimony except possibly the name Herod at Isaiah 53:6. (Rambsel, HNJ, 45) The Apostle Philip as well as his son and James of Alphaeus (Luke 6:14) died at Hierapolis in 34 c.e. and the trial of Pontius Pilate was in 37 c.e. His son Judas Thaddeus had gone to Edessa. However Apostle Philip was brother-in-law to two other Herod Philips because he married the Other Mary. (Mary of Cleopas, Matthew 28:1) Those two were also called Cleopas (son of a famous father=Herod the Great) The Deacon Philip was father-in-law to his brother Prince Herod Philip (the rich young ruler, Luke 18:18 ff). Prince Philip married his daughter Salome. Deacon Philip was the Good Samaritan (Luke 10:25 ff). He and Stephen the man beaten and robbed (Schurer, HJP. 1.2. 172) were of the Seven. (Acts 21:8,9) The Deacon had served as a substitute for Herod Archelaus and possibly for his brother in Iturea. When the Deacon died, it was assumed that the prince had died, so the kingdom of Prince Philip was given to Syria which was also occupied by Rome. (cf Josephus, 3) Prince Philip went to Rome in 37 c.e. As a student in Rome he had been friends with the household of Caesar. At the end of the trial that never happened because of the death of Tiberias, Prince Philip went to Gaul. His ex-mother-in-law Herodias and Herod Antipas had been exiled to there. They had met in his home in Rome. Prince Philip sent Joseph of

Arimathèa to the **British Isles** from Gaul in 60 c,e, (McBirnie, STA, 124- 128, 213)

In Cave I at Qumran there was a manuscript called the Genesis Apocryphon written in Aramaic. Nine times the wording of this testimony and of the apocryphon are alike. (Fitzmyer, SBNT, 98-99) Adam, the star of Genesis, was the first man to be created by God. God is One. Prince Philip was the first to be called to become a disciple, but he made the excuse of going to see his father (Herod the Great). (Bromiley, ISBE, III, 833) It is more likely that he wanted to have the Apostle Philip sit for him as the Deacon Philip had sat for Herod Archelaus. The Apostle had sat in at Gamla on behalf of Agrippa. (Schurer, HJP, 1. 2.200) He returned to Jesus in time to be one of the Seventy. (cf Luke 10) The Gospel of Philip is extant (Schneemelcher, NTAS, I, 188-209) although allusions to the Gospel of John, the Book of Revelations and First and Second Corinthians seem more pertinent. Because references are copius within the Gospel of Philip, reference to the comparison with Jesus shall be given herein by numbers. The overall clue word is first or one. Part One has its clue words Herod and multitude.. A summarizing verse of inspiration is II Kings 17:29.

Isaiah 62:1 may give light to the phrase Lamp of the Lord. In Greece Jewish slaves were given a lamp made of baked clay which held enough fuel for ten hours. Then they would work in the silver mines until the lamp extinguished. At Paneas which was in Herod Philip's territory, lamps were made of baked clay and smashed to set the light free. This glorified Pan, the god who protected shepherds. The Samaritan wife of Herod Malthace gave birth to two sons, Herod and Philip. (Josephus) In Rome where she and the younger son lived, she was known as Cleopatra of Jerusalem for her dancing. (cf Josephus, 357, 366, 463) The older son was known as Herod Philip husband of Herodias and father of Salome. (Josephus, 388, 479) Salome married her uncle, Herod Philip's brother Herod Philip who moved to Rome. There he was the best friend of Drusus who was expected to become emperor of Rome someday. The third Herod Philip and possibly the son-in-law of Herod and Malthace by marrying their daughter Mary, also sister of the two Philip's. General Herod Philip was son of Jacimus whose name means Alcemis, the name of the Wicked Priest. (Josephus, 263) He was commander of troops for Agrippa and Herod Philip. To complicate things further, when Herod Philip was educated in Rome, he was host to Herod Antipas when he met Herodias. At the time Antipas was married to the daughter of Aretas IV, Queen of Edom. Herod Antipas fell in love with Herodias, the ex-wife of the older Herod Philip.. John the Baptist objected. Salome, Herod Philip's wife, danced for Herod Antipas which led to the beheading of John the Baptist.

Samaritans feared that they would beforgotten in history. They erected three great stones (the three Steles of Seth) on which they recorded history and a hymn. (Charlesworth, OTP, II, 607)

To recap Herod the Great and Malthace (Cleopatra of Jerusalem) had three children which shall hereafter be designated as the uneducated Deposed Herod Philip, the Young Ruler Herod Philip and their sister Mary, the wife of Apostle General Herod Philip. The Deposed was never a disciple. The Young Ruler Herod Philip was called to be one of the Twelve Disciples but left and returned to be one of the Seventy, and General Herod Philip who became one of the Twelve. He was the grandson of Obodas I (Costobaris) of Edom and was educated at Bathyra by Gamaliel. The testimony herein is from the Young Ruler Herod Philip.

The Young Ruler's kingdom would include more, but this testimony is related to Samaria and Qumran. The analysis of his testimony is in three parts. Part One is an encomnia about Primal Adam the first man and Jesus of Nazareth, the firstborn son of God. Sethians who were Samaritans called the Second Adam. Supplemented with notations from the Gospel of Philip, the Gospel of John, both Corinthians and the Book of Revelations the comparison of the first man Adam and first disciple can be made. Although it is seldom considered, Adam was at first an androgeous man. His son Seth (substitute or another) was created as Adam was. Part Two has the clue word 'father' which may allude to the name Cleopatra (pater=father). Part Three relates the teachings of Jesus as Philip understood them to the Ten Commandments.

Unlike references in the other testimonies, the ones in this show influence of the Sethians rather than dependence. Seth thought God was unknowable except through the spirit. What seems to be animosity to Jews in the work of Marcion may reflect that Christianity was a radical change. If God is unknowable, the Old Testament is not valid.

The Samaritans had a work entitled Teachings of Marqah which might have influenced the Sethians, (Bromiley, ISBE, IV, 304)

PART ONE: STATIONS OF THE CROSS

Sethians claimed that God the Creator was invisible and unknowable except by revelation. Often he was similar to the Third Person of the Trinity. God was unknowable to man except when the Spirit chose to reveal itself. The god Pan was worshiped in the area near Caesarea at Banias as the source of light.. Negative words underline the concept of unknowable.

At Paneas near Caesarea Philippi, which was in the territory of Herod Philip, lamps were broken as the worshipers asked the god Pan to heal. Candles are often used in Christian worship. A statue of Jesus was placed there to honor Jesus after he healed Bernice, a member of the Herodian family. (Dalman, SSW, 203)

SUBJECTS (Luke 6:39-46, first, one, ,good, brother, Edenic Covenant, Genesis 2:8-9) Fitzmyer found that Luke 6:44=IQapGen 20:15. Alan notes that Luke 6:46=13:25. When Prince Philip first met Jesus, he went to tell his friend Nathaniel of Cana. Either Nathaniel and Bartholomew were twins, each deserving to be called Thomas or they were different names for the same person. Nathanael asked if any good thing could come out of Nazareth. (John 1:46) One may wonder if the occasion that inspired Prince Philip was changing water into wine at Cana. (John 2)

The Apostle Philip was said to be the uncle of the Virgin Mary. Her father was called Joakim (Jacob) and the Apostle Philip's father was the Babylonian Jacimus (Jacob). (Josephus, 263) Jacimus (Alcimus c 159 b.c.) was called the wicked priest at Qumran as well as the Righteous Priest. The words 'heres' and 'sheres' differed by a dot beneath the first letter.. (cf Jeremias,, 182, 186) The name Jacob appears in the lineage of Jesus as the father of Joseph of Nazareth. (Matthew 1:16)

FAMILY (Luke 2:1-20[10], multitude, firstborn, Gospel of Philip 80, 83, I Corinthians 4:6, John 1:14, Revelation 14:6, Genesis 1:3) Aland notes that Luke 2:5=1:26. Jesus is almost presented as a priest of Melchisedek who was without family. (Genesis 14:18) Philip writes that those born of the spirit, have spirit. They are like their father. Jesus's parents had to go to Bethlehem for he would be descended from his father David.

The presence of the light had meaning to the Sethians who were named for Seth. He was the son given to Adam and Eve after Cain killed Abel. His name means substitute or other. Mary tells no other.

GENEALOGY (Luke 20:27-44 [34], first, no father, Abraham, Isaac and Jacob, Gospel of Philip 83, 99B, I Corinthians 6:16, John 2 wedding at Cana, Revelation 22:19, Genesis 3:4) Philip writes that God created animals first, then Adam. He provided food for their needs. Genesis tells that Eve led Adam to eat of the tree of knowledge.

In gospel times, the Sadducees in particular stressed genealogy. They were not above reminding others that the Tribe of Benjamin, the ancestor of David, might be impure. Back in the days of Shiloh, the Benjaminites were depleted of people. They were given permission to attend the feasts at Shiloh. They could date-rape-marry single women there from other tribes. Perhaps with the secrecy involved they may have even rape-married onlookers who were pagans. (Judges 21:21)

The genealogy of Herod the Great was of great embarassment to him. Rumors said that either he or his father Antipater had been slaves for a time. Mary was related to Elizabeth who was possibly sister or sister-in-law of Escha (Joeph's first wife who had died). Elizabeth was descended from Aaron.

SERMON (Luke 4:14-30, others, idea of multitude, 'first' stand up, Isaiah 61:1,2, John 4:44) Fitzmyer finds that Luke 4:25=IQapGen 2:5. Aland finds that Luke 4:24=3:23. The word 'poor' may be an allusion to Qumran. Jesus preached quoting Isaiah and fulfilling Deuteronomy 18:18. The reader should note that he does not complete the part of Isaiah about violence, a point of interest to the Apostle Philip. As a military man from Gamla, this would have been reported at once if he had given the full quotation. Adam was the first man, and the Adamic nature could only be overcome by Jesus, the Second Adam.

Herod Antipas went to Machaerus to celebrate his birthday. His wife escaped going to her father Aretas IV. Herodias persuaded Salome, the wife of Herod Philip I to dance for her lover Herod Antipas. She told her to ask for the head of John the Baptist if he let her ask for something. Salome danced and asked. Some defended Antipas's deed in that an ancestor of John the Baptist (Fabatus) had beheaded one of his own ancestors. (cf Josephus, 464)

MARVEL (Luke 9:5-26 [13] other, brother, multitude, three, Herod, order implies a first, Gospel of Philip 94, 92, I Corinthians 1:27-28, John 6:1-14, Revelation 3:17, Exodus 16:4) At Qumran, the rite of baptism and of communal meals were held sacred. However, communal meals at Qumran were based on one dish. In the territory of Prince Herod Philip, the Apostle Herod Philip could have been on military duty for Agrippa. Jesus changed five loaves and two fishes into enough food for thousands. Therefore there is the possibility that all three Philip's were present.

Herod Antipas heard about the miracles and wondered if Elijah had indeed returned or if John the Baptist had returned. Sethians thought that miracles were revelations of the Spirit's presence. Their concept of God was more like that of the Holy Spirit than of the other two persons of the Trinity, unknowable except by revelation at the spirit's will.

The word 'dust' could allude to the creation of Adam. Samaritans read a book called Book of the Hidden Power. It had references to the secret or Hidden Adam. (Eisenman, JBJ, 366) At Qumran two works were studied not readily available to others, Jubilees (Charlesworth, OTP, II, 52-142) and Life of Adam and Eve. (Charlesworth, OTP, II, 271-275)

FAME (Luke 13:6-17, immediately=first, fig tree, Isaiah 5:1-7, 36:16, I Corinthians 6:20, Genesis 2:9) Fitzmyer found that Luke 13:13=IQapGen 20:16,26. Aland noted that Luke 13:14=6:7. At Gamla where the Apostle Philip studied scripture and warfare, an issue was the correct position for prayer. (Charlesworth, H & J, 427-457) Jesus heals her and then she can pray 'correctly'. Jesus blames Satan for her health problem. Another possibility is that he proves matters of spirit are superior to matters of the flesh. Even if a person can not control what happens to the flesh, his spirit can overcome.

As darkness and light are the same to a blind man, goodness and evil are not discerned by mankind except by revelation. God told Abraham to be perfect, a term used at Qumran in the evaluation of residents.

PROPHECY (Luke 19:28-44, multitude, another, Herod, many, John 12:12-19) Aland notes that Luke 19:32=22:13, Luke 19:38=2:14 and Luke 19:44=21:8.

The Adamic curse resulted from disobedience. Jesus prophesies his own death as prophesied by Isaiah and the Psalm 22 of David. Jesus wept over Jerusalem for it had not accepted him as the Messiah.. .

The ass was considered as appropriate for a coronation. Solomon had ridden to his coronation on his father David's ass. The Virgin Mary had been told by an angel that her son would sit on the throne of David.

LAST WEEK (Luke 23:1-16 [4], not-one, multitude, Gospel of Philip 41, 24, I Corinthians 5:7, John 5:10, Revelation 1:16, Genesis 2:15) After they ate of the tree, Adam realized that he and Eve were naked. God provided clothing for them.

Herod Agrippa not Antipas was curious about Jesus. He wanted Jesus to perform miracles as parlor tricks. Jesus would not nor would he answer the questions that Herod Antipas posed. The Romans had taken all the royal and priestly robes into their custody. They allowed them to be checked out for special occasions. Herod Agrippa, not Herod Antipas, had a shining robe which was put on Jesus along with a crown. Then the Herods and their soldiers mocked the King of the Jews. Pilate or Antipas put the sign above the crucified Jesus to mock Jesus. Agrippa had ruled over Philip's territory three years before he died suddenly. (Josephus, 412)

DEATH (Luke 13:22-35 [32], Herod, perfect, first do, Pharisees, Gospel of Philip 71,76, I Corinthians 15:45, John 33:20, Revelation 9:20. Genesis 1:27) Aland notes that Luke 13:33=9:22, 31. Herod Antipas is called 'that fox' because the word for fox sounds like Saul. (Marshall, L, 571) Saul tried to protect his crown from David. David, however, was not trying to kill Saul. (cf II Samuel 1:15) Although Luke does not mention the split in the temple veil here, he mentions it in Luke 23:45. Jesus did as he had said.

The skull of Adam was believed to have been buried beneath the spot on which the cross of Jesus stood. (Hall, TSAA, 594) Genesis records his death.

AFTER THE DEATH (Luke 24:16-27, one, pass, third, people=many, Gospel of Philip 21, 42, I Corinthians 14:34, John 19:25, Revelation 19:10, Genesis 19:25) Aland notes that Luke 24:21=2:38. After the death of Adam, Adam was remembered through his progeny.

After the Resurrection, one of the two called Cleopas (sons of Cleopatra of Jerusalem?) walked and talked with Jesus on the Road to Emmaus.Cleopas not only means 'son of a famous father', but it can be a nickname for Cleopatra of Jerusalem. Some sources call her Mariamne the Boethusian and others Malthace. (cf Josephus, 366)

According to Josephus, Cleopatra of Jerusalem had two sons. (Josephus, 357, 463) Mary of Cleopas (Alphaeus) would have been her daughter who married Philip, the son of Jacimus who became the Apostle Philip. (cf Matthew 28:1 where she is called the Other Mary.) Legend says that she lived with Hannah and Joakim when the Virgin Mary went to live in the Temple. This was prior to her marriage to Joseph.

PART TWO THE LORD'S PRAYER

The key word in Part Two is the word 'father'. Philip asked Jesus to show him the father, and Philip was rebuked. (John 14:8) The name Cleopatra contains two syllables which have a similar sound to 'pater' (father).

OUR (Luke 10:14-24, father, many, hell,Genesis 3:9, cf Exodus 18:25 for 'seventy', Isaiah 14:12-19) Fitzmyer notes that Luke 10:17-24=IQapGen 10:21. Near Banias, there was a waterfall whose basin was so deep it was said to end in Hell. (Dalman, SSW, 203) Jesus called another group of disciples after the Twelve and they were called the Seventy. The serpent motif is also found in the service of the Apostle Philip. At Hierapolis he stopped a dragon in a cave and saved the king's son. Napthali's territory was at Bethsaida, Capernaum and Chorazin. (Bromiley, ISBE, 490) Two of the Philip's were born in

Bethsaida.Father Abraham was claimed by all Jews, but the promise of salvation is what is important here. Philip objects to the Holy Spirit as a father, for as he said all know the spirit is female.

FATHER (Luke 9:51-62, father, first, another, not, I Corinthians 4:11, John 14:8, Revelation 12:47, Genesis 3:12) Eve blamed the serpent and Philip blamed his father. Probably he wanted to return to his father-in–law Deacon Philip to have him substitute as the ruler for a while. Few knew him personally for he had lived in Rome and received the kingdom while still in Rome. (based on Hastings, DOB,III, 835 fn and Kraeling, TD, 49)

Aland found that Luke 24:21=2:38. The father-in-law herein called Deacon Philip was a farmer, poor and uneducated, so his wife Herodias had left him. Salome would remain in Samaria for a time with her father. Then she would desert to marry Aristobulus by whom she had three sons. His brother herein called Prince Philip is accused of returning to his kingdom after Jesus called him to be a disciple. (cf Bromiley, ISBE, III, 833) He said he wanted to return to his father, but Herod the Great was dead. However, Deacon Philip had sat on the throne for Agrippa, so Prince Philip may have returned to ask Deacon Philip to sit on his throne. In time Prince Philip became one of the Seventy disciples. The Apostle Philip had been commander of Agrippa's army for a time. He would have known about the lookout called Elijah's Roost or nest. As stated above his own father was Jacimus. (Josephus, 358, 10, 491, 497)

Herod the Great was father to Deacon Philip and Prince Philip by Cleopatra of Jerusalem. (Josephus, 357) Deacon Philip stayed in Samaria and married Herodias. His brother Prince Philip went to Rome where he studied Greek and was friends with Drusus. At the time Drusus was heir apparent to the throne in Rome. Eventually Philip received his own kingdom which consisted of Gaulonitis, Trachonitis (neck) and Paneas. When his substitute died, it was thought Philip had died. The kingdom was given to Syria. (Josephus, 366-367,382)

NAME (Luke 3:1-9, one, father, vipers, good, multitude, II Corinthinians 9:8,10, John 1:46, Revelation 3:17, Genesis 3:17, 4:11, Isaiah 40:3-5, 52:10) Fitzmyer found that Luke 3:4= IQapGen 19:25. Aland found that Luke 3:1=9:7,8 and Luke 3:6=2:30-31. Of all the Philip's only Prince Philip spoke Greek. He spoke to the eunuch about Jesus. (Acts 8:27) He could not be in two places at once. (Acts 8:37) He was asked by Greeks if they could see Jesus. (John 12:20-22) After Prince Philip baptized the eunuch, the Apostle preached in the cities of Azdotus. He died at Hierapolis in 34 c.e. so he could not have been the Philip who went to Southern Russia with Bartholomew (whether Nathanael or Thomas). It had to be Prince Philip. The Book of Revelation usually attributed to John has a Sethian approach to God. It describes seven churches of Southern Russia.

Isaac Pinas was known as a maker of needles, for his scriptural arguments hinged on very fine points. Jesus ben Sira spoke of the Covenant of Phinehas (serpent's mouth, Bromiley, ISBE, IV, 529, Joosephus, 171). The irony is that Prince Philip welcomed Greeks to Christianity, but Phinehas wanted to kill 'foreign' wives of Jews in his day. The Zealot movement included Ishmael ben Phiabi, the disciple of Phinehas. (Hengel, Z, 353) Zealots intended to restore purity, faith and the role of the Temple to earlier times. (Hengel, Z, 67) Sometimes they are called Purist Sadducees.

KINGDOM (Luke 18:18-30, first do this, father, good, rich, one, ten, I Corinthians 8:6, John 18:20, Revelation 3:17, Genesis 18:20) Aland notes that Luke 18:18=10:25 and Luke 18:29=9:23, 14:27. Because of Prince Philip's contacts in Rome, he well could have been visiting Herod Antipas in France when he sent Joseph of Arimathea and his son Simon Zelotes to what is now Great Britain in 60 c,e. (McBirnie,STA,213) At age 87, Prince Philip of the seventy was hung. He had preached twenty years.

The Apostle Philip married Mary of Cleopas (making her wife of Alphaeus=one) who was one of the Twelve. He went to Hierapolis where he faced a serpent in a cave. Poisonous vapors were in the cave from which he took the king's son. Also the serpent (dragon) was in the cave, but Philip killed it. He healed many other animals.

A faithful leopard and the kid went to prison with Philip. Mary, Philip's sister, had made friends with Nicanora. After forty days, he was buried at Hierapolis with the leopard and the kid. Those who had heard him preach built a church where he was buried. (Kraeling, TD, 55) He had four daughters who were pioneer-nuns. He served as an evangelist at Ephesus near John. He had been commander of the armies of Agrippa I and II. (Eisenman, JBJ, 630) People often remarked about his powerful hands. (Josephus, 358) Thieves often had their hands cut off. He grew up at Bathyra where Gamaliel was a teacher and Saul a student. Perhaps he was the Philip who asked Jesus to see the father. He might have wished to embarrass the Young Ruler Philip. (John 14:8)

The death of Deacon Herod Philip was a cause for embarrassment. Prince Philip, the Rich Young Ruler, was not dead, but the Roman government assumed he was and gave the kingdom to Syria which they also controlled. (cf Edersheim, LTJM, I, 219, 672,673) Trachyonitis (neck) was the name area where John Hyrcanus built his retirement estate. He ran out of money and killed himself. The estate lay idle on the border of the country many years. Then Herod the Great invited 500 Babylonian families to move there. In exchange for defending his border, there was no charge for the land which was to remain taxfree forever. They agreed to setting up a military academy, and then added a scriptural academy. Two professors of note were Hillel and Gamaliel.

To the north in Trachyonitis was Caesarea Philippi (Nahr Banias), a city associated with Prince Herod Philip. Herod the Great built a temple dedicated to Augustus Caesar there. Herod Philip renamed the city. Its residents had once worshiped Baal, but in gospel times Pan the god of the shepherds. After Jesus healed Bernice and the daughter of Jair, someone put up a statue to honor Jesus at Caesarea Philippi. It was probably not a disciple of Jesus.

EARTH (Luke 20:1-26, [3], one, father, first, another, power, I Corinthians 12:13, John 1:33, Revelation 22:17, Genesis 2:10-17) Aland notes that Luke 20:4=3:3 and Luke 20:20=11:54, 6:7. Herod Antipas changed the procedure for paying taxes to Rome. Taxes were collected by Jews who turned the money over to him. Then he sent it to Rome. The Jews liked that better. Earlier armed Romans collected taxes. However, no tax rate existed so some tax collectors charged whatever the traffic would bear.

Jesus was accosted by some who wished to trap him. High Priest Annas refused to allow faced coins in the temple at Jerusalem. It was against the commandment concerning images. They asked Jesus to give his opinion. He said, "Render unto Caesar what is Caesar's and unto God what is God's." Coins were made in Philip's name.

John the Baptist had come to prepare the way for Jesus. (Isaiah 40:3-5) If the people accepted him, they needed to accept that Jesus was the answer to prophecy. (Deuteronomy 18:18). The father sent servants (prophets) but they were killed. He decided to send his son. Jesus was both the prophet and the Messiah to come.

BREAD (Luke 14:15-27 [16], not yet a father, one, many, another, I Corinthians 7:33, John 15:6, Revelation 22:17, Genesis 3:12, Isaiah 35:6, Isaiah 5:1-7) Aland would note that Luke 14:15=13:29 and Luke 14:26=9:23, 18:29. Bethsaida was built or restored by Prince Herod Philip tetrarch and Bethsaida was the hometown of Philip the Son of Jacimus. Jesus called himself the bread of life.

At Qumran most meals consisted on one dish. Their festive communal meals foreshadowed the great banquet that would occur when the Messiah came. Jesus told a parable about a host who invited three men to his banquet. The first claimed he had bought property which he had to inspect. However, Jews were not allowed to buy property except through relatives of their own tribes. The Deposed Deacon Philip could not buy. The second (Apostle Philip with strong hands) said he had to prove 5 yoke of oxen. Proving was like coaching, learning to interact while working. Even the strongest hands like those of General Philip could barely prove three yoke of oxen. The third Prince Philip said he had married and could not come. The Law allowed a newly-wed man to impregnate his wife before going into battle. The host had not planned a battle.

After Prince Philip married his brother Deacon Philip and Herodias's daughter Salome, the Sanhedrin forbid intercourse on the grounds of incest. These were likely the over literal interpretations of law attributed to Isaac Pinas (clean platter).

EVIL (Luke 14:25-35, father, multitude, good, first, I Corinthians 4:5, John 15:6, Revelation 1:1, Isaiah 30:15) The Apostle Philip escaped from Bathyra (Gamla) with two women. (Eisenman, JBJ, 538) The city was like a fortress on top of a mountain. The tower there was incomplete because John Hyrcanus ran out of money. Houses were built on either side of the path leading to the top. When the Romans attacked, they noted the flat roofs and how narrow the path was. They and their horses got up on the roofs. The added weight caused the houses to fall like dominoes. The well-trained Jews of Gamla (camel) won the battle. (Josephus, 522) Philip ben Jacimus once escaped the Romans at Jerusalem wearing a wig that looked like a woman's. (Josephus, 3)

The Deacon Philip was sitting for Agrippa when Varus killed the messengers he sent to Bernice and Agrippa. Prince Philip had used his father as an excuse. Even so, the Young Ruler Prince Philip became one of the Seventy. Jesus assured him that his name was written in heaven. Rulers often put their names on monuments to be remembered. He also told him that many had wanted to see and have truth revealed as it had been revealed to him. He had power over evil serpents. The importance of this is receiving mercy after baptism as well as at the time of baptism. Salt was a source of his income.

FORGIVE US (Luke 9:57-62, first, father, another, I Kings 19:20, I Corinthians 4:11) General Herod Philip would have related to Elijah's Roost (nest). The Apostle Philip wanted to have it all. He went to get his father-in-law Philip to substitute on his throne while he traveled with Jesus. The father-in-law had been deposed, but this gave him a way to forget Herodias who blamed him for his poverty.

AS WE FORGIVE (Luke 10:25-37, good, pass by, idea of other, I Corinthians 8:1, John 4:9, Revelation 22:19, Genesis 4:9) Aland notes that Luke 10:25=18:18. Prince Philip needed to forgive his brother Deacon Philip, the Good Samaritan. Jesus praised the Good Samaritan who helped a man who had been robbed. Deacon Herod Philip helped refugees from both sides in the battles between Aretas IV of Edom and Antipas of Israel. Perhaps Prince Philip the Young Ruler thought that his father-in-law (Deacon Philip his brother) had cheated him. A story in Josephus says that whoever was in charge of Agrippa's estate tried to cheat Deacon Philip while he was away from the country. (Josephus, 3-4)

AMEN (Luke 17:11-19 [1], father implied, one, ten, 'other', many, I Corinthians 15:52, John 3:16, Revelation 15:4, Genesis 11:35) Aland notes that Luke 17:11=9:51, 13:22, 9:52 and Luke 17:13=18:38 and Luke 17:19=18:42. Philip's gospel has a saying about an ass who is pulling a grindstone round and round. He gets nowhere. Jesus tells about healing ten lepers. Only the Samaritan returns to praise God and thank him. The other nine do as told and go to Jerusalem where priests will declare them cured. That is, they were not changed inside when healed outside.

When the Jews went into exile in Babylon, many of the Samaritans were left behind. They farmed the deserted land and lived in the deserted houses. When the Jews returned, they refused to let Samaritans worship as equals. Jesus sent the healed leper to the Temple at Jerusalem, but it was revealed to him that he should thank Jesus, the Son of the God of both Jews and Samaritans.

PART THREE THE TEN COMMANDMENTS

Residents at Qumran were dissidents who called themselves the poor or the many. The difference between 'heres=wicked' and 'sheres' was a dot beneath the word. Fitzmyer found that Aramaic usage at Qumran was identical to phrasing of parts of this testimony. (Fitzmyer, SBNT, 98-99)

ONE GOD

(Luke 12:1-15, first, many, hell, Isaiah 28:15, Deuteronomy 32:22, I Corinthians 4:5, nothing, John 1:32-33, Revelation 20:13, Genesis 19:3) Many Jews thought of Jehovah without the spirit. Only one son of Cleopatra received a kingdom in his own name. The entrance to hell was said to be near Banias. (Dalman , SSW, 203) Reference is made to the Book of Hidden Power which would have been known to the Samaritan Deacon Philip. The Apostle Philip was tried at Hierapolis.

IDOLS

(Luke 8:1-8, Isaiah 49:15, many, others, good, I Corinthians 7:1, John 19:26, Revelation 19:7-9, Genesis 3:5) Because Eve ate the forbidden apple, all women were suspected of evil. Jesus however was called a Bridegroom. He turned water into wine at a wedding in Cana. Jesus healed Mary Magdalene, Joanna, Susanna and probably the Other Mary (of Cleopas). He forgave their sins.

Women are associated with fertility. His parable about the seed lists 'idols' that prevent seed from developing. The fowls of the air suggest Assyrians (homonym for sparrows). The Rock may suggest Bathyra, Tyre or Petra. Thorns would suggest the Cantheras family of Greek lineage. Some seed fell on the good ground and produced a hundredfold.

HOLY NAME

(Luke 21:8-19, 'many', one, I Corinthians 11:13,15, John 16:2, Revelation 6:5, Genesis 3:4) Aland notes that Luke 21:18=12:7 and Luke 21:12-15=12:11-12. Again there is a mention of hair. Eve was deceived in the Garden of Eden and many will be deceived in the end times. Jesus urges his followers to believe in His name and be patient.

SABBATH

(Luke 6:6-11, another, good, one, II Corinthians 9:8, John 2:25, Revelation 12:10, Genesis 31:29) Fitzmyer found that Luke 6:7=IQapGen 21:13. Aland notes that Luke 6:8=5:22, 9:47. Laban was father-in-law to Jacob with the power to hurt him, but he did not. Jesus healed a man's withered hand on the Sabbath. An outstanding feature of the Apostle Philip was his strong hands. Josephus tells of a man who cut off his own hand. Perhaps the man was Mark Kolobodactylis who invited Christians to Pella when Jerusalem was captured around 70 c.e.

PARENTS

(Luke 2:25-38, many, one, perfect, I Corinthians 1:23, John 17:23, Revelation 14:13, Genesis 17:1) Aland notes that Luke 2:38=24:21 and Luke 2:30-31=3:6. Simon ben Boethus was the High Priest who held the infant Jesus. He could have been the maternal grandfather of the brothers Philip. Some have said that Herod Philip's mother was Mariamne the Boethusian (Cleopatra of Jerusalem). Herod the Great had made Simon High Priest so that he would not be ashamed of her Alexandrian (Greek) background. (Jeremias, JTJ, 69)

KILL

(Luke 11:45-12:1, [45], many, one, multitude, I Corinthians 13:5, John 6:64-65, Revelation 22:19, Genesis 4:8) Aland notes that Luke 11:54=6:6-11, 20:20. Perhaps Philip was present when Silas was arrested at a birthday banquet for Agrippa I. The charge was that Silas pretended to be an equal to Agrippa I. Later Silas may have been executed, but not immediately. (Eisenman, JBJ, 538)

Jesus warns the disciples that some will be betrayed by their own families. Herod the Great did not eat pork, so it was said that it was better to be his pig than his son. Jesus says to listen to the Holy Spirit which will tell them what to say. They should not fear enemies that can only kill the body, but fear God who can send them to hell.

ADULTERY

(Luke 3:16-22, many, one, other, Herod, II Corinthians 6:10, John 12:36, Revelations 1:18, Genesis 3:6) Aland notes that Luke 3:19=9:7-8. The Samaritans sought to know god in terms of epiphanies. Herod Antipas believed in the Jewish god, but Herodias misled him. His pride was too great for him to go back on his word. He had John the Baptist beheaded so he was duped by a woman just as Adam had been. Philip knew that Herodias and Antipas was living together openly. Many believed the Savior whom they thought would be Elijah would come. It would be the day that no sin was committed in all the land. This teaching made Herodias angry enough to want to kill John the Baptist. She knew that Antipas feared God and needed to be tricked into doing that. She used Philip's wife Salome, her daughter.

STEAL

(Luke 19:11-27 [13], first, good, not, ten, another, I Corinthians 15:25, John 1427, Revelations 19:11,21) Aland notes that Luke 19:17=16:10. Jesus tells a parable with several synonyms: Cities (minyehs), coins (minas), worship quorum (minyahs) and curses (minim). The General Philip was given ten, the ruler five and the father-in-law one. He owned a small insignificant plot of land. When he died, he had nothing and it led to the ruler also having nothing. (Josephus, 329 has acomparable story.)

LIE

(Luke 16:1-13, other, light, one, no, [9], II Corinthians 6:10, John 12:36, Revelation 19:17) Aland notes that Luke 16:10=19:7 and Luke 16:10-12=19:17-26. Costobaris was a Samaritan who under-reported the balsam crop. He wanted Cleopatra to accuse Herod the Great of skimming, for he was the one who sent the 'profits' to her at Cos. (Josephus, 319) As a Herodian, Young Ruler Prince Philip would have been on his father's side of this. As a ruler himself who let his brother Philip substitute for him, he would have feared under reporting.

Adam did not answer God in the Garden of Eden. He hid because he felt guilty. When Jesus healed Ptolemy (or his brother), he said that his sins were forgiven. It was called a lie or blasphemy because the accusers said that only God could forgive sin. His friends had dug through the tiles to lower him down before Jesus. He had been ill 38 years. .

What seemed like a shining waterfall from a distance at Hierapolis was the accretion of salt from its strong mineral water. Tourists came there to be healed. Others came to dye cloth. The Apostle Philip compares God to a dyer who first bleaches then refreshes.

COVET

(Luke 12:13-15, not, one, I Corinthians 3:8, John 3:27, Revelations 4:2, Genesis 16:5) Before the Young Ruler became a ruler, he was a student in Rome. He would have been covetous toward Agrippa who was his 'brother' and had a throne. After the Young Ruler had a 'kingdom', he did not want to share profits with his brother, the Apostle Philip who was substituting for him on the throne.

PART FOUR BIBLIOGRAPHY

Aland, Kurt et al. trs. The Greek New Testament. American Bible Society (New York:1975)

Ausubel, Nathan. Book of Jewish Knowledge. Crown Publishers (New York:1964)

Bromiley, Geoffrey W. The International Standard Bible Encyclopedia. 4 vols. William B. Eerdmans Publishing company (Grand Rapids, Michigan:1988).

Carrington, Philip. The Primitive Christian Calendar. University Press (Cambridge:1952)

Charlesworth, James, and Loren L. Johns, eds. Hillel and Jesus. Fortress Press (Minneapolis:1997)

Charlesworth, James and Loren L. Johns, eds. Old Testament Pseudepigrapha. 2 vols. Doubleday & Copany (Garden City, New York:1985)

Dalman, Gustaf. Sacred Sites and Ways. Society for Promoting Christian Knowledge (London:1935)

Edersheim, Alfred. The Life and Times of Jesus the Messiah. Wm. B. Eerdmans Publishing Company (Grand Rapids, Michigan:1976)

Eisenman, Robert. James the Brother of Jesus.Viking Press (USA:1996)

Fitzmyer, Joseph A. Collected Aram aic Essays in The Semitic Background of the New Testament. Pb. Willaim B. Eerdmans Publishing Co mpany (Grand Rapids, Michigan: 1997), pp. 98-99.

Hall, Manly P. The Secret Teachings of All Ages. Pb. Penguin (New York:2003)

Hastings, James, ed. A Dictionary of the Bible. Charles Scribner's Sons (Edinburgh:1908)

Hengel, Martin. The Zealots. T & T Clark (Edinburgh:1989)

Jeremias, Joachim. Jerusalem in the Time of Jesus. Pb. Fortress Press (Philadelphia:1969)

Josephus. Complete Works. Tr. By William Whiston. Kregel (Grand Kraeling, Emil G. The Disciples. Rand McNally & Company (n.a.:1966)

Lawlor, John Irving. The Nabataeans in Historical Perspective. Pb. Baker Book House (Grand Rapids, Michigan:1974)

Marshall, I. Howard. Commentary on Luke. William B. Eerdmans Publishing Company (Grand Rapids, Michigan:1979)

McBirnie, William Steuart. The Search for the Twelve Apostles. Pb. Tyndale House (Wheaton, Illinois:1977)

Rambsel, Yacov. His Name is Jesus. Pb. Word Publishing (Nashville:1999)

Robinson, James M. The Nag Hammadi Libray. Harper & Row (SanFancisco: 1978)

Schneemelcher, Wilhelm, ed. New Testament Apocrypha. 2 vols. John Knox Press (Westminster:1991)

Schurer, Emil. A History of the Jewish People in the Time of Christ. 5 vols. Hendrickson (Peabody, Massachusetts:1994)

XX. ANDREW BAR JONAH-ESAU-JESUS

The name Andrew is found to begin in ELS for Isaiah 53:4 as 'Andrew fears God'.

Other ELS originating there are 'to one finding my spirit', Zion and Esau. (Rambsel, HNJ, 7, 28) One recalls that Esau was the older brother of Jacob. Perhaps Andrew was the older brother of Peter, but Peter gained more fame over time than Andrew. St. Andrew's cross is a slanted X. He was revered in Russia and Scotland.

The name Andrew can mean 'the manly one'. The unifying word for this testimony is man (or woman). When the Apostles Creed was formed, Andrew was associated with the Virgin Birth. (Hone, LB**B, 91**) **Andrew was an Encratite Christian which was like being a monk. They believed in dualism but condemned marriage, eating meat and drinking wine. At Communion they used water. (McClintock, CBTEL, III, 188 and I, 222-223) The text of Jubilees used for information about Esau can be found in Charlesworth's Old Testament Prophecy, and the numbers are pages in his book. (Charlesworth, OTP, II, as given below)**

PART ONE STATIONS OF THE CROSS

These are notes to be used in a dual biography about Jesus and Esau. The unifying words are "man" and "fear."

SUBJECTS (Luke 4:1-13, man , spirit of fear, Jubilees 92) Abraham the grandfather loved Jacob more, but Isaac the father loved Esau more. Esau was tempted because of hunger, and the devil tries to tempt Jesus because of his hunger. Esau sold his birthright, and Jesus was a step closer to his birthright.

FAMILY (Luke 2:8-20, man, fear, Genesis 26:4, Jubilees 112) Aland notes that Luke 2:14=19:38. The Holy Family saw a heavenly host in the sky. Isaac, the father of Jacob and Esau, had been told that his seed would be as numerous as the stars in the sky.

When the family split, Esau went to Mount Seir, and Jacob sends Rebecca and Isaac to the Tower of Abraham.

GENEALOGY (Luke 1:5-38, man, spirit of fear, Malachi 1:2, Jubilees 122-123) Aland notes that Luke 1:15=1:41 and Luke 1:26=1:45. Malachi pronounces a curse against Edom. According to him, God hated Esau. Yet Jesus would say later to hate the sin and love the sinner. John the Baptist (Yahya ben Phabes) was a Mandaean and possibly an Edomite descended from Aaron. Romans 9:13 refers to Malachi, but adds, "I will have mercy on whom I will have mercy and I will have compassion on whom I will have compassion."

Rebecca is concerned that Esau might harm Jacob. She makes him promise Isaac that he will not. Still afraid, she encourages Jacob to go to stay with her family. He is said to be looking for a bride.

SERMON (Luke 11:14-28, man, sign, spirit, fear, Genesis 27:34-40, Jubilees 122-123) Aland notes that Luke 11:27=1:28, 48. Esau was jealous of his brother, and Jacob took advantage of his hunger. Esau reasoned that if he died, he had no use for his inheritance. Jesus teaches that evil is in the world. He asks if he can cast something out, how could it be stronger than he is. After Jacob leaves, Esau takes everything that Rebecca and Isaac own. Jacob learns that they are in the Tower of Abraham without food or money, so he sends gifts back to sustain them.

MARVEL (Luke 8:22-25, man, spirit of fear, Genesis 24:29, Jubilees 124) Esau sells his birthright. Isaac learns he has been fooled. Isaac was angry because Esau did that, but also because Jacob and his mother had put fur on Jacob's arms to fool him. When Rebecca pleads for him to do so, he makes both sons swear to fear God.

Sometimes waves are said to be angry. God through Jesus stills the angry waves.

FAME (Luke 9:10-17, man, spirit of fear, I Chronicles 1:35, Jubilees 102) Hunger can cause hatred and war. In contrast to that Jesus provides freely for those who come to listen to him. He takes 5 loaves and 2 fish to feed five thousand. There is even some leftover. The location was Bethsaida, the native home of Philip, Peter and Andrew. (John 1:44, 12:21)

PROPHECY (Luke 21:25-34, man, spirit of fear, Genesis 25:23, Jubilees 106) Aland notes that Luke 21:32=16:10-12 and Luke 21:34=17:27. Among the Jews the younger sons served the elder son. In turn he would receive a double portion of the inheritance and help his brothers if they ever needed him. Esau was the older brother, but he sold his birthright. Jesus was the younger brother to four brothers.

After Jacob left for his uncle Laban's home and married his daughters, Esau married the daughter of Ishmael. (Genesis 28:9) This separated the brothers even more. Esau swore he would kill Jacob when their father Isaac died.

LAST WEEK (Luke 21:5-24, man, sign, spirit of fear, Genesis 33:16-17, Jubilees 103) Jesus warns his followers that there will be trouble. They need to seek shelter in the mountains. Isaac's family restores the wells that Abraham's servants dug. Isaac wants to remain where he is.

DEATH (Luke 22:1-13, men, fear, Genesis 33:16, Jubilees 126-128) The time for Passover was near. Jews celebrated the flight from Egypt. The last of the plagues involved the death of sons. The blood painted on the Jewish doors kept the plague from entering and killing their sons.

Jesus sends Peter, Andrew's brother, and John into Jerusalem to prepare for the Passover. They found everything as Jesus said it would be. They did not see that the chef priests and scribes were plotting to kill Jesus.

After Isaac's death, Esau's sons attack Jacob, but Jacob is victorious. Esau's four sons leave their father Esau's dead body as they retreat.

A.D. (Luke 23:39-49, man, fear, spirit, Genesis 18:23) Aland notes that Luke 23:48=18:13 and Luke 23:49=8:2-3. Once Abraham asked if God would destroy the righteous with the wicked. One of the thieves (wicked) asked Jesus for mercy. He was given a promise. Jesus (righteous) was crucified. Even the centurion Longinus said that Jesus was a righteous (innocent) man.

Eve was blamed for evil by the Encratites of which Andrew was one. Even so, Jesus said "Receive my spirit" just as she had. ("Life of Adam and Eve" in Charlesworth, OTP, II, 295) Esau died with hate in his heart.

PART TWO: THE LORD'S PRAYER

Mark 13:3 indicates an interest in signs. Philip the Good would in time found the Order of the Golden Fleece which honored Andrew. (Kraeling, TD, 40) Esau was promised that he would live by the sword until he broke Jacob's yoke off his neck (Genesis 27:40) The words 'generation' and 'seed' are the unifying words of Part Two.

Abraham was called the Father of Mankind, so father is substituted in places for generation.

OUR (Luke 1:46-65, generation, seed, fear, signs, father=man) Aland notes that Luke 148=11:27. Samuel was promised to God by his mother Hannah. (cf I Samuel 2:1-10) The Virgin Mary repeats Hannah's Song. God has promised to bless Abraham's seed forever.

FATHER (Luke 11:39-41) A legend says that Peter and Andrew had served as chorizontes (singers of psalms) in the Temple at On. Jonah with a silent J has a similar sound to On, so the name Simon bar Jonah may reflect that or their mother's name Joanna. Joanna's husband's name was Chuza, Herod's steward. Possibly Chuza was son of Joseph Herod Philip Costobaris, Herod the Great's uncle. (C=CH)

Hidden in this passage is the name Isaac Pinas (clean platter). Isaac Pinas was well-known for his overly technical interpretations of scripture. Isaac Pinhas was one of the five early Hebrew poets. He was associated with letters like the Kabblists. (Kahle, CG, 35, 300)

NAME (Luke 9:23-27, any man sounds like Andrew, idea of a generation) Aland notes that Luke 9:24=17:33 and Luke 9:26=12:9. Joanna (Luke 8:3) was said to be the mother of Peter and Andrew, but Luke cites Chuza (Jug), Herod's steward, as her husband. His name could be a reference to Hazor. (Ch=H) It was the place to which the Benjaminites returned after captivity. (Neh. 11:33)

Andrew evangelized in Greece, Macedonia and Scythia near the Black Sea. (McBirnie, STA, 81) He arrived in Russia during a storm just in time to save Matthias from cannibals. He is beloved in Scotland and in Russia. His death involved St. Andrew's cross shaped like the letter 'X'.

KINGDOM (Luke 13:18-19, man, seed) Mustard seed (sinapis) is similar to the name of a seaport in Russia, Sinope. Seneca's son Nova would become a Christian bishop there. Andrew as a fisherman would have been pleased with Sinope. Jesus called him to be a fisher of men, a term used by Mandaeans. The fowls of the air may have referred to Assyrians (sparrows) or Arabians (orebim) in exile there.

EARTH (Luke 3:17-20, generation, father=man, wheat=seed) Andrew was a follower of John the Baptist before he followed Jesus. Andrew refers to the winnowing of wheat. Chaff drops out, but the good seed is harvested.

BREAD (Luke 17:22-33, generation, man, sign) Aland notes that Luke 17:27=21:34.

This teaching agrees with the teachings of the Encratite Christians. When life gets too easy, people tend to become self-centered, wanting luxury and forgetting God.

EVIL (Luke 13:20-30, woman, idea of father, leaven) Evil came into the world by Eve in the Garden of Eden. It was the beginning of dualism in the mind of mankind. The word 'measures' may refer to the tombs of the Maccabees at Modin. Bodies were placed on a shelf at the top of a tower so the birds could carry the flesh to heaven. All leaven was considered evil so a Jewish woman had to clean thoroughly before Passover. Encratites thought Eve's evil had spread throughout the world.

FORGIVE (Luke 22:21-30, man, father) Andrew may have been the older brother, but Peter was recognized as a surperior leader. Jesus taught that the one who serves is superior. The allusion to meat may be lost until one recalls that Andrew was a vegetarian. Even just before the crucifixion, the disciples were unsure of themselves and each other. Jesus reassured them.

AS WE (Luke 20:27-38, man, not fathers, seed) Sadducees wanted Jesus to affirm their beliefs about genealogical rights. Jesus said there are no marriages in heaven. That would have pleased Andrew who did not believe in marriage. Jesus added that marriages are for the living on this earth. Andrew may not have been pleased with that.

AMEN (Luke 12:1-12, man, spirit, fear, leaven) Hypocrisy was feared by the EncratiteCommunity. They abstained from everything that they thought might separate them from God. Jesus said a sin against the Holy Spirit would separate men from God. One hypocrisy is associated with gossip often tinged with envy or ignorance.

PART THREE; THE TEN COMMANDMENTS

ONE GOD

(Luke 2:36-38, man=husband, spirit of service) This woman could have been Anna or her mother. The timing is such that her husband could have been Governor of Edom at one time. She gave thanks for what she believed was happening.

IDOLS

(Luke 18:1-8, man, spirit of fear) Aland notes that Luke 18:5=11:7, 8. Anna and Elizabeth had not received property of their own after the deaths of their husbands. Nabatean (Edomite) law allowed women to retain property after marriage and to inherit property. Jewish law said that two witnesses had to come forward testifying they had seen the dead body. Felix helped Elizabeth regain her property. When Andrew died, a golden urn was prepared for the head of Andrew. It was smashed by a fellow encratite. (McBirnie, STA, 84)

HOLY NAME

(Luke 11:11-13, man, spirit) Jesus wanted to encourage believers to pray. He said a father would not give his son a serpent (tannaim is a homonym for scribe) if he asked for a fish (Christian). If he asked for an egg (the black nothing before creation), he would not give him a scorpion (whipping).

Jesus told the disciples to ask in His name. Parents are asked by their children for help. The fish was the sign of a Christian, for alpha looks like a fish. A stranger who was a Christian would draw a fish in the sand. If the other person were also a Christian, he would draw omega beneath the fish. A small omega looks like a wave. Then he would erase the sign with his foot. One name for the Trinity is Alpha and Omega with Now understood as the third party.

SABBATH

(Luke 13:10-17, woman, spirit) The proper procedure for prayer was an issue. Hillel made his pronouncements. The woman could not pray correctly because she could not stand up straight and lift her hands. (cf Charlesworth, H&J, 431 and Deuteronomy 6:7) Jesus healed her.

PARENTS

(Luke 2:40-52, man, spirit) Aland notes Luke 2:40=1:80, 2:52. Peter and Andrew could have been children during that Passover.

KILL

(Luke 20:9-18, man, spirit) Andrew healed many. Among those he healed were the son and wife of King Aegeates. Perhaps the wife accepted Andrew's celibacy and became celibate herself and his friend. Aegeates ordered death for Andrew. (Kraeling, TD, 38)

The owner of a vineyard leaves it in the hands of husbandmen. He sends messengers and they kill the first, second and third messengers. He decides to send his son and they kill him too. (cf Josephus, 3) Mosaic Law allowed a life for a life.

At one point Aegeates wishes to kill Andrew's enemies. Andrew begs for their lives so that he can evangelize them. (Kraeling, TD, 38)

ADULTERY

(Luke 8:2-3, woman, spirit) Aland notes that Luke 8:2-3=23:49. Mary Magdalene did not wear clothes. Although that is not adultery, Andrew's prejudice against women might have caused him to accuse her of adultery. Jesus healed her. Peter never accepted her as forgiven. Andrew did not accept women. Their only hope was to become androgenous.

STEAL

(Luke 18:9-14, man, wrong spirit) Aland notes that Luke 18:14=14:11. Some encratite people become self-centered and boast of their religious deeds. The publican boasts that he is not guilty of extortion (stealing). Other encratite people become more humble as time goes on. They outlive their sins.

LIE

(Luke 5:17-26, man, spirit) Someone, perhaps Ptolemy or his brother Nicodemus, is brought to Jesus for healing. Jesus begins by saying his sins are forgiven. Those present say he lies, for only God can forgive sin.

COVET

(Luke 12:13-21, man, spirit of fear) Jesus tells someone, perhaps Malchus, to beware of covetousness. God wants to bless his children. Life does not consist of things. A rich man, perhaps Nicodemus, considers tearing down his barns and building bigger ones. The Law though forbids storing more than two-and-a-half years of produce. Any more than that belongs to the widow, orphan and stranger. Jesus warns that there will be no secrets. Christians should fear God who can cast them into hell rather than fear those who kill. The spirit will teach God's people what to say when others are covetous.

BIBLIOGRAPHY

Aland, Kurt.The Greek New Testament. United Bible Societies. (New York:1975)

Charlesworth, James and Loren L.Johns, eds. Hillel and Jesus. Fortress Press (Minneapolis:1997)

Charlesworth, James and Loren L. Johns, eds. Old Testament Pseudepigrapha. 2 vols. Doubleday & Company (Garden City, New York:1985)

Hone, William. The Lost Books of the Bible. Bell Publishing (New York:1979)

Kahle, Paul E. The Cairo Geniza. Frederick a Praeger (New York:1960_

Kraeling, Emil G. The Disciples. Rand McNally and Company (USA:1966)

McBirnie, William Steuart. The Search for the Twelve Apostles. Pb. Tyndale House Publishers (Wheaton , Illinois:1977)

McClintock, John and James Strong. Cyclopedia of Biblical, Theological and Ecclesiastical Literature. 12 vols. Baker Book House (Grand Rapids, Michigan:1981)

Rambsel, Yacov. His Name Is Jesus. Pb. Word Publishing (Nashville:1999)

XXI. MARCUS RUFUS PUDENS-SAMUEL-JESUS

Yacov Rambsel did not find ELS for Mark, but he did find ELS for two words in Mark 2:15-17, "pass" and "physician".. The overall pattern uses two unifying words "behold" (pun for Edom) and "pass" or Passover. (Rambsel, HNJ, 34, 35,45) The name Mark means "shining" and it is used three times. The word "physician" is also used three times. Rufus means "healer" or physician. Marcus Rufus Pudens was a Roman Senator, the son of Imma Shalom (the mother of Saul) and of Simon of Cyrene. ELS for Simon begins at Isaiah 52:14. As a descendant of Samuel, he had the right to live at Bethany. Bethany is mentioned three times. (McBirnie, STA). The Gospel of Mark is accepted in contemporary bibles. Perhaps this section refers to a written document rather than oral testimony. ELS from I Samuel 1:2 spells out "his writing of Jeshua" (Rambsel, HNJ, 212). Once Rufus and Gratus (Alexander his brother) led 3000 Syrian men which they turned over to the Romans. (Josephus, 371, 473-4) Some say that Mark is not accurate. He depended on what Peter told him. Before being imprisoned in Rome, Peter lived in the home of Pudens. (McBirnie, STA, 284)

PART I. STATIONS OF THE CROSS

The name Mark also may refer to "maraq" which means sword, polished or shining in II Chronicles 4:16 He was descended by his mother from

Samuel. Samuel and his heirs were given an estate at Bethany which was once called Nob Hill.

SUBJECTS (Luke 2:41-42, behold, pass, I Samuel 3:19) Aland notes that Luke 2:51=2:19. The Gospel of Mark does not mention the boy Jesus. Samuel's mother placed him in the temple to assist Eli. The Virgin Mary and Joseph took Jesus to Passover. He stayed behind to talk with the doctors. They were amazed at his understanding. Eli was amazed at Samuel when he reported to him the sins of his sons. Mary accuses Jesus of worrying them. The family of High Priest Boethus lived at Bethany where Samuel and his heirs had been given an estate. Samuel was taken to High Priest Eli at Shiloh because Eli's sight was failing.

FAMILY (Luke 2:8-20, behold, pass, shine, I Samuel 1:20) Aland notes that Luke 2:9=24:5 and Luke 2:19=2:51. Before Samuel was born, Hannah and Elkanah had plans for him to serve God. Hannah tells of her plans, but the Virgin Mary keeps hers in her heart. Syrians called their holy men shepherds.

GENEALOGY (Luke 1:39-56, behold, pass, I Samuel 2:1-10) Mark had ties with Alexandria where the Septuagint Bible was translated. The Jerusalem text said that the Messiah would be born of a young woman. The Septuagint: said she would be a virgin. The Virgin Mary sings a hymn composed by Hannah, mother of Samuel. Her own mother was also named Hannah.

SERMON (Luke 4:14-23, return=pass, found=beheld, glory, cf. I Samuel 3:17, Mark 1:21) Jesus preaches on the text of Isaiah 61:1-2, but omits a part of the last verse which was about violence. As a boy, Samuel was told by Eli not to leave out anything.

Matthew's version of this sermon differs from Luke's in that the. chiasmus is better preserved in Luke's. Chiasmus is a pattern of clue words or synonyms given in one order. Then the order is reversed. In this sermon, synagogue, stood, delivered, opened, Lord, preach, sent. (line without such a word), send, proclaim, Lord, closed, gave it back, sat down, synagogue. (Lund, CNT, 236=237)

FAME (Luke 9:35-43, pass, can not behold, glory, I Samuel 3:2, Mark 9:2-8) Aland notes that Luke 9:35=3:22. Samuel was helpful to

Eli whose eyes were failing. Jesus helped a blind man by restoring his sight. He immediately praised and told others.

PROPHECY (Luke 17:11-24, pass, behold, shine, glory, I Samuel 17:12, Mark 13:21) Aland notes that Luke 17:11=9:51, 52, 13:22. Luke 17:12=18:38 and Luke 17:14=5:14. God told Samuel that theboy David was his chosen. Jesus proclaims that God's Will is made clear, but God chooses the time.

When the Jews returned from exile in Babylon, they did not accept the Samaritans as their equal. They could contribute to the funds, but not worship within the temple. When Jesus sends the lepers he has healed to the priests at the temple, the Samaritan does not k now what to do. Then he recognizes Jesus as being from God and bows down. Perhaps this is a teaching about universality of God's Will as expressed by Jesus.

LAST WEEK (Luke 22:7-13, behold, Passover, Mark 14:12-21, I Samuel 8:1) Aland notes that Luke 22:13=19:32. Samuel judged Israel. After his death, he made his sons judges over Israel Jesus said that even nature would judge those who tried to prevent his being recognized as the Messiah. At the Last Supper, Jesus tried to prepare his disciples for service toGod after his death. After Paul's death, Marcus had him interred in his own home. After Marcus's death, the home became the Church of Saint Pudentia. (McBirnie, STA, 285).

DEATH (Luke 23:5046-56, behold, preparation refers to Passover, Mark 15:37, 42-47, I Samuel 28:3) Samuel died and was buried at Ramah. Jesus died and was buried in the tomb of Joseph of Arimathea, also a son of Imma Shalom but not of Simon of Cyrene.

A. D. (Luke 24:1-5, 50, behold, pass, shine, Bethany, Mark 16:1-8, I Samuel 21:1) Nob Hill (Bethany) was the place that David was hungry and ate the showbread. After Samuel's death, Saul tried to consult him about his problems. After the death of Jesus, two men in shining garments asked, "Why do you seek the living among the dead?" Then in due time, Jesus went to ethany and he arose.

OUR (Luke 5:30-32, physician, Mark 2:16-17, I Timothy 1:15) After serving in the military, Marcus Rufus Pudens took his nephew

Timothy to Rome. Rufus was brother-in-law to Seneca the Elder's wife who was a Christian.

FATHER (Luke 23:24-29, idea of passing by, Mark 15:22-32) Imma Shalom of Bathyra was a relative of Hillel and Gamaliel. She married Eleazar ben Hyrcanus by whom she had Jair. She married Simon of Cyrene by whom she had Rufus and Alexander (Gratus). She married Simon of Arimathea by whom she had Domitilla, Saul (Paul), and Joseph of Arimathea. Sylleus was also said to be her son. Simon of Cyrene carried the cross for Jesus when he was on his way to crucifixion.rehad . It is said that Mark (Rufus) went to Alexandria and established the Christian church there. (Hastings, DOB, III, 248) After the death of his father, Mark established a church in Cyrenaica. (McBirnie, STA,252) Simon Boethus's second wife was Mariamne, daughter of Herod the Great. He had been High Priest 22-5 b.c. One Simon Kantheras would be High Priest in 41 a.d. (Jeremias, JTJ, 194, 196) Mark's Hebrew name was John, and his mother's name was Mary (Imma Shalom). (Acts 12:12)

NAME (Luke 4:23, physician, Mark 2:17) The name Rufus means healer or physician. Colobodactilus can mean an amputated or withered hand, foot or penis. Mark was sometimes called that. It is believed that the present ending of the Gospel of Mark was not written by the same author as its beginning.

Moreover, it is said that he was harmed in battle in Syria.. (Hastings, DOB, III, 247) Ironically, after Jesus healed the problem, his hand wrote one of the books of the New Testament. Since Luke uses Mark but Luke is usually dated 65 a.d., the theory of Urmarkus could be true.

Paul was tried by Rufus's brother-in-law Gallio. Then Paul went to Rome for trial and was imprisoned in the home of Marcus Rufus Pudens.

KINGDOM (Luke 2:2, II Samuel 8,10) King David was victorious against the Syrians. The similarity of the name Simon of Cyrene and Cyrenius, the governor of Syria should be noted.

EARTH (Luke 9:27-36, behold, pass, glistering=shining,I Samuel 3:1-10, Mark 9;28) Aland notes that Luke 9:31=9:22, 13:33 and Luke 9:35=3:22. God speaks saying that Jesus is his beloved son..

BREAD (Luke 22:14-23, behold, Passover, II Samuel 7:14, Mark 14:18-26) Aland notes that Luke 22:16=13:29. The Last Supper may have taken place in Mark's home. (Hastings, DOB, 247) One legend is that Mark was seen running naked. Among some Jews, frequent baptism was practiced. God's mercy is that he promised David.

EVIL (Luke 16:19-31, behold=lift up eyes, pass, Mark 7:28) Lazarus was brother to Mary and Martha. Jesus restored him to life after his death. A waterfall over a cave was said to be the entrance to hell. Mark displeased someone, for it was said that all he said was second-hand. Later he separated for a time from Paul, but they were reunited in Rome.

FORGIVE (Luke 9:37-45, behold, pass, Mark 9:14-29) Aland notes that Luke 9:44=18:32. Jesus heals the only son of a man, perhaps Marcus Rufus's brother-in-law. He was the father of Timothy. Then Jesus warns that he will be killed. Marcus ignores the warning and feels that he could have done something.

AS WE (Luke 10:25-37, behold, pass, Mark 12:28-34) Jesus teaches that the one who showed mercy on the Samaritan was on the way to eternal life. Legend states that Mark was one of the seventy sent out by Jesus during his lifetime. If he returned early, it would be a foreshadowing of the time he left Paul. They were both ill, but Mark returned home and Paul continued on. One should note that the word 'shaul' means 'wolf'. If Mark had left the seventy earlier, one can be sure Paul remembered.

AMEN (Luke 18:31-43, behold, pass, Mark 10:46-52) Aland notes that Luke 18:32=9:44..Baba ben Buta was Herod's physician. When Herod became angry with him, he ordered that his sons be killed in his presence. Then he should be blinded. This man could have been Baba. Jesus healed him.

PART III. THE TEN COMMANDMENTS

Qumran has a name that sounds like 'rise up'(Qumah).

ONE GOD

(Luke 3:21-23, look up=behold, pass, Mark 1:9-11) Aland notes that Luke 3:22=9:35.This passage reflects the Trinity of Father, Son and Holy Ghost. Since Mark was Peter's amanuensis, it is said that an y errors belong to Mark. John Mark and Barnabas were kin to each other, and Peter's wife was kin to Barnabas. Therefore, Mark would have heard this directly from Peter. Rechabites were to live intents until the Messiah came. Peter knew that the Messiah stood before him. Moses and Elijah were discussing Jesus's impending death. The need for making Rechabite tents was over.

IDOLS

(Luke 4:30-37, came down=pass, hold for behold, Mark 1:23-26) The distinction between devils and idols is not clear. Jesus is called the Holy One of God by the devil.

HOLY NAME

(Luke 10:17-20, return=pass, behold, Mark 16:18) When the seventy returned after their mission, Jesus blessed them by saying their names were written in heaven.

SABBATH

(Luke 6:1-5, pass, Nob=Bethany, I Samuel 21:1, Mark 2:23-28) A second Sabbath was created to allow those who missed the first to make it up. This usually applied to feasts. As David ate the showbread, he not only worked on the Sabbath, but he ate consecrated bread at Nob Hill (Bethany).

PARENTS

(Luke 8:40-56, behold, pass, physician, rise up, Mark 5:21-43) Aland notes that Luke 8:42=7:12, Luke 8:52=7:13 and Luke 8:54=7:14. Peter was present when Jesus healed the daughter of Jairus, but Salome was healed on the street. Mark could have seen that. Jesus told her to rise up. Rechabites were not to eat meat until the Messiah came. Jesus told her parents to give her meat.

KILL

(Luke 22:35-39,, behold, pass=take up, Mark 6:8-9) Jesus knows that he will be killed, so he makes preparation. Isaiah 53:12 states that he will be reckoned with transgressors. He makes sure that his men have at least two swords. The words translated as swords and words are homonyms. Then he goes into the Garden of Gethsemane which belongs to Joseph of Arimathea. There he prays, but the disciples go to sleep.

ADULTERY

(Luke 7:36-50, behold, go in peace=pass, Mark 14:3) Aland notes that Luke 7:48=5:20, Luke 7:49=5:21 and Luke 7:50=17:19.. One superstition was that the Messiah would not come until the Holy Land was sinless for a day. Herod Antipas although married was sleeping with his ex-sister-in-law. The Simon in this story may have been any one of many Simon's. The woman, although a sinner, anointed Jesus for his burial.

STEAL

(Luke 19:11-27, behold, pass, Bethany, Mark 13:34, 4:25) Aland notes that Luke 19:17=16:10 and Luke 19:26=8:10. Several puns exist in this parable. They are minas (coins), minyahs (quorum for worship), minyehs (villages) and minim (curses).

LIE

(Luke 5:17-26, behold, pass, Mark 1:40-44) Aland notes that Luke 5:20=7:48 and Luke 5:21=7:49. Perhaps the lie is Luke 16:10, but this seems to fit the code better. Jesus is in a situation where it is tempting to lie. Instead he challenges his accusers to tell the truth about John the Baptist.

COVET

(Luke 20: 9-18, went=pass, beheld, Mark 12:1-12) The vineyard recalls that Joseph of Arimathea tilled the balsam groves while married to Herod's sister Alexandra Salome. Philip and Bernice went somewhere, so Varus decided he would take over the groves. Marcus Rufus Pudens fought for them. Philip and **Bernice returned and took over the groves. (Josephus, 3)**.

BIBLIOGRAPHY

Aland, Kurt, et al. The Greek New Testament. United Bible Societies (New York:1975)

Hastings, James, ed. Dictionary of the Bible. 5 vols. Charles Scribner's Sons (New York:1909)

Lawlor, John Irving. The Nabataeans in Historical Perspective. Pb. Baker Book House (Grand Rapids, Michigana: 1974)

Lund, Nils W. Chiasmus in the New Testament. Pb. Hendrickson (Peabody, Massachusetts:1942)

McBirnie, William Steuart. The Search for the Twelve Apostles. Pb. Tyndale (Wheaton, Illinois: 1977)

Rambsel, Yacov. His Name Is Jesus. Pb. Word Publishing (Nashville:1999)

XXII. ANDREW JESUS ESAU

The names of Esau and Andrew are found in ELS from Isaiah 53:4. Also from that verse the ELS for "Andrew fears God" and "the one finding my spirit". (Rambsel, HNJ, 7, 45, 28) God fearers were those whose backgrounds were not Jewish, but they believed in the God of the Jews. Mount Seir was given to Esau. (Deuteronomy 2:5), If Andrew and Peter were descendants of Korah, they worked at the Temple. One job was being a chorizonte, leading a speaking choir. The Psalms of Korah are numbers 42, 44, 46, 47, 48, 49, 85, 87, and 88. There is a monastery in Cyprus called Apostolos Andreas Monastery. Peter's wife had a family background in Cyprus. Andrew became the patron saint of Scotland and Russia. Andrew's cross is shaped like an "X" rather than a "T". The cross is thought of as being crimson as a reminder of the blood of martyrs. Also Edom means red. Andrew is associated with miraculous military maneuvers and the presence of God through angels.

Andrew allowed several people to talk to Jesus perhaps as an appointment clerk. Descendants of Esau refused to permit the Jews to cross his land in order to return to Israel. (Numbers 20:18) One of his sons was named Korah. (I Chronicles 1:35)

As Esau was the older brother of Jacob, Andrew was the older brother of Simon Peter. Both were fishermen, and dried salted fish were exported to Cyprus for the miners.

All holiness groups have in common a belief in the presence of God in worship. Quakers wait silently, but John Wesley's Holiness Club sang. Charismatics even faint. Feelings and emotions are considered necessary to respond to the Holy Ghost.

The overall unifying word is man, and the name Andrew means "manly". The unifying word for Part I is "fear", for Part II is the Holy Ghost, and for Part III is spirit.

PART I THE STATIONS OF THE CROSS

In this context, fear can mean "awe" as well as the state of being afraid.

SUBJECTS (Luke 18;2-8, fear, man, Psalm 34:9) Aland notes that Luke 18:5=11:7-8.

Herod the Great's father Antipater killed the husband of the Queen of Edom. Then he ruled Edom on behalf of Mariamne the Hasmonaean's mother. Perhaps Anna (Luke 2:36-38) was her daughter. Edom had matriarchal rule, but Herod persuaded Rome to appoint his sister Alexandra Salome Queen of Edom instead of appointing Anna. (cf. Josephus, 316 for she is called Alexandra rather than Anna there.)

FAMILY (Luke 2:1-20, afraid, men, Psalm of Korah 85:10) Aland notes that Luke 2:9=24:5 and Luke 2:17=2:10-12. Korah defied Moses because he thought Moses should disqualify Aaron. The reason was the Golden Calf incident. Moses commanded him to go out and the ground swallowed him up. God gave Mount Seir in Edom to Esau. It may or may not have been called Zohar, the Book of Shining Radiance. (Barnstone, OB, 707-718) The location of the Levitical School of the South is not known. It is known that descendants of Korah were temple servants. One job was singing or chanting. (Numbers 16, 26:9, 58, 27:3)

Because of the census it is known that Jesus was descended from David by Joseph of Nazareth and Mary.

GENEALOGY (Luke 1:26-38, fear, man, holy, Daniel 2:44) Arabians and Muslims attribute to angels most of what Christians attribute to the Holy Spirit. The angel Gabriel spoke to Mary telling her that she would bear a child of the lineage of David. <u>When she protested that she had not known a man, he told her that Elizabeth who was post-menapausal would also bear a son.</u> Both births were seemingly impossible.

According to Aristeas, Esau was fifth in line from Job. (Charlesworth, OTP, II, 855, 856)

SERMON (Luke 12:4-40, fear, Goodman, friend, Psalm of Korah 49:16, Daniel 4:31) Aland notes that Luke 12:2=8:17, Luke 12:4=9:26, Luke 12:7=21:18 and Luke 12:32=22:29. Jesus preached a sermon against the entanglement of riches. He speaks of "treasure" which is what Samaritans and Edomites called the scriptures.

The treasure which Esau was to inherit was his birthright. He was hungry so he sold it to his brother Jacob for a mess of pottage. Pottage was reddish brown. Esau's hair was red and the name Edom means red.

MARVEL (Luke 20:19-26, fear, man, I Peter 2:13, 17) Aland notes that Luke 20:19=22:2.

Jesus was tested concerning two commandments, the Mosaic one about idols and the Roman one about citizenship. He replies that each has its place in time. The people marveled.

FAME (Luke 5:17-26, fear, man, Psalm of Korah 49:6-7) Aland notes that Luke 5:20=7:48, Luke 5:21=7:49 and Luke 5:22=6:8, 9:47. The name Esau means "hairy". To fool his father Isaac, Rebecca ties fur to the arms of Jacob. Isaac gives Jacob the blessing intended for Esau. Isaac is so blind he can not recognize either son by sight. (Genesis 25:29)

Jesus is blindfolded to test him for his divinity. (Luke 23:62-65) Gods are thought to be omniscient.

PROPHECY (Luke 9:37-50, fear, man, II Peter 1:16) Aland notes that Luke 9:46=22:24, Luke 9:47=6:8, 9:47 and Luke 9:50=11:23. Jesus is tested regarding the superiority of his healing. A possible explanation is that this was a genetic problem.

Isaac was asked by Esau to give him a blessing also. He said, " Behold, thy dwelling shall be the fatness of the earth, and of the dew of the heaven above, and by they sword shalt thou live, and shall serve your brother, and it shall come to pass when thou shall have dominion that thou shall break his yoke from off thy neck." (Genesis 27:39-40)

Jesus knew there was strife over status. He said that he came to serve. (Luke 22:25-27)

LAST WEEK (Luke 9:26-36, fear, man, II Peter 1:16, 17) Aland notes that Luke 9:26=12:9 and Luke 9:5=3:22. The descendants of Esau were cave-dwellers. Some Edomites lived like Rechabites in tents. They had sworn to do so until the Messiah came. Andrew among others were convinced by the appearance on the Mount of Transfiguration. If Jesus were indeed the Messiah, tents could be replaced with houses.

DEATH (Luke 22:1-6, 21-23, fear, man, younger, Psalm 41:9, I Peter 5:5) Aland notes that Luke 22:2=20:19, Luke 22:24=9:46 and Luke 22:29=12:32. Esau vowed to kill Jacob who had betrayed him with their mother's help. Judas will betray the identity of Jesus because his relatives Joseph Caiaphas and Annas bribe him to do so. The Rebecca begs Isaac not to allow Esau to kill Jacob. Jacob goes to a far country.

AFTER THE DEATH (Luke 24:1-7, afraid, man, II Peter 1,11) Aland notes that Luke 24:5=2:9. The two men standing by the tomb would have been called angels by Andrew. In the Book of II Enoch, man dies and becomes like the angels, the angels become like men (the Resurrection) for a time. Then they return to heaven as angels.

Jesus appeared to the disciples, including Andrew, after the Resurrection. (Luke 24:36)

PART II THE LORD'S PRAYER

The unifying term is the Holy Ghost.

OUR (Luke 1:39-64, Holy Ghost, woman, Psalm 103:17) Aland notes that Luke 1:45=12:20, Luke 1:42, 48=1:28, and Luke 1:59=1:68 and 2:21. Peter and Andrew were born in Bethsaida and lived in Capernaum later. They did not know Jesus until they were grown.

FATHER (Luke 2:25-38, Holy Ghost, man, I Peter 2:7) Aland notes that Luke 2:21=1:31, 59. Obviously this does not refer to the father of Peter and Andrew, but to the father of Jesus. If Anna is Joanna, calling Peter Simon bar Jonah is a possibity. (Luke 2:36-38) If so, (Luke 8:3 and 2:36-38) The name Hani-Oannes-John appears in Mandaean belief. (Mead, GB, 16) In one sense, Jesus replaces him.

As to the prophecy of the sword. Andrew healed the wife of Aegeas. When he first saw the sword of Aegeas he knew it would kill him some day. Out of gratitude to God, she became celibate. Aegeas put Andrew in prison. It was there that he made his farewell address. " O Cross, trophy of the victory of Christ over the foe! O cross planted upon the earth and havingthy fruit in the heavens!" (Kraeling, TD, 39)

.NAME *(Luke 6:6-19, spirit, man, touch, I Peter1:2) Since this is the only place in Luke where the name of Andrew occurs, this has to be placed here. Aland notes that Luke 6:7=13:14 and Luke 6:8=5:22, 9:47. Andrew became a God-fearer before Simon Peter. He took Peter to see Jesus. Sometime later at the Lake of Gennesaret, they were called to be disciples (Luke 5:1).*

KINGDOM (Luke 3:1-17, Holy Ghost, man, I Peter 3:16, II Peter 1:17) Aland notes that Luke 3:7,12=7:29-30. In Edom, the Mandaeans awaited the Messiah. John the Baptist was their leader in gospel times. They spoke of being fishers of men and called the scriptures a treasure. (Mead, GB, 71, 86)

EARTH (Luke 1:67-80, Holy Ghost, Psalm 106:48) Aland notes that Luke 1:68=1:59, 7:16. Zacharias describes the covenant that God gave to Abraham. Edomites and Jews claimed Abraham as their progenitor.

BREAD (Luke 11:5-13, Holy Ghost, friend, Psalm 35:12) Aland notes that Luke 11:7-8=18:5. Andrew healed Exoos. Exoos was then disinherited so that he was not entitled to an inheritance when his father died. Exoos was offered the money anyway. At first Exoos refused the money, then he opted to give it to the poor for bread. (Qumran?)(Kraeling, TD, 37

Peter is often described in relation to crowds, but Andrew to individuals. Even when living with Laban, Jacob sent gifts of food to his parents. Esau neglected them. (Charlesworth, OTP, II, 112))

EVIL (Luke 4:1-13, Holy Ghost, man, Psalm 91:11-12). Jesus is tempted by the temptations most feared by the Rechabites and the Poor. He answers each temptation with scripture.

FORGIVE (Luke 1:12-25, Holy Ghost,man, Daniel 8:16, 9:21) Aland notes that Luke 1:20=1:45. Edomites did not appreciate Jews. They sometimes fought. When Elizabeth escaped to the desert with John, the leading of the Holy Ghost led Andrew to accepting a Jew (John the Baptist) as a messenger of God. In time, Andrew also accepted Jesus.

AS WE (Luke 12:1-3, 12, Holy Ghost, man, Psalm 19:14, I Peter 2:13) Aland notes that Luke 12:12=21:12-15. When a judge is accusing Sostratus falsely, an earthquake happens and the judge(Andrew?) falls off his bench. (Kraeling, TD, 33) This may suggest that Andrew rushed to judgment in some cases.

AMEN (Luke 3:21-23, Holy Ghost, genealogy of a man, Psalm 116:16) Aland notes that Luke 3:22=9:35. The Virgin Mary has called herself a handmaiden. (Luke 1:38).

PART III. THE TEN COMMANDMENTS

The unifying word is "spirit".

ONE LORD

(Luke 7:1-10, 19-23, spirit, man, friend, Psalm 40:7, I Peter 2:8) Jesus healed the son of a centurion. Andrew healed the servant of Demetrius who was an Egyptian boy. (Kraeling, TD, 33) The transition of following John and then Jesus must have been difficult. However, there is only one Lord that both served.

IDOLS

(Luke 11:14-23, spirit=Satan, man, Psalm 106:37) Aland notes that Luke 11:23=9:50.

When Andrew and his companions meet the Russian army, they are afraid. Andrew prays. Some say they saw angels touch the swords of the Russians. Then thesoldiers fell down before them. (Kraeling TD, 35)

HOLY NAME

(Luke 4:31-44, spirit, man, holy, Peter's mother=Andrew's, I Peter 3:12) Aland notes that Luke 4:33-34=8:28 which does not appear in this testimony. Andrew could have seen Jesus cast devils out of a man at Capernaum.Peter and Andrew considered Capernaum their home.

SABBATH

(Luke 13:10-19, spirit, man, Peter's mother=Andrew's Daniel 4:12, 21) Aland notes that Luke 13:14=6:7 and Luke 13:16=19:9 Jesus corrected the over-literal interpretation of Mosaic Law. If the author of Luke did not wish to duplicate the healing of their mother, this story has the added point about the Law.

Mustard seed (sinapis) sounds like Sinope, a city on the Black Sea in what is now called Russia. Andrew went to Sinope located near the place where the Apophagi (cannibals=man-eaters) lived. He was answering the call of Matthias (Zacchaeus) for help. Although afraid on the ship going, he ate bread and fell asleep. He arrived the next morning on the shore. He believed angels had steered the ship. Together with Matthias, they converted the people and taught them precepts before they left. (Kraeling, TD, 30)

PARENTS

(Luke 7:11-18, fear, man, Psalm 86:16) Aland notes that Luke 7:16=1:68. Andrew restored another only son in a similar way He did not ask for pay, but the mother gave Andrew the son he had saved. (Kraeling, TD, 33)

KILL.

(Luke 21:10, fearful, spiritt of patience, man, friend, hair, I Peter 4:12-14. Aland notes that Luke 21:12-15=12:11-12. Jesus warns his disciples that they might be betrayed, but they should continue to serve and to have faith. Philip the Good honored Andrew and Gideon by establishing the Knights of the Golden Fleece. (Unger, UBD, 404))

ADULTERY

(Luke 7:29-50, spirit, man, touch, hair, friend, I Peter 5:14) Aland notes that Luke 7:29-30=3:7, 12 and Luke 7:50=8:48 Andrew arrived at a port where a pre-wedding feast was in progress. Unfortunately the bride and groom were near Andrew refused to marry them for that reason. (Kraeling, TD, 36).

It is assumed that the sin of the woman was adultery. Herod the Great had married several women, and they could have been considered adulterers by remarrying.

STEAL

(Luke 19:9-32, 45-48, fear, man, Psalm50:17, I Peter 4:10, 11) Aland notes that Luke 19:26=8:18, Luke 19:9=13:16, Luke 19:32=22:13.

(Luke 22:13 refers to Peter.) Jesus told the Parable of Ten Pounds. It uses word play in the form of homonyms. They are Minyehs (villages), minas (coins), minyahs (quorum for worship) and minim (curses). The Decapolis was a cluster of ten cities in Galilee. They had been rebuilt in 65 b.b. by the Romans. Scythopolis and Kanatha may have been visited by Andrew.

LIE

(Luke 8:40-56, spirit, man, touch, I Peter 22 Aland notes that Luke 8:42=7:12 andLuke 8:48=7:50 The people tell Jesus not to bother for the daughter of Jairus is already dead. Nevertheless she survives..

COVET

(Luke 16:19-17:6, torments=fear, man, Psalm of Korah 46:1-3) The words "mustard seed" are used in 13:19 and 7:6.One rumor is that Salvador persica is meant, for it sounds like the salvation of Persia. (Unger, NUBD, 1140)

Andrew's own salvation included joy over the success of his brother Simon Peter.

Thr people of Bithynia near the Black Sea in Russia greeted Andrew bearing olive branches. They chanted, "Our salvation is in you, o Man of God." He baptized many and appointed Callistus to bebishop. (Kraeling, TD, 34)

BIBLIOGRAPHY

Aland, Kurt, et al., eds. The Greek New Testament. American Bible Society (New York:1975)

Barnstone, Willis, ed. TheOther Bible. Harper Collins (San Francisco:1984)

Charlesworth, James and Loren L. Johns, eds. Old Testament Pseudepigrapha. 2 vols. Doubleday (Garden City, New York:1983)

Josephus. Complete Works tr. By William Whiston. Lrege; (Grand Rapids, Michigan:1985)

Kraeling, Emil G. The Disciples. Rand McNally (USA:1966)

Mead, G. R. S. The Gnostic John the Baptizer. John M. Watkins (London:1924). ,

Rambsel, Yacov. His Name Is Jesus. Pb. Word Publishing (Nashville:1999)

Unger, Merrill F. Unger's Bible Dictionary. Moody Press (Chicago:1978)

XXIII. CONCLUSION AND THEORY ABOUT SENECA'S FAMILY

The thrill of finding hidden treasures is to be followed by deciding what to treasure and what to think it means. Most of these eyewitnesses were in Rome when Pontius Pilate was tried in 37 c.e. for breaking the pax romana. The first trial of him was by Tiberius over the trouble in Israel when John the Baptist died. The second trial was over trouble when Jesus was crucified. If Jesus taught Judaism, which was legal according to Rome, then Pilate was in more trouble than just breaking pax romana. The Senate would decide. Seneca the Elder would interview eyewitnesses and prepare a brief. The second trial did not occur because Tiberius died suddenly. If the brief was properly prepared before the trial, Nero had it destroyed along with every other document that contained the name of Tiberius. However, Seneca the Elder was sentenced to commit suicide. His sons asked him to write five books before he died. A glib translation of the title would be the Great Battle. Of course, there are five books in the Pentateuch. According to M. D. Goulder, each of the synoptic gospels including Luke is arranged in the order of the Pentateuch. Seneca the Elder had knowledge if not access to the brief he had prepared. In 57 c.e. his wife was executed for externa superstitio, probably for being a Christian. (Scullard, FGN , 379)

Seneca's oldest son is known as Gallio of Achaia who became proconsul in 52 c.e. When Paul came before him to be tried, his father's work had not been published. It was the best evidence about Jesus available to him. He called the religious squabbles "words and names". He had been adopted by Lucius Junius Gallio but his birth name was Marcus Annaeus Novatus. He had been in Rome during the reign of Tiberius.(Bromiley, ISBE, II, 393).

Seneca's second son had made "corrections" to his father's manuscript. (Griffin , SPP, 418) Above it is explained that ELS patterns from Isaiah are used in the Gospel of Luke to identify the source. One should note that Secundum Luke only took ELS from Second Isaiah.These tags are called "corrections" for the scribes once used them to correct their copies of scripture. Jesus used chiasmus based on his sermon in Nazareth. If he used "catchwords" to aid memorization, Seneca could have felt justified in using ELS to protect the identity of eyewitnesses. Even the Torah used "catchwords" to identify the source of recorded information. When Seneca the Younger left the script to Gallio, he inscribed it "Librium secundum Lucan Lucan". That can be translated, "the writing of Second Luke for Luke". (Hastings, DOB, III,162) He was possibly baptized just before his death. (Lucas, SET, 45)

Seneca's third son Mela was called Tertius. He was a Roman governor of Sinope on the Black Sea. Some think the last stage of editing the Gospel of Luke occurred 64-67 c.e. He did not publish either but in 74 c.e. left the manuscript to his anti-Jewish nephew Marcion of Alexandria. After editing out what he considered Jewish or a miracle, he published Marcionite Luke. (Farrar, SAG, 21-22) When Marcion died about 117 c.e., the Alexandrian document was found which does not differ from the contemporary Gospel of Luke.

Seneca's wife's brother-in-law was Marcus Rufus Pudens, the Procurator of Judea prior to Pontius. He did not return to Rome until he was appointed to the Senate. He took Timothy with him. The Gospel of Mark was written in the Pudens home.. (McBirnie, STA,257) Fragments of Mark's Gospel have been found at Qumran which were written in 50 c.e. (McBirnie, STA, 251) If Marcus served Herod the Great in the military as Rufus, he would have been getting very old. It is said that the errors in Mark were caused by Mark who was Peter's amanuensis. Is "errors" a homonym for "corrections"?

Words hidden in full sight for centuries do not necessarily contradict the teachings of the church. History is know to be a slanted knowledge of truth at its best. What still exists and can be found is the testimony of eighteen eyewitnesses, one secondhand witness for Mark repeated what Peter said and the accused Pontius Pilate.

BIBLIOGRAPHY

Bromiley, Geoffrey, ed. Et al. The International Standard Bible Encyclopedia. 4 vols. William B. Eerdmans Publishing Company (Grand Rapids, Michigan:1982)

Clark, Donald Lemen. Rhetoric in Greco-Roman Education. Columbia University Press (New York:n. a.)

Farrar, Frederick William Seekers After God. A. L. Burt (New York:n.a.)

Goulder, M. D. Evangelists Calendar. SPCk (London:1978)

Goulder, M. D. Midrash and Lection in Matthew. SPCK (London:1974)

Griffin, Miriam T. Seneca: A Philosopher in Politics. Clarendon Press (Oxford:1976)

Hastings, James, ed. Dictionary of the Bible. 5 vols. Charles Scribner's Sons (New York:1909)

Hastings, James, ed. Encyclopedia of Religion and Ethics. 12 vols. Charles Scribner's Sons (New York:n.a.)

Lucas, F. L. Seneca and the Elizabethan Tragedy. Haskell House (New York:1969)

Scullard, H. H. From theGracchi to Nero. Methuen & Company (London:n.a.)

INDEX OF SUBJECTS, NAMES AND CHRISTIAN GROUPS

BIOGRAPHY

Louise Banner Welch loves her God and mysteries, but not on the same level. When she studied under Dr. William Farmer many years ago, he challenged the class to come up with a new explanation for Q. He allowed her to use a work of Rudolf Bultman that Bultman had made notes upon concerning the repetition of words. The current study "The Key to the Original Luke Found". This theory" is the result, but not the answer. Evidence of her curiosity is that she has obtained three Master's Degrees, one each from Southern Methodist University, Texas A & M at College Station and Western Illinois University at Macomb. Her family has had a star named for her, the star in the forehead of the Constellation Lynx. She is a descendant of Philip Boehm who founded three of the earliest churches in America.

Reverend Welch taught English in Texas high schools before becoming a local pastor in the United Methodist Church. She is a member of the Society for Biblical Literature. Previously she published a paperback "Luke's Twelve Eyewitnesses" and she has had a third book "Decoding the Gospel of Luke' on the internet.

When she was ten, she had a neighbor Pastor Lindley who was blind. He spent his days studying Luke in Braille and trying to figure out patterns in Greek. Reverend Welch took a shortcut on that by using a work published by the American Bible Society called "the Greek New Testament." She had found patterns of testimony before Yacov Rambsel published his findings about Equidistant Letter Sequencing in the Bible. His findings in the Isaiah and hers in the Gospel of Luke came together. What does it mean? It means that scholars who are Christian have new reasons to be amazed at the way God works.

He is the greatest mystery of all.